THE MANY FACES OF WAR

There is just one final target: victory and peace. But there are many targets in between.

The target may be a bridge in the North, defended by the most intensive flak a plane has ever been called upon to fly through. Or it may be a ripple of movement in the high elephant grass in the South, or a junk on the Mekong, or a group of thatched huts, or a VC force no more than fifty yards from friendly forces, or even the jungle itself.

To hit these targets the most extensive force of air weaponry ever assembled is being employed in Vietnam. Without these varied instruments of destruction, the war would be impossible to win. With them, the balance of power has been shifted. Most of the time they strike home. Sometimes they miss.

This is the on-the-spot story of the war they are waging. It has never been told before in full.

AIR WAR—VIETNAM

Books by Frank Harvey
published by Bantam Books, Inc.

THE LION PIT
NIGHTMARE COUNTY

AIR WAR- VIETNAM

BY FRANK HARVEY

For Maj. George Weiss, U.S. Air Force, a top pro,
a valued friend and a man who will no doubt take
violent exception to some of the things in this book.

AIR WAR—VIETNAM
A Bantam Book / published July 1967

*The publisher wishes to acknowledge that this book is adapted
and expanded from an article that originally appeared in*
FLYING MAGAZINE, © *1966 by Ziff-Davis Publishing Company.*

Library of Congress Catalog Card Number: 67-25661

All rights reserved.
Copyright © *1967 by Frank Harvey.*
*This book may not be reproduced in whole or in part,
by mimeograph or any other means, without
permission in writing.*

Published simultaneously in the United States and Canada

*Bantam Books are published by Bantam Books, Inc., a subsidiary
of Grosset & Dunlap, Inc. Its trade-mark, consisting of the words
"Bantam Books" and the portrayal of a bantam, is registered in the
United States Patent Office and in other countries. Marca Registrada.
Bantam Books, Inc., 271 Madison Avenue, New York, N.Y. 10016.*

PRINTED IN THE UNITED STATES OF AMERICA

Contents

1 Dixie Station, *1*
2 Shore Leave, *17*
3 Saigon, *23*
4 Tan Son Nhut, *34*
5 Into the Delta, *43*
6 Those Mysterious Black Boxes, *52*
7 The Death Bringers, *54*
8 Village Sick Call, *63*
9 Night of the Dragon, *70*
10 —Meanwhile, on the Ground, *73*
11 Patrol with the River Jets, *86*
12 Vinh Long, *96*
13 "The Muttering Death," *101*
14 North of Saigon, *108*
15 Intercontinental Bombers
   vs. Jungle Hideouts, *123*
16 Just around the Corner, *127*
17 R and R, *130*
18 The Out-Country War, *139*
19 The Flying Marines, *154*
20 The Jolly Green Giants, *158*
21 Yankee Station, *163*
22 Gott Mit Uns, *179*
23 The Haves vs. the Have-Nots, *181*

1 DIXIE STATION

On the night before first combat, briefings were held in *Constellation's* various ready rooms to acquaint pilots and crews with the details of the upcoming strikes.

The big carrier was steaming in a race-track pattern about 80 miles off the coast of the Delta of South Vietnam. There was no moon. The jets were hard, black shapes outlined against the stars. There was a kerosene smell of jet fuel; warm drafts of air swirled up out of the carrier's ventilator exhausts; and a soft pervasive hum came from the buried activities in the ship's hull.

The carrier was blacked out, but a lot of people were not sleeping. Little groups of sailors were gathered on the catwalks to escape the heat of their compartments, talking or staring at the running lights of the planeguard destroyers that kept pace with *Constellation* about a mile away to port and starboard. Overshadowing the rest of the activity was the ominous presence of the jet fighters and bombers, tied and spotted topside, ready for the morning launch—the first one "in anger" of this cruise.

Round-the-clock feeding had now begun and would continue night and day during combat, except when the ship came off the line for R and R (rest and relaxation) in Manila's Subic Bay, Hong Kong or (as the crew was lusting for) Australia. Anyone on board could get hot chow, coffee, cocoa, sweet rolls and juices at any hour. The food on *Constellation* was very good and some of the officers and men were already developing pot bellies. No one could really blame them. Chow and movies are about the only amusement, except of course for James Bond, that they have.

The movies shift very frequently, however. The *Connie* trades movies with *Ranger* and *Ranger* trades with *Oriskany*, which trades with *Intrepid*, and so on. The films are flown back and forth by the ship's COD (carrier on board delivery) plane, a twin-engine Grumman.

If tilted on end, the *Constellation* would be taller than the Empire State Building. Two ocean liners the size of the *Queen Mary* could be placed side by side on her flight deck. Originally designed for a crew of 4,200, the carrier now had more than 5,300 people aboard because the complexity of her newest jets had made it necessary to bring an army of trained technicians to keep the electronics equipment, or black boxes, peaked out. All staterooms were full to capacity. People were sleeping in spare bunks in Sick Bay and in compartments intended for parts storage. Many of the rooms were covered with the wallpaper of the Vietnamese war: full-color pictures of voluptuous girls in the near-nude, cut out of *Playboy* and other magazines. It was a welcome relief from gray steel.

Dixie Station had a reason. It was simple. A pilot going into combat for the first time is a bit like a swimmer about to dive into an icy lake. He likes to get his big toe wet and then wade around a little before leaping off the high board into the numbing depths. So it was fortunate that young pilots could get their first taste of combat under the direction of a forward air controller over a flat country in bright sunshine where nobody was shooting back with high-powered ack-ack. He learns how it feels to drop bombs on human beings and watch huts go up in a boil of orange flame when his aluminum napalm tanks tumble into them. He gets hardened to pressing the firing button and cutting people down like little cloth dummies, as they sprint frantically under him. He gets his sword bloodied for the rougher things to come.

On Yankee Station, some hundreds of miles to the north, the shoe is definitely on the other foot. When you fly into North Vietnam against the triple-A and the SAMs (surface-to-air missiles), when the air is so full of flak bursts you can't see how you possibly can go through them unhit, the experience earned on Dixie stands you in good stead. Warm-up lasted a week to 10 days before you steam north into the real hell.

An aircraft carrier is probably the most spectacular fighting machine in the world. Its 4½-acre flight deck is the scene of concentrated sound and fury unmatched on any airfield. The number-one place to watch the action is from Primary Flight Control, a glassed-in control tower that juts out over the flight deck from the middle of the island. The air officer sits in a high padded chair inside this fishbowl where he can see the planes landing and taking off merely by turning his head. In my opinion, the air officer, and not the commander of the air group, has the most interesting job on a carrier. CAG is always the hero in the movies because he drives an airplane. But the guy who really has the blowtorch on his neck is the guy who drives *all* the planes—from that padded seat in Pri-Fly: the air officer, or air boss.

During flight quarters, when the steel parking area is a howling madhouse, when one little goof-up can snowball with dreadful speed into a major catastrophe, it's the air boss who unravels it all safely—or doesn't—depending on how cool, quick and experienced he is. Let's take a look at Pri-Fly on *Constellation* and let you watch a very cool and capable air boss, Comdr. Ken Enny, in action.

It's dark. The night launch is about to begin. Below, on the flight deck, an RA-5C Vigilante, configured as a long-range recon plane instead of a bomber, is buckled on the waist catapult. The wire-rope bridle that connects the plane to the takeoff shoe is taut. The holdback cable, with its sheerable link, has a high strain on it. The catapult crew has hooked up this monster and rolled out from under her belly. The last man out, who had to wait while the big bird built up a hard fury on her engines, tosses a final, casual thumbs-up, almost like he was throwing it away.

Now the lucite wand of the catapult launch officer does a brief pinwheel in the dark. There is a moment when nothing happens. Then the two tailpipes of the Vigilante glow like fiery eyes and there is a massive jump in the sound level, even through the double-paned glass of Pri-Fly. The RA-5C stabilizes in afterburners for an instant, then leaps down the catapult track and off the deck trailing gray steam, its twin tailpipes glaring in the night. Tatters of steam flutter and seethe backward, looking like clouds of red neon in the ship's battery of blood-red lights shining down from high on the island.

These red floodlights, incidentally, are new since the last war, when carrier decks were spooky wells of darkness lined with two strings of dull orange beads. A landing pilot used to get the disorienting sensation, as he sank down into that pit, that the deck wasn't really there, or that the carrier had suddenly reared up on end or performed some other weird gyration. The sensation is known as vertigo, and at times it made pilots suddenly fling the stick hard over and dive into the drink. But the red lights that now outline the deck in a ghostly glow orient the pilot much better, and since in the Tonkin Gulf and the South China Sea there is nobody coming out in an airplane to bother you, you might as well see what you are doing.

The Skyhawks follow the Vigilante onto the cats in the hissing thunder of the dark flight deck. These tiny, delta-winged, subsonic jet fighters have cockpits so small a big man is cramped. They were designed by Ed Heinemann, one of the great aircraft designers of our time, when he worked for Douglas, and are known by such names as "Heinemann's Hot Rods," "Tinker Toy Bombers," or aboard the carriers recently as "scooters." At one time these little planes were thought to have outlived their usefulness and were seen sitting forlornly down at the end of the ramp with canvas covers over their canopies, and if you walked up and kicked a tire, a bird might fly out of the gun port. Now the A-4 Skyhawks are not only out of mothballs, but a new version that uses the J-52 instead of the old J-65 engine is being widely used in Vietnam. The Marines also fly Skyhawks out of Chulai, south of Danang.

Skyhawks scoot off the deck like balsa gliders shot with a rubber sling. And here, of course, is where the air boss's headaches can begin. If an A-4 has to be moved off the catapult for some reason, and taken forward out of the way or shunted down to the hangar deck, the beautiful sequence that Ken Enny has been reeling off may start "going to worms," which is what they say in the Navy when an operation starts screwing up. There may not be another A-4 waiting to launch. There may be an F-4 waiting, which requires readjustment of the catapult steam pressure below decks to handle its greater weight. Then, after the F-4 is launched, it may have to orbit the carrier waiting for the other planes in its flight, which are buried in flight-deck traffic. By the time all of them join up and get started toward the target, there is a serious discrepancy in fuel aboard.

So Comdr. Ken Enny up in Pri-Fly likes to launch planes of the same kind in a flock. It simplifies the work of the catapult crew, and also works well for the pilots who are going out on a mission, since all of them start out with approximately the same fuel aboard.

After the Skyhawks get launched, Ken Enny watches his F-4s build up to fury, cut in their ABs and wallow, nose high, off the deck into the night. Suddenly, down below, the darkness is empty. Enny picks up the mike and speaks to the flight deck over the amplifiers. "Launch complete. Clear the decks and stand by to recover aircraft. . . ."

The previous flight is up there in the darkness waiting to come aboard, and very soon they start coming up the groove, slamming down hard and going to full blasting power as soon as the wheels touch the deck. You might expect them to pull off the power. The reason they don't is because if they get a "bolter" (the tail hook skittering over all the arresting wires without catching one), they need full power to get airborne again. Particularly with the F-4. To get on the power late— even a second late—in an F-4 is extremely dangerous. In the event of a go-around this big heavy plane will not rotate quickly once the nosewheel slams down. The night before I came aboard, *Constellation* lost a pilot and radar man in an F-4 on a night go-around attempt. All he did was hesitate with his power on a long landing—and when he finally got to it, it was too late. They went into the water with full burners. Neither survived.

The tensest time for the air boss is when he starts to recover his aircraft after a combat mission and everybody is coming in screaming "low state!" on his fuel. Maybe the situation is complicated by somebody with battle damage, and then, suddenly, there's an accident aboard and the air boss gets a foul deck. This is where he can either use his head, think quick and cool, and bring everybody aboard or get rattled and put them all in the water.

The air boss has lots of options. He has tankers stacked up above the carrier for people who get really critical. They can plug in and get a drink. He also has Tilly, the pushmobile, which can shove a badly garbled plane over the side if necessary. If he thinks far enough ahead, he can bingo some of the incoming planes to nearby Danang, on the Vietnamese mainland. But whatever he does, he has to do it fast and he has to do it right.

Running a carrier deck is like trying to hold a rubber horse under water. If you get the foreleg under, the hind leg tends to pop up, and so on. Every decision has to be based on all the planes in the air, not just on the one that's screaming bloody murder. You can't be a nice guy, and Ken Enny isn't, at least when he's working. He can be caustic as lye, and often is. Some of the pilots hate him with a passion. He doesn't mind. If he has to send a "nastygram"—a curt reprimand—to anybody, on deck or aloft, he doesn't hesitate. He would rather have people dislike him—but bring all his planes aboard instead of losing some at the bottom of the South China Sea—than be voted Mr. Wonderful. This, of course, is why they chose him for air boss in the first place.

Hundreds of things can screw up a launch. Sometimes the bridle gets stuck in the groove and the cat crew huddles around it like frantic bugs, prying and cursing. Or, as happened one day when I was watching Ken Enny run a launch, somebody can forget to put enough boilers on the line to keep up a big head of steam. It takes an enormous belch of steam pressure to hurl a steel monster like an F-4 from zero to 140 knots in a couple of hundred feet. And you don't dare fire unless you've got full pressure, or the plane dribbles off into the drink. The name for this embarrassing (and usually fatal) mishap is a "cold shot."

The most fearful accident I have ever seen on a flight deck (although it was mild compared to some I heard about) happened on the way down from Japan to Subic Bay. An F-4, with a 600-gallon auxiliary fuel tank mounted on its centerline, was being launched from the port waist cat. It was a hot day and the plane was grossed out at max, so it was necessary to go to full afterburners during the holdback. The burners were roaring and belching flames when the big F-4 broke her sheer link and leaped down the deck. But the massive G-loads of the catapult were too much for the teardrop tank, and it came apart like wet paper, spewing raw jet fuel over the men on the deck and in the catwalk. Some were drenched. A fraction of a second later the blazing afterburners torched the fuel and the whole forward part of the deck was a rolling cloud of fire. Out of it raced human torches, screaming in agony. The whole sequence occurred—from everything normal to a sickening horror—in about a tenth of a second.

Comdr. Ken Enny fully earned a year's pay in the next 10 seconds. Men were screaming at him over the phones to pull the chain and flood the place with seawater, lest the whole carrier turn into a torch. At the same time, an A-4 Skyhawk was sitting on the adjacent catapult, completely enveloped in fire, engine pulling full power, with the pilot not knowing if he'd be launched any second.

But Ken Enny didn't panic and pour tons of saltwater on the fire, since the fuel was going to burn out very quickly by itself anyway. Besides, the seawater could have done so much harm to the catapult mechanisms as it poured down the groove to the insides of the ship that the waist cat would have been out of commission for weeks. So Enny sat tight. Then he picked up his mike and began giving his orders— calm, deliberate, positive.

He told the A-4 pilot to hold full power lest he be accidentally fired off the cat in the excitement. He told the below-decks crew to secure all launches immediately. He called Damage Control and Sick Bay and told them to move in on the double. Because he was cool and deliberate, he did not make any mistakes and he got off all his messages fast and ungarbled. What might have turned into a real nightmare was stopcocked in a few critical moments. Thirty-two men were burned, four of them seriously, but nobody was killed.

Later, an A-4 pilot in the Blue Tail Fly Squadron, who saw the fire from 15,000, told me he thought there'd been a deck crash of major proportions and that the whole ship might start burning. But the carrier was relatively undamaged and flights ops went forward as soon as the burned men were evacuated below.

It is fascinating to watch seasoned flight-deck directors as they move with their jets while these firebreathing monsters taxi and turn. The director runs alongside a deadly, invisible furnace of fire, with his head maybe a foot or so to the side. He stays in close, like a bullfighter to a bull. When the plane pivots, he ducks under and bobs up on the other side. It is a little like watching a ballet dancer whose partner is death. The front end of a jet, too, is lethal. When an F-8, for example, with its low intake scoop, goes to full power, anybody standing close to it can be snatched in and crammed down the maw of the monster. This has happened more than once. Or a tug, racing to hook up to a downed plane, can run over your foot, or over you. Or you may be standing around minding your own business, and a jet may turn up suddenly and blow you off the edge of the deck. (The drop to the sea is more than eight floors.) Add to all this the fact that the deck handlers—directors, fuel gang, damage control, ord-nance, maintenance, arresting gear, catapult, plane captains—work very long hours indeed. The directors work the longest and hardest of them all. The average, I am told, is about 15 hours a day, once the carrier reaches Yankee Station and starts its furious tempo of raids against North Vietnam.

I spent time with Damage Control, the rescue squad aboard a carrier, and was issued my own red jersey and red cloth helmet with its bulbous Mickey Mouse ear defenders. On *Constellation* they have two big, rugged youngsters in aluminum suits, who lower their fire-proof helmets with their glass observation windows and wade into the flames to rescue people. Damage Control is in charge of Tilly, the monster yellow pushmobile with the man-high rubber tires, which can shove a burning jet over the side if need be. The leading petty officers wear portable transceivers inside their red helmets and can talk back and forth with other key people on deck—including Comdr. Enny up in Pri-Fly.

One of the most frightening hazards of being on the flight deck is the breaking of an arresting cable. When this happens, the loose ends of the cable curl fiercely backward, dragged by the automatic retraction motors, and lash around like nightmare snakes. If they hit your legs they cut them off like a big knife. Several ghastly accidents were described to me where men lost legs or were cut in half above the hips. I was told of one very cool head who did not try to run. He waited for the cable and in the fraction of a heartbeat when it slashed at him, he hopped nimbly up in the air, and the steel razor whizzed past underneath.

On Dixie Station, our task force consisted of six carriers: *Constellation, Intrepid, Oriskany, Ranger, Hancock* and *Yorktown;* two missile-firing cruisers: *Chicago* and *St. Paul;* and a number of destroyers. An ammunition ship, *Sacramento,* came alongside at regular intervals and replenished the carriers with ordnance. The bombs, tanks of napalm, pods of rockets and other explosive weapons were hauled across on a pulley that moves on ropes between carrier and ammo ship. Helicopters are also used to transfer the ordnance.

An attack carrier the size of *Constellation* carries two 14-plane A-4 Skyhawk squadrons, two 14-plane F-4 Phantom squadrons, one 12-plane A-6 Intruder squadron, one six-plane Vigilante squadron, a four-plane tanker outfit composed of modified Douglas Skywarriors, a twin-engine Grumman COD plane for transporting people and mail, three Kaman UH-2B helicopters, and—last but not least—a detachment of new Grumman E-2A Hawkeyes, an advanced radar picket plane used to sweep the skies for attacking aircraft and give the ship's Combat Air Patrol sufficient time to leap off and make an intercept far from the ship.

The E-2A Hawkeye is a vastly more sophisticated follow-on to the older Grumman WF-2 radar picket plane that was known as the "Willie Fudd." Quite naturally, the new plane is called the "Super Fudd." It is a twin-engined propjet that looks like a flying pancake, because of the 24-foot radome it carries on its back. The entire radome rotates at six rpm. The Super Fudd can orbit at 30,000 feet, and its 11,000 pounds of airborne electronics gear is the most sophisticated for its size in existence. Some enthusiastic Grumman engineers say that the E-2A can do everything the carrier's entire Combat Information Center can do. (The CIC is a place the size of the Waldorf Ballroom and is filled with every kind of radar and radio available.)

The Super Fudd's job is to keep a sharp radar watch on everything within reach of its electronic eyes and to act fast if it sees something it doesn't like. If it spots attackers approaching, it can instantaneously provide information on altitude, course, range and speed, and even name the best weapon for counterattack. It can handle many bogies at a time. The Super Fudd can also double in spades as the director of a fighter-bomber strike into the land mass of Vietnam. By fixing its own position in reference to a known landmark, it can direct Skyhawks to a distant target whose coordinates are known. The little birds can't drop their bombs—target unseen—on remote signal from the E-2A. However, they can be set up close to the target, with good accuracy, and can then "punch down through the glue" (penetrate the cloud cover) and hit by surprise. Or, on a clear day, the little jets can be guided in at treetop level and told when to pop up, take a fast look, roll in, hit and jink like hell for safety.

Thus the E-2A is an airborne control platform for both defense and offense. But like its sister plane, the Grumman A-6, it needs top maintenance on the black boxes to be effective. A final plus for this odd-looking bird: It is stressed like a fighter and turns on a dime. The F-4, which can fly rings around it as far as speed goes, can't turn sharply enough to get on its tail in a rat race. Which is something nice for the Super Fudd guys to think about if the MiGs ever start coming out over the water looking for them.

The McDonnell F-4 Phantom, the huge pot-bellied jet fighter powered by two General Electric J-79s, looks as if it had its horizontal stabilizer mounted upside down. I went to Mach 2.15 in the back seat of an F-4 out of NAS Oceana, in Virginia, back in January, 1962, when the F-4 was fairly new in the Navy's inventory. Now, of course, the Air Force has swallowed its pride and bought the F-4 in large numbers too. The F-4 has proved it can do things—bomb, strafe, take pictures, you name it—better than almost anything. It can also fight, which is nice, since it was designed as a fighter.

I talked to Maj. Paul Gilmore and Bill Smith, his rear-seat pilot (not navigator! Smith said if I called him a navigator he'd fly to New Jersey and wipe me out!) at Danang later in my trip about their MiG-21. It was the first one knocked down in combat and was important because people had been saying (even as they said of the MiG-15 in Korea) that it was a very good airplane and probably more than a match for the F-4. Gilmore and Smith described their fight in detail and from what they told me, history seems to be repeating itself. The MiG-15 could out-climb the F-86 in Korea, but the F-86 pilots could out-think and out-fly the MiG-15 pilots and clobbered them at a rate of six to one. Gilmore and Smith out-thought and out-flew this guy in the MiG-21, and knocked him down with a heat-seeking missile. Later, while I was in Danang two other members of the 480th Tactical Fighter Squadron out-thought and out-flew two more MiG-21s and shot them down.

The RA-5 Vigilante is one of the classiest-looking aircraft flying anywhere. It looks like a barracuda, or a vampire bat with its ears laid back. It drills through the air like a cutting bit. It was originally designed by North American as a bomber, but the RA-5 has now been largely modified as a recon plane.

The RA-5 takes films of much greater sophistication than was possible with its forerunner, the Ling-Temco-Vought F-8U Crusader configured for cameras. It has cameras that look ahead, down and to the sides. It takes pictures in color, black-and-white, infrared and radar. It can fly low over a SAM site at over 1,000 knots and stop the action so dead with its synchronized high-speed cameras that you can see the worried expressions on the faces of the ground crew.

The RA-5 can also fly high enough to photograph half of North Vietnam's Red River Valley on one negative, but it doesn't, because at that altitude its chances of dodging a SAM aren't too good. In fact, even down low, several Vigilantes have been lost. It is a very touchy bird to get back on the ship. It lands hotter than anything else—about 165 knots at touchdown—and if you come in a little too fast you can blow a nose gear. There are also severe control problems close to the deck, when you get in the island burble, and only the old pro instructor pilots really feel at home in the groove. (One guy who *never* feels at home in the groove is the camera operator in the back seat. He's got only two small portholes to look out of, and all he can see is sky. The only way he knows if they made it is if no water comes in after the RA-5 stops moving.)

One of the squadrons aboard the *Constellation* had a skipper I liked. His name was Comdr. Jim Morin, and he was a fresh-faced Boston Irishman with a twinkle in his eyes. If you looked close you saw the squint wrinkles and the flat stare that came when he meant business, and you knew that this man had been around the bases. He was 38 and on his last tour of combat. He was commanding officer for the Silver Foxes, who flew A-4 Skyhawks with the new J-52 engines. Also, he had a sense of humor. One day we were sitting in his Ready Room when the typist hidden somewhere in the bowels of the carrier, whose job it was to type commands that then appeared on a large yellow luminous screen in all the ready rooms, began one of his "unpredictable voyages of discovery," as Jim referred to his madly garbled transmissions. You might think the Navy would pick a good typist for so important a job. But no. The boy started out briskly: PILOTS MAN YOUR. Then there was a pause. Then, for some reason, four dots appeared, followed purposefully by a single letter L. Another pause. Four more dots. The man seemed to be working up to something. Suddenly, in a staccato burst, he typed PILOY. There was a somewhere longer pause as the typist gathered himself for a supreme effort. It came out in a dynamic single burst: PIHOTS MAN YOUR PLANQB.

Comdr. Morin looked at me. "I think he's trying to tell us something," he said gravely. "I'm pretty sure that's it."

I asked Jim Morin once if he was worried about going into combat over North Vietnam. Was he afraid of the heavy flak there? "Afraid, my good man?" Morin asked. "I don't know the meaning of the word. I'm utterly fearless and always have been." Then he said, a bit grimly, "Sure I'm scared of the flak. We all are until we get in it. Then we're too busy."

"How about SAMs?"

"No big thing," Comdr. Morin said. "But a fellow usually bends his bird around rather smartly when he sees one coming up."

One Air Force pilot I talked to at Danang showed me the wings of his F-4. They were ragged, as if they'd been shredded with a giant grater. "That happened during a turn," the pilot told me. "The turn was brought on when I observed a SAM coming." He grinned. "It got my attention," he said.

Lt. Comdr. Pete Garber of the A-6 Squadron was the *Constellation's* toughest veteran. He had the blocky build of a football player and a butch haircut that made his weather-beaten face look even more rugged. This was his third tour of bombing North Vietnam.

Some people go into combat because they are ordered to do so, and are relieved when it's over. But Pete Garber lived for combat. Furthermore, he had a fixation. He was after the Than Hoa Bridge, which he said was the "big status symbol" target in North Vietnam. This is an open-work steel bridge, quite narrow, constructed on massive boulders hewn to fit like a great "dry wall." Navy and Air Force planes have been after it for some time. They've missed it by 10 feet with 3,000-pounders and it didn't so much as quiver. They have tossed 2,000-pounders through its steel girders but the bombs blew up too late and the trucks were moving the next day. All in all, Garber said, just about every gung-ho pilot in both the Air Force and Navy had taken a crack at the Than Hoa Bridge. Some had dive-bombed it. Some had tried flying up the valley and skipping bombs against the piers. But they didn't all get off without getting hurt because the Than Hoa Bridge is surrounded by masses of big and little guns that sprouted like steel asparagus. That spelled excitement to Pete Garber. "That bridge belongs to me," he said. "I've got a system that'll drop it for sure."

"What's that?"

"I'm going there with a max load and I'm going to come down the highway about 15 feet off the deck and salvo them at a slight angle with the bridge so I walk them through it."

Nobody in the room argued. Pete Garber had done things like this before. He paid no attention to flak. When he got on a bomb run, all he could see was the target. Now he had the airplane for the job, the Grumman A-6 Intruder, which was, at the moment, under the spotlight. Grumman wouldn't admit it, but they had sent the top people in their black-box department to make very sure the A-6s were calibrated to the closest possible tolerances and held there. Scuttlebutt had it that if the A-6 did well on this tour there would be a very big Navy buy and maybe even serious consideration by the Air Force.

Pete Garber's squadron was only the third to use the A-6 in combat. It's not a very pretty airplane. It has a lump of a front end and a skinny tail that gives it the appearance, in the air, of a huge flying tadpole. The plane comes aboard, however, with its funny wing-tip flaps out, like a great big Piper Cub. McDonnell's F-4, on the other hand, comes aboard like a truck falling off a cliff. It ramrods through the burbling air thrown off the island structure without much displacement. The A-6 wallows and bucks like a Cub, but hits the deck with far less impact than the F-4. The A-6 is a subsonic airplane in a supersonic war, but it's built to fly on the darkest nights, in rain, clouds and fog, and its black boxes can deliver the bombs almost as accurately under these conditions as other planes can in daylight. Of course, it takes a staff of genuises working full time to keep these boxes on the money, and it takes a bomber-navigator (who sits up front beside the pilot in the big plexiglass cockpit) with a year's hard study and practice to be able to use the system.

The two Pratt & Whitney J-52 engines buried in the Grumman's tadpole belly are little jewels; they are reliable, have the power and aren't at all greedy about fuel. This funny-looking plane can carry 7½ tons of bombs (the biggest payload for a plane of its power), and can go almost anywhere you want.

Regarding the A-6, Pete Garber says, "I have a simple solution to this war. We just take all the other planes off the carrier, and load it with A-6s. We keep them in perfect bombing shape. We wait for dark nights and heavy rain. We go out and wipe out the targets. We come home and land and spend the rest of the time in Singapore on R and R."

Pete Garber was kidding, but there is a certain amount of truth in what he says. It is admitted, even by those who are not partial to the A-6, that it could run a carrier dry of bombs faster than the ammunition supply ship could lug them out from the beach for the "unrep" (underway replenishment).

A few days before the first Dixie Station strike against "warm-up" targets in the Mekong Delta, an Air Force major named Young had come out to *Constellation* from Saigon to brief the pilots on what to expect if they had to bail out over South or North Vietnam. Maj. Young had been shot down over Germany in World War II and had successfully escaped and evaded, so he had earned the right to speak.

"I'm not going to fuss at you chaps about roots and tubers and that sort of thing," Young said in his British accent. "Fact is, you won't be able to escape and evade very well in this war. If you go down, one of two things will happen rather quickly: Either we'll get to you—or they will."

But the odds that American rescue helicopters would pick them up, Young assured them, were very high indeed, and the most important survival tool was the radio. "If I were going out," Young stated, "I'd not worry about these little medical doodads and those pearl-handled .45s you're all so proud of. I'd hang two extra radios round my neck just in case I banged one up in my landing."

Young pointed out that the radio beeper would bring American rescue aircraft to the spot if the pilot or his wingman got out a position report that was reasonably accurate. Once the rescue helicopters and their escort planes were overhead, the pilot could direct his own rescue by using a two-way radio.

A smaller proportion of battle-wounded Americans are dying in Vietnam than in any war in our history, in spite of the steaming, disease-ridden jungles in which they must fight. Why? Because of the revolutionary application of the airplane to the saving of soldiers' lives.

The essence of it all is the speed with which men are brought to fully equipped hospitals after they are hit in combat; and the medical facilities—doctors, antibiotics and even surgery in the planes and choppers while they are lifting the wounded out of the field.

The sequence begins with helicopter pickups, often right in the middle of a jungle fire-fight. At least four out of five wounded men are picked up almost immediately after they're hit, and airlifted to a field hospital within a few minutes. After treatment, they are airlifted to a transfer point where a C-123 medevac plane takes them to a big base hospital. If they need specialized care and can travel, they go directly from the transfer point by C-130 or C-141 to the Philippines, to Hawaii, or even back to the States.

No war in history has seen such efficient, prompt and skillful handling of the sick and wounded. A very small percentage of men with treatable wounds die in Vietnam. If you're hit, you're usually out of there inside the hour and in the capable hands of skilled surgeons who are all geared to get you through.

Maj. Young displayed a device he called a "forest penetrator" that drops down from the rescue chopper on a cable. It looked like an enormous steel punch, which is what it really was. Three little fold-in stubs could be pulled down out of its body and used for seats after it had punched down through the treetops.

Young said that some downed pilots, agitated by the sound of Vietcong bullets snicking through the foliage, don't wait to deploy the seats. They leap at the penetrator, wrap arms and legs around it, and shout at the winch man in the chopper to hoist away. "They lifted one chap nearly two miles high in this manner, before they reeled him in," Young said. "A VC automatic weapon was making Swiss cheese out of them and they were anxious to be off."

Young had been lecturing on survival for many years and had developed an interesting and often humorous delivery, salted with funny—and obscene—stories. There was one simple doctrine to follow if you were hit anywhere near the sea. If the plane would fly at all you stayed in it and tried to make the water. Even if it was burning brightly. Even if parts were falling off. If, Young said, you could cross the controls, lean forward, stroke your St. Christopher's medal or perform any other useful emergency procedure, you stayed in the airplane until you were sitting there flying the seat. The South China Sea was your friend. Everybody on the ground in South or North Vietnam (when you floated down in a parachute, at least) must be considered an enemy.

Grumman twin-engine amphibians (HU-16s) are based in Danang. One of them is always on station over the Tonkin Gulf waiting for a mayday. If you could bail out at least a mile from shore (preferably five, since enemy shore batteries shoot at you like mad), your chances of being picked up without injury were good. The HU-16 Albatross lands beside you, hauls you aboard and takes you to the hospital at Danang. If you needed a specialist, medevac planes would take you to Clark Field, in the Philippines, or all the way back to the United States on a new Lockheed C-141 Jet Starlifter. So actually, even if you're sitting in the South China Sea, you're only hours from home.

The flight surgeon then spoke about new antimalarial tablets being introduced to combat an especially dangerous form of malaria found in the highlands around Pleiku; about a new super-wonder drug called Tetracycline that, in ointment form, can cure the dreaded trachoma; about the fact that a cloth sack of Bull Durham chewing tobacco, soaked in water and dripped on a leech, will cause him to let go; and about a new system being taught on snakebite. The old system involved putting on a tourniquet first, then cutting an X over the bite, and then applying a suction cup to the wound. Common sense should have come into this picture long ago and now, apparently, it has. The thing to worry about is the poison. The more of it you can remove from the bite the better. The longer you fool around fixing tourniquets and getting out razor blades, the more chance the poison has to circulate in the body, which it does with fearful speed. So the thing to do, if you're bitten on the arm or hand or any part of the body within reach of your mouth is grab that bitten place and clamp your mouth over it *instantly* and suck, suck, suck, like you were trying to pull the marrow out of your very bones. If you are very quick you can get a lot of the poison out in the first few seconds before it has a chance to go anyplace.

One interesting thing Young brought out is that a man can go for a long time with no food at all, if he has water. Young said not to spend a lot of time fiddling with deadfalls and snares. If you were down in Vietnam and the VC by some miracle had not found you, never mind hunting for food. Get to the highest ground in the neighborhood and stay in the deepest tangle of vegetation and, if your radio wasn't working, climb a tree and wait until you saw a plane, which should be soon because we have so many planes of all types flying around this relatively small country. Try to zap the pilot in the eye with your signaling mirror. If it's an overcast day or growing dusk, and he can see your flare or tracer fire from your pistol, take a chance and let loose. You may bring the VC, but if you get the pilot's attention, he'll bring choppers and A-1 Skyraiders to suppress ground attacks on you, and he'll do it quick—by radio.

Typical of the pilots in Maj. Young's audience who were about to get their first taste of combat was Lt. "Zap" Zlatoper, of the A-6 Intruder Squadron. I had met Zap first in the Officers' Club in Yokosuka, Japan, when *Constellation* had stopped there to get briefed by the pilots of the *Kitty Hawk*, a sister carrier that had returned from Yankee Station that week. Zap had the pink, unlined face of a happy teenager and his nickname quite appropriately was "Baby-San." He entertained us once in Yokosuka by singing several delightfully unprintable Navy songs like "Shagging Riley's Daughter." And a middle-aged woman in the audience, when it was explained to her that Zap would eventually go forth into the sleet storm of steel over North Vietnam, was heard to say, "That boy is too young and sweet to go there." Zap, on the evening before his first Mekong Delta strike, didn't consider himself young and sweet at all. He explained, a bit testily, that he was 25 years old, and it wasn't his fault if he looked 15. "I know you want me to tell you how scared I am and all," he said to me. "I know you want to put that in your story. But I have to tell you the truth. A couple of other guys and I are just going to the room to play some bridge."

2 SHORE LEAVE

All the Navy ships operating the South China Sea between Vietnam and the Philippines go back into Subic Bay from time to time for resupply, minor repairs, and to give the crew a chance to relax on the beach before going back to the action. Before a ship like the *Connie* goes into port, the chaplain usually gets on the public address system, which is turned to the complete circuit of speakers so that his words can be carried to every part of the ship, and makes a little speech about the temptations you may expect to find ashore, and how it's a good idea, both as a God-fearing Christian and a VD-fearing sinner, to watch yourself. Don't get drunk, fight or fool around with the girls. It's likely to bring you grief. Then the chaplain quotes some statistics of casualties from brawls and other unfortunate preventable incidents and prays for his 5,300 charges and click, you're on your own.

I personally enjoy shore leave—even as an aged, white-haired correspondent—almost as much as the sailors. The truth is, you may only live once, and like the man said, "If that frail machine known as the human body, which can and does dish out liberal helpings of light, intermediate and severe pain, can give you some pleasures—grab them. You may never pass this way again." I am past the age when girls are a problem but I do enjoy six or eight scotches and if the noise level in a club reaches the volume of a moderately active fire fight, and a couple of little fist fights break out here and there, well, it does break the monotony. Not to be bested by the some 5,300 officers, enlisted men and tech reps on the *Connie,* I got a fistful of funny money at the gate of the Subic Bay (Philippines) Naval Base gate and fared forth with several friends into a town called Olongapo, which is well known to seafaring men who ply Asian waters. There are perhaps 20,000 people in town. About half of them wear a passion flower behind one ear, and this doesn't include the "Benny Boys" who cater, it was said, to the homo trade. The action is very wild. I was told in sober sincerity that people have had their wallets stolen while gripping them inside their pants pockets.

The town is mainly a couple of main drags—mud streets that are solidly jammed with American jeeps that have been somehow obtained by local Philippine owners and painted as insanely and colorfully as human imagination plus buckets of bright-pink, poison-blue, passion-purple, lettuce-green, blood-red paint can make them. These jeeps have an entry step in the rear and you sit on benches facing each other. The only limit on passengers is how many people can be crammed in. Some vehicles featured fringe on the roof, and others were spectacularly named: "Luis's Limping Leopard"; or carried an ad for a popular combo: "Hear Mamba Sam and the Shit Kickers! No cover! No minimum! Hottest girls in town!"

There may be no cover and no minimum but the prices they charge per drink in these places (shrewdly gauged by how drunk you are and what kind of folding money you fumble up out of your billfold) are sometimes astronomical. If you get confused about the change, you don't have time to present your case—the waitress is long gone and nobody understands your problem if you try to bring it up with the management. Of course the bar girls drink shots of tea or colored water, which you pay for at the rate of a dollar a shot on the theory that you are buying them scotch. If you ask to taste the shots, the girls get on the ball and drain them, and if you persist, they may tell you to get lost. There are plenty of customers who aren't chincy about wanting to taste their drinks!

The girls, as might be expected, aren't bashful. You sit down at a bar stool in the middle of an empty bar and 10 seconds later a soft voluptuous arm creeps over your shoulder and you get a whiff of some kind of powerful perfume and look sideways at a girl or a woman. She could be gorgeous (if you are a young, handsome sailor) or she could have been around for quite awhile and show it. She could, in fact, be so rugged looking you might scream with fear at the sight of her purple, semi-toothless lips drooping invitingly six inches from your own.

I went into a cafe with some friends off the *Connie*. They said they always came here and were known and so we didn't have to worry about being rolled or gypped except on the drinks, which was standard everywhere. It was a second-floor place with great open screens where the palm trees rustled. Except you couldn't hear any sound less powerful than a machine gun when we topped the stairs, because the orchestra was beating out a rock 'n' roll tune as if they were intent on smashing their instruments instead of playing them. The dance floor was crowded but one couple really stood out. In fact, they were so spectacular that the other sailors, who normally ran around aggressively, trying to start fights by accidently-on-purpose ramming an elbow in your ribs, were giving them space in the center of the floor to do their stuff. The girl was about 16, I would judge, with a body that was encumbered by only the mere vestiges of clothing, skin the color of warm honey, and so shapely only the queers were drinking: everybody else was bug-eyed, staring. The sailor was young, blond, handsome; he was high as a kite and thoroughly engrossed in his work. The lovely young girl had spread her thighs widely and semi-wrapped them around the boy, and he had sort of crouched down and was holding her buttocks tightly with both hands. It seemed, on first look, that they were actually having sexual intercourse. Come to find out, when the music ended, they hadn't been. The sailor's fly was buttoned. So it was just a normal dance (as I found out, since many others were performing in a similar manner; their physical charms were less spectacular but their interest in their work was just as dedicated).

We took our seats at a table and a woman who seemed to be the madam of the place, about 45 or so, with gold teeth and beautifully frizzed hair, sat down beside me and said, "H'lo Papasan. You want a drink?" I said I'd like a drink, and my now-firmly-esconced girl friend waved grandly to the waiter to bring me a scotch and her a brandy. Well, I took this to mean two things: (1) Madam knew a big-spending sucker from America when she saw one; and (2) I'd made a mistake in ordering a drink. Now it would be a little difficult to shake Gold Tooth without disrupting the happy little gathering of girls who had appeared from different directions and had drawn up chairs beside my several Navy friends. These were girls who offered a fairly wide range of charms. If you liked them thin and lithe, with a beauty mark and a spit curl, there was one like that. If you liked them plump with bee-stung lips and breasts bulging massively up out of their low-cut dress, there was one like that. If you wanted a mere child of say 14, there was a mere child of 14 with large eyes and a TB-looking pallor. If you wanted a pretty Negro girl, you could have her. The table was surrounded by an extravagance of riches. To rise and take flight would have been, in a sense, a retreat in the presence of the action.

"Papasan," Madam said, rubbing her thigh against mine, "you like Olongapo, eh?"

"It's pretty active," I said.

"Akteev?" Madam said, putting her hand on my leg. "Who is thees word akteev?"

"Look," I said, retrieving my privacy as best I could by moving my chair away a couple of inches (all the room there was), *"No quiero amor. Yo tengo una mujer."*

"Señor!" Madam cried, entranced. *"Usted habla español!"* (She then let loose a long volley of Spanish that I couldn't understand.)

"Un poco," I said. *"Yo hablo un poco. Pero yo no entiendo mucho."*

"Yes, yes, yes!" Madam cried. "You can speak a little but you cannot understand it. *Verdad?"*

"Verdad."

"And you have a wife at home and do not want to make love."

"That's it."

"Don't worry, *señor,"* Madam said magnanimously. "I

married too. Have childs. *No necessario,* love. We drink, eh?"

"Good," I said, gladly willing to settle for the dollar-a-shot tea as the price of escaping the roving hands, the gold teeth and the delightfully frizzed hair.

My friends, in the meantime, had managed somehow to offend several of the girls who had ringed us in and were sitting in chairs they had pushed up for that purpose. Several of the girls rose haughtily and left. A couple of others were glaring at my friends. But my friends weren't concerned. One of them, a CPO, had selected the buxom girl with the bee-stung lips. The other chap, a young sailor who appeared almost as lost in the place as I was feeling, had apparently become stuck with the 14-year-old TB victim.

Drinks for everybody were naturally being hustled in by the alert waiters. The band was again assaulting its instruments. Pandemonium reigned. A bill in local currency for what turned out later to be eight dollars was thrust into my hand. Madam squeezed my wrist and smiled encouragingly. I paid the bill. My own drink, when I tasted it, might or might not have been scotch. It seemed mildly alcholic. I drank it slowly. At these prices even rich Yankee suckers can't get too carried away.

I hung around about an hour, and the GIs bought a couple of rounds and I bought a couple of rounds, and Madam made one more effort. She said she had a house not far from there. It was all fixed up with pictures and rugs. She wanted to take me there and show me the lovely pictures and rugs. It seemed to me the reverse switch on the Park Avenue lad who invites the young thing up to his penthouse to see his etchings. I replied that I would love to see the pictures and rugs but that I had to meet a friend, and by jingo—I looked at my watch—I was late now! Whereupon I dragged myself up to my feet and saw Madam looking at me, and saw that suddenly, in the moment it had taken me to rise, she had dismissed me as a prospect, as a human being, as existing at all. She was staring with professional interest at another old sucker who'd just come in. I leaned over and told my friends I was leaving, and made my way through the bedlam to the stairs and down to the street, where I was accosted by a pimp who offered me "young girl, virgin, clean, beautiful—20 dollars."

I guess everybody has a breaking point, and I'd just been

hustled out of 20 or so dollars for absolutely nothing, and my head ached. "Beat it, bub," I said, and my tone was not exactly friendly. Neither was his reply. I know enough Spanish to know what he called me in Spanish. "You're a little son-of-a-whore, yourself," I said, and we parted. I don't mind paying, but like any other normal ugly American, I don't like my nose rubbed in it. But I hasten to add that I do not in any way blame the folks in Olongapo for their little con games, their purse snatching, their whoring, their pimping and their lack of morals. Nobody forced me off the ship and into the streets of Olongapo. And if I were a Filipino and lived in Olongapo, I might very well work me up a nice little purse-snatching business of my own. After all, those Americans can spare it. Everybody knows the bloody streets in the United States are paved with gold!

An exciting climax awaited me on the Navy bus, which transports men inside the Navy base from the gate to the ship. I had been aboard the *Connie* for weeks and everybody knew I was a writer gathering material on the air war in Vietnam, and I suspect (although I could be wrong) that my friends, the sailors, put on this event for my benefit. At any rate, an argument started over something so trivial I can't remember what it was. It quickly burgeoned into a shouting and gesticulating session, all hands on their feet. This, in turn, while the bus was rolling along, became a wild free-for-all, with curses, thuds of fists and shrill, excited sounds from the native driver. I myself am naturally timid, in addition to being old and out of shape, so I scrunched down in my seat, put my arms over my head and hoped I didn't look like a combatant. Nobody actually struck me, although several sailors fell on me rather heavily. Then a face appeared down by my feet, under the mass of struggling bodies, with roguish eyes and a certain amount of nosebleed.

"Hey, sir!" the face yelled happily up at me. "Getting lots of material for your book?"

A few moments later, the driver stopped the bus and the shore patrol surged in and dragged a lot of my buddies away, cursing happily. I was sorry to see them go.

My most memorable contact aboard *Constellation* was Damage Controlman First-Class Williams. I had unofficially joined the Red Shirts (who are the rescue squad on the flight deck of a carrier), been issued my own red shirt, red helmet and flight-deck shoes, and Williams more or less took me in hand lest I get squashed by a tug or blown off into the ocean by a swiveling jet. He was known to everybody aboard the ship, including the captain, as "Sweet Willie." He could out-work, out-fight and out-curse anybody aboard. When his hot brown eyes focused on you, and his fearsome mustache quivered, and he took a deep breath and bellowed, "LISTEN, YOU MOTHER———!" (his customary way of getting your attention), you braced yourself to dash and do it, whatever it was—and quick. By this I do not intend to imply that Williams obtained obedience merely through fear. Fear accounted for only 98 percent of it. There was at least two percent of sincere love and devotion to this inspiring leader.

Willie was seen at 7:00 in the morning, the first day we docked at Subic Bay, leading a loyal little band of damage controlmen through the gate in the direction of Olongapo, shouting something deathless like, "Last man stoned out of his mind gets four extra sea watches!" When visions of admirals and generals fade, and the captains and the kings depart, I will still remember Sweet Willie with his ferocious mustache, burning eyes, and cool, tough, on-the-ball comportment on that hellish concentration of sound-and-fury known as a carrier flightdeck. A fine man to go on liberty with if you like to be where the action is. And don't mind taking on a dozen or so blokes off some destroyer, on the spur of the moment, with no holds barred and last man standing buys the drinks.

3 SAIGON

In the good old days BAS (Before Arthur Sylvester), newsmen wishing to write stories about the U. S. Air Force could count on a free ride to the location involved on any aircraft that might be going there. But due to loud complaints by commercial airlines hungry for cash sales of tickets, this delightful mode of travel had been eliminated by Mr. Sylvester, Assistant to the Secretary of Defense for Public Affairs. I was sitting on the aircraft carrier *Constellation,* about 60 miles off the coast and about 100 miles as the crow flies from Saigon, but I could not hop on the COD plane that left almost daily to land at that city for conferences and such. No, I had to take that selfsame COD plane 300 miles back to Subic Bay, then work my way to Mánila by boat, fight the battle of the visas (very difficult in Manila) and purchase a ticket on Air France for Tan Son Nhut in Saigon—all of which took, instead of less than an hour, nearly a week! This is not a disgruntled blast at Mr. Sylvester, now retired and who, despite many opinions to the contrary, this reporter believes did a very difficult job very well. It was just the way the ball bounced.

When I arrived at Tan Son Nhut on an Air France jet from Manila I was, as most new arrivals usually are, nervous about being blown up by a terrorist's grenade. I came down the steps from the plane alertly, eyes peeled for the little flicker of motion that would mean a tossed bomb, ready to hit the deck with my arms over my head. The airport was jammed with people. Nobody seemed alarmed in any way. It was hot and muggy. I noticed several persons sleeping on the airport benches. Customs, to my surprise, was quick and uncomplicated, and in a few minutes I found myself duly "signed in" and ready to start working on my story. I felt scared, lonely and disorganized. All I had to show anybody was an invitation from my friend, Maj. George Weiss, USAF, who presumably was hidden somewhere in this frightening place.

I went into a booth presided over by a middle-aged lady in one of those natty uniforms that ladies who look after lonely boys newly inducted into the armed services usually wear. She was, at the moment, involved with two or three such boys, and was talking earnestly into a phone. She glanced at me in a harassed way, made some sort of motion I took to mean she'd be with me as soon as she could, and said into the phone, "I can't imagine what happened to it. I sent it with the Vietnamese driver two hours ago. . . . Yes, I know it's only 10 minutes over to your building. . . ." From outside was heard the approaching freight-train roar of a taking-off jet, and the rest of the lady's words were drowned out. I spied a phone on the wall and went over to it. Three phone books hung on chains beside the phone. All of them were curled over and greasy from having been thumbed at. I examined them and found that they all seemed to be different, yet all seemed to be concerned somehow with Tan Son Nhut.

A big sergeant with a paratrooper patch on his sleeve was sitting nearby reading *Stars and Stripes*. I told him I was trying to get in touch with Maj. George Weiss, and he grinned. "Fella," he said, "we probably got four or five Maj. George Weisses around here. What outfit's he with?"

"Air Force Public Information."

The sergeant, who was an old hand, did not try to explain it. He rose, thumbed through one of the phone books, came upon the number we wanted, dialed it and handed me the phone. In a moment a voice said, "Seventh Air Force Public Information, Sergeant Shonyo speaking." I explained who I was and asked for George Weiss. Weiss wasn't there. Where was he? On leave in Kuala Lumpu, be back in a week—but Col. O'Hara was there.

Dave O'Hara is a friend of mine from years back, when he was a captain, and when he came on he said, "Hey, Frank, where the hell are you?"

"Standing here in the Tan Son Nhut passenger terminal," I said.

"You got hotel reservations?"

"No. I just got off the plane."

"Hang tight," Col. O'Hara said. "We'll pick you up in a couple of minutes."

Col. O'Hara was filling in for Col. McGinty, who had gone on TDY, and he introduced me to Maj. George Larrieux, a photography officer in the building, who shared an apartment with George Weiss. Larrieux took me there through the streets of Saigon in an Air Force staff car. The streets of Saigon had been built to handle a city of 100,000. Now it had grown to 2,500,000. A few blocks outside the Tan Son Nhut gate was "Chicken Corner," a place where a number of streets intersect. There was no traffic light. No policeman stood there to direct which street had the right to disgorge its avalanche of bicycles, cyclos, taxis, jeeps, six-bys and miscellaneous vehicles. If you were timid you could wait at Chicken Corner for 10 minutes hoping to get across—if you could tolerate the uproar of tooting horns behind you, urging you onward. The secret of driving in Saigon is to drive as if you intended to go through a place and as if you *could not see* the other vehicles involved. Don't slow up. Don't hesitate. Ram it ahead as if you were on an empty street—but with due regard to personal survival in one respect: Never argue the right of way with a vehicle larger than your own!

George Larrieux admitted he was a very cautious driver. He said he never drove at all except in an emergency, but rode a bicycle back and forth to work. Just at the moment, he said, we had almost run over a man riding a bicycle with two little kids on the back. George jammed on the brake and we avoided disaster, but his sudden braking had caused an emergency behind us. I looked back. A cyclo (the most common means of transport in Saigon: a small motorcycle or bicycle pushing a two-wheeled gondola car in which two people sit) had found it necessary to run up on the sidewalk to avoid ramming us. In turn, a couple of bicycles had been displaced (they had been in use on the sidewalk) and had stopped inches from a mass of black-market goods. The space behind us, which the cyclo had vacated, was now filled with another cyclo. Behind him was a solid mass of machinery—bicycles, cyclos, taxis, jeeps, people pushing carts—as far back as I could see. Nobody seemed upset. This kind of thing apparently happened all the time. In fact, Larrieux said there were serious accidents and deaths happening almost hourly in Saigon traffic.

I believed him. The bicycles seemed to operate as if the riders did not care if they lived or died. They turned suddenly in front of oncoming cars. The cars applied the brakes. The bicycle swooped clear. The traffic zoomed through. It was split-second stuff, and after I had been in it for 10 minutes watching George drive I saw why he hated driving. And yet I couldn't see why George Larrieux's rode a bicycle to work. If I had my pick I'd rather run over somebody than get run over myself, selfish as that may sound.

"You can roll down your window," George said, "it's getting a bit hot in here."

I looked at the window doubtfully. Thousands of people pressed close to the line of traffic—which often stopped for long periods—and an open window, it seemed to me, was an invitation to some Vietcong terrorist to pull the pin on his hand grenade and toss it in my lap. Larrieux, who knew the little nervous tendencies of newcomers, said, "You don't have to worry about a grenade. You can roll down your window."

Reluctantly, I rolled the window down. Larrieux explained that the chances of being blown up by a VC grenade were about the same as getting struck by lightning. Saigon was an enormous city and bombings were few and far between. They got a lot of publicity in the press and TV back home, so most people who had just arrived expected to be attacked. No sweat.

"Great," I said, sweating.

"Of course, we had an incident outside the gate at Tan Son Nhut," Larrieux went on. "They set off a Claymore mine during the rush hour. Everybody who could move ran like mad away from the blast—and ran into the second mine, which was triggered to go off in their faces. If you ever do hear a blast, hit the deck and stay down until you're sure there isn't a second one coming."

"I will," I said.

George Larrieux and George Weiss shared an apartment with two other officers at the dead end of a dirt alley. Three or four soldiers with guns occupied a small open shelter near the entrance to the building. They smiled at us and nodded when George spoke to them. He explained that they were "Nungs"—professional Chinese soldiers frequently hired as bodyguards in Vietnam (also hired as combat soldiers, they are said to fight like tigers). Larrieux said that several civilian tenants in the close vicinity had chipped in with the GIs to hire the Nungs as night-and-day guards, and that it had worked out well. Nobody had been robbed, stabbed or assaulted in this alley as yet. But you had to be careful about identifying yourself at night. The Nungs really didn't fool around. "They *like* to shoot people," Larrieux said. "That's what makes them such good guards."

We let ourselves in and climbed steep concrete stairs to the two upper floors that were occupied by the Air Force officers. It was a comfortable and charming place. A painting of rain falling on bamboo huts beside a canal adorned one wall. It was done in oil, with restraint and imagination. You got the feel of rain, growth and warmth. Larrieux explained he'd bought it (for a rather substantial amount). Later on, when he got back to the States, he would look at it and recall how he had felt in Vietnam.

I sat down at George Weiss's desk while Larrieux made us some coffee by filling a cup with instant coffee and water, dropping a heating unit into it and plugging the unit to the wall. The unit got so hot that it boiled the coffee in a few seconds. Larrieux said that the heating unit would burn up and be ruined very quickly if you plugged it in without water around it. While drinking the coffee with Preem and sugar I looked at the objects Weiss had on his desk. There were: a guide book to Hong Kong, a Funk and Wagnalls dictionary, a book called *Quataban and Sheba* by Wendell Phillips, a *Gourmet* cookbook and *The Complete College Reader*. A large color picture of a plane dropping napalm was fastened to the wall over the desk, and an Air Force garrison cap with gold leaves on it hung from one corner. Several bottles of medical aids stood in a row beside a pipe rack full of pipes. Meclizine for motion sickness. And a bottle of pills labeled: *Two capsules every four hours as needed for pain*. There were partly full bottles of Cherry Heering, Benedictine, Paul Masson brandy, Gilbey's gin and Vin Rosé Sec. A pressurized can labeled "Slug-a-bug" sat beside Weiss's portable typewriter.

"You guys have it pretty cozy," I said to Larrieux.

"You should have been here when we had the rats," he replied. "I don't know what happened but suddenly the whole building got full of rats. You'd be lying in your bed and they'd run across your body in the middle of the night. Weiss, as you know, is not the sort of guy who puts up with things like that, and he solved our problem."

"Poison?"

"No. They get in the walls and under the floor and stink if you poison them. George closed all the doors and windows and plugged up all the holes he could find and went looking for the rats with a club. When he flushed one out of a closet or from under the bed, he chased it until he caught up, and then he flailed away until he smashed it. Pretty exciting around here for awhile, but we got rid of our rats."

I would like to state here that it was Maj. George Weiss's page-and-a-half letter that brought me to Vietnam. If he hadn't written it I would not have gone. I had no stomach for the war, felt we shouldn't be in it and didn't see how going there could help anything. Weiss convinced me differently. He said a writer who'd spent nearly seventeen years following the Air Force around the world, as I had, and who knew the planes and the guys as well as I did, was really obligated to go there and report it. Weiss is a hawk. His letter was a glowing tribute to our aviators. It was not only convincing; it was moving. And not only because he writes well, which he certainly does, but because he happens to be a PIO officer who doesn't just send out newsmen on the mission: he goes out himself into the fire fights, so he really knows what he's talking about. He flew seven Ranch Hand missions (the Ranch

Hand planes are the heaviest-hit of this war); eight FAC missions (he was hit repeatedly); night missions with Puff, the Magic Dragon (where the plane was hit); dive bombings in Skyraiders; close-in observation of a B-52 drop. In short, Weiss is a gung-ho guy, a top pro and a man I am proud to call my friend—even though I am not a hawk myself. I am sure he will not agree with some of the things I say here. But then, I don't agree with a lot of the things George says, either.

When it got dark we went up on the roof of the apartment to, as Larrieux put it, "watch the war." Warm orange flashes appeared in the darkness on the outskirts of the city, followed in a few seconds by a heavy boom. Larrieux explained that they were long-range guns shelling the Vietcong off in the distance someplace. A plane kept circling overhead, making raucous noises that Larrieux said was Vietnamese music, highly popular at the moment. Then the music would stop and a frantic chattering would come down from the sky. This was propaganda, Larrieux said, calculated to convince the people that the VC were no good and they should come over and join our side. The music and the voice were, to me, almost as annoying as fingernails on a blackboard. It occurred to me that if I were a VC I would have a double reason for pot-shotting at the plane; and the *first* reason would be to shut off that awful noise.

From time to time a jet would take off from Tan Son Nhut in afterburner, ripping a hoarse blowtorch roar through the night. Helicopters kept circling with their red warning lights winking on and off like blood-red fireflies. Off in the distance, from time to time, a bright-white light would glare, like a miniature sun, and sway gently as it sank, making white reflections on the clouds: a flare dropped to illuminate some suspected VC hideout. And once we saw furious firing coming down from the sky—a kind of pink curtain, which Larrieux said was a Dragon Ship firing its guns at the Vietcong.

"It seems to be inside the city limits," I said.

"Distances are deceiving at night," Larrieux said. "That's more than 10 miles away."

I had gotten a good look at Saigon and its environs when the Air France jet came down to land (it did not make the usual long, gradual descent we are used to Stateside; it came down in a steep spiral from 15,000 feet, staying high until the last moment, to escape snipers on the approaches to the

runway, and this gave me a really thorough look at the city).
I therefore knew that even 10 miles out there were apt to be
lots of houses, and I said so.

"Yes," Larrieux said, "there may be houses where that
Dragon Ship is firing. That's one of the damned things about
this war. We all wish it was a clean-cut thing, like Korea—
where you had a perimeter and trenches and stuff like that.
There's no front here."

I turned my attention to other houses in the vicinity, which
were open to view from our high vantage point. Close to us,
in a courtyard, an old man was taking a bath in a sunken
tub. Across the street, in a lighted window, a man with a
green eyeshade was laboring over what appeared to be a set
of accounting books. Out of the corner of my eye, in the
darkness on a smaller roof that adjoined ours, I saw a motion. I turned and peered. A dark figure was crouching there
with a gun. "George," I whispered to Larrieux, "don't look
now, but there's a guy over there."

Larrieux chuckled, "It's one of our Nungs," he said. "He
likes to hide up there in the dark—waiting for somebody to
try to pull something."

Breathing more easily, I began to look around at the roof-
tops themselves. The city was dotted with lighted penthouses.
I saw gardens of flowers, lovely tiled patios, pools, people
dressed in high fashion (or bathing suits) taking their ease
with drinks, high above the streets. The streets were pretty
messed up. Driving from Tan Son Nhut I had noticed piles
of garbage as high as a man's head and blocks long. Many
buildings (notably those occupied by Americans) were pro-
tected by piles of sandbags further supplemented by rolls of
accordion wire (barbed wire in springy helices that are impossible to get through quickly). And in particularly sensitive
areas there were Vietnamese soldiers or American GIs,
armed and ready to shoot. The Vietnamese policemen, small
men dressed in white (called "White Mice" but highly respected), patrolled the streets and did not take any nonsense
from anybody. A White Mouse was killed by the Buddhists
the day I got to Saigon; such killings were said to have
helped turn the people against the Buddhists, and caused an
end to the rioting.

"If you get in a jam when you are out on your own," Larrieux said to me, "don't hesitate to call a White Mouse. He'll
help you."

On the way back to the base the next morning, Larrieux alerted me to get my *piastres* ready to give to the boy from whom he habitually bought his morning newspaper (printed in English). I spied the boy ahead and he must have been pretty alert, because he stepped quickly to the side of the road and hailed George (whom he presumably was accustomed to see arriving on a bicycle), and we bought a paper. He grinned at us. "Okay, Number One!" he said enthusiastically, using the standard phrase I was to hear several thousands of time from urchins like him in the course of my travels.

"Clean-cut-looking kid," I said to Larrieux.

"We're old buddies," Larrieux said. "I wouldn't dare pass him without buying a paper."

The Vietnamese were, of course, taking advantage of the American affluence. Cab drivers overcharged outrageously. Landlords had hiked their rents double, triple, five times— anything they thought they could get. And, of course, the GIs were trying to outwit the Vietnamese. One trick (it worked) was to direct your taxi to the part of town you wanted, and then, when you were nearly there, order the driver to stop near a White Mouse. Pay him what is on the meter. If he gave you any trouble, call the cop. He usually departed— with, of course, a few well-chosen Vietnamese words of farewell to you. But words couldn't hurt you—particularly if you can't understand them.

Headquarters of Air Force Information for Vietnam was a small concrete building across the street from the Officers' Club at Tan Son Nhut. In this two-story structure were housed specialists in radio, TV, newspaper, magazine, photo; general assistance was available to anybody who came there with the proper accreditation to cover something or other in the country. The shop was headed, when I was there, by Col. William McGinty, USAF.

McGinty is the kind of information officer you find sitting at his desk, looking disgustingly healthy and bright-eyed, when you drag in at 9:30 with red eyes and blue fingernails after a hard night "interviewing" at the club. He informs you at once how glad he is to report he was able to clear all those little requests (Oh God, *what* requests?) you made at the bar last night. Hastily you move your cotton lips to say you didn't really mean—but Mac is ahead of you.

"At 10 sharp," he announces briskly, "you will be making

a high-speed low-level attack in the back seat of an F-100. At two in the afternoon I've got you aboard Maj. Ralph Dresser's defoliation plane. Ranch Hand is going to spray a real hornet's nest down in the Delta. And tomorrow, if I get final clearance—I'm sure I will!—you can go on a night patrol with the Marines, and they assure me—" At this point, if you have any sense at all, you slump over and simulate a heart attack.

Some newshawks, of course, preferred to get the "curt word" at Lt. Col. Jack Keeler's "Five O'Clock Follies," as Keeler's everyday briefing in the MACV (Military Assistance Command, Vietnam) Building is referred to by the press. (As far as anyone knows, nobody has yet been wounded while sitting in Col. Keeler's air-conditioned room, watching him point at a map.)

Between Bill McGinty and Jack Keeler, the horde of aspiring Pulitzer Prize winners poking around Vietnam were in good hands. Whether you wanted to go out and really see the war, or lush it up in the Caravelle bar, the "Mac and Jack Show" could take care of you nicely.

I spent a few days in the office at Tan Son Nhut reading back issues of the *7th Air Force Times,* which McGinty supervised, and which contained a lot of hard news that was well worth reading. Of course, the *7th Air Force Times,* like all service newspapers, was inclined to Accentuate the Positive. If the colonel was talking about his flight crew, he described them as the finest, most dedicated, bravest bunch in the Air Force. The crew, in turn, spoke of their colonel as the greatest leader since Genghis Khan. (Actually, if you looked into it, you might find that these sterling fellows all hated the colonel, the colonel hated them and they hated each other.) But you'd never find this out from reading *7th Air Force Times.*

Another thing these newspapers are addicted to is Teamwork. "Tell me," the Air Force interviewer always says, "how do you account for that superb hit you made in the middle of the oil dump after going through that hellish skyful of flak?"

"Well," the pilot replies in print, "it isn't just me who deserves the credit. I owe it to the devotion-to-duty and the tireless efforts of that great gang back at the field. The crew chief, the tech reps, the fellows who do the routine work that nobody hears about, but who are just as essential to the final result as I am. In this war it's teamwork that counts!"

One sometimes wishes that *Mad* magazine would take over on this particular story. When a pilot was asked how he could account for the success of his bombing raid through the hellish flak, etc., wouldn't it be wonderful, for once, if the pilot replied, "How did I get that superb hit in the middle of that oil dump through that hellish skyful of flak? I wish I could answer that question, mister, but I can't. The truth is, I don't rightly know. I had my goddam eyes shut at the time."

There has been a lot of criticism in this war of President Johnson and some of his top advisors who, the public feels, have been less than candid in reporting the true situation from time to time. The bomb shortage was a case in point. Attempts to present a rosy picture of the progress of the war at times when it was going pretty badly, are another. In fact things got so serious they added up to what newsmen began to call "The Credibility Gap," a polite way of saying that a lot of people no longer believed what they read or heard out of Saigon.

However, the censors (that's what they are, even though they are known as "spokesmen") have their side to the story. News *is* a weapon. Secrets divulged by irresponsible newsmen *can* give aid and comfort to the enemy. Even an completely honest report, if quoted out of context, can present a damaging impression. People who are trying to discredit a point of view do not hesitate to print stuff out of context. People who approve of a story, but want to make some point of their own, quote it selectively so that the overall intent of the piece is distorted. For example, when sections of this book were first printed in *Flying* magazine, I mentioned our use of CBUs and napalm, and described the civilian casualties I saw in the Delta. These sections were excerpted from my long story and consolidated into what appeared to be a censure of the American effort in Vietnam. They were reprinted in the United States and abroad and used by peace groups to show the brutality of American arms. I do not retract those sequences. In fact, in this book I include them and enlarge upon them. But I want to point out that they are not the whole story and that censors do, indeed, have their headaches. If they want to be completely safe they *must* sometimes throw the baby out with the bathwater. Because if they leave in sections (true ones!) that may be cleverly excerpted, they leave in ammunition that can, and usually is, used in a way they wish to prevent.

I am not a dove. Neither am I a hawk. I am a reporter. The

purpose of my trip to Vietnam was to observe events there as carefully as I could, and then to report them as truthfully as I could. I know I am bound to offend *both* my friends in the Air Force and my friends who oppose our presence in Vietnam at all. But I did not go to Vietnam to launch a personal popularity program. I just went there to try and get the facts.

4 TAN SON NHUT

Tan Son Nhut Airfield in Saigon is a steaming cauldron in which the ingredients of war are mixed and stirred and blended in preparation for a multitude of missions in support of the Vietnam war. The field is dominated by a single 10,000-foot strip, and during the morning and evening rush hours it is close to a madhouse. Tan Son Nhut is the busiest airfield in the world—busier than Kennedy, busier than O'Hare.

Everything is designed to clear the planes off the runway in a few seconds. Spaced along the main strip are three feeder strips angled into the runway. Sixty planes are sometimes waiting in these three lines, engines running. Often two planes take off together—either in formation or in tandem, one after the other. As one lifts off, it turns sharply to make way for the one behind it. Takeoffs and landings are often taking place simultaneously. The FAA wouldn't like it, but it sure gets planes up and down in a hurry.

Pipers, Cessnas, Beeches, DC-3s, Caribous, Grumman HU-16s and other smaller aircraft line up at the 5,000-foot turnoff while C-54s, C-118s, Connies and the like wait their turn at the 7,500-foot mark. Heavy fighters—F-100s, F-102s, F-104s, F-4s, F-5s—and lumbering jet transports such as the Lockheed C-141 lock their brakes and spool up to takeoff power down at the far end.

A light plane may land long and wheel off quickly around the banked racetrack curve at the end of the runway while a jet comes in hot behind—landing short and popping its chute at the beginning of the strip. A C-130 full of ammo turns on short final and squeezes in front of a Pan Am 707 on a long, straight-in approach.

Emergencies occur almost hourly. A squadron of choppers, down to their reserve fuel, flail toward the field. An RF-101 Voodoo touches down gingerly on battle-damaged landing gear. A B-57 limps in all shot up, and they lift out the wounded pilot after he shuts it down and rush him to surgery.

A Kaman HH-43 helicopter lugging a large red fire bottle on a cable under its belly stands by constantly for just such emergencies. As the wounded ship comes on final and touches down, the chopper flies alongside ready to douse any blaze instantly. Crash trucks and a mobile derrick are always at the ready too. If a crash occurs, the trucks race out, spray foam on the damaged plane and the mobile derrick muscles it off the runway. With the wild stackup that's usually overhead, the field can't afford to close down even for a few minutes.

Tan Son Nhut is the most active American air base in Southeast Asia. Around the field are rows of ramps and concrete parking areas where planes are outfitted for every conceivable kind of mission. In addition to being a marshaling yard for the goods our cargo planes bring in from overseas, Tan Son Nhut is an operational base for search and rescue, defoliation, in-country supply redistribution, air defense fighters, helicopter salvage work, bombing missions, day and night reconnoissance, VIP air taxis, spotters, medevac, troop transport—and a host of other activities.

You see here a greater variety of aircraft than has ever been assembled on a military field. It's a regular air show to watch them come and go. To visit Tan Son Nhut, to wander about the field and see the number and variety of its aircraft, and the multiplicity of missions they are engaged in, is to have brought home to you the absolutely central role of air power in the American involvement in Southeast Asia.

The largest planes in the Air Force, giant Douglas C-133 Cargomasters, are working hard out of Tan Son Nhut. There are clusters of various sorts of helicopters, which are used for every conceivable purpose. There is a row of handsome little North American T-39s, including the American Ambassador's personal VIP jet. Cessna 310 Blue Canoes dart in and out on their never-ending ferry flights back and forth across Vietnam.

One sees light transports, such as the de Havilland Dove and the C-123, and the Army Beavers and Caribous. A strange-looking French STOL propjet with two boxy kite-like tails floats out of the field buzzing like an angry bumblebee, yet hardly seems to be moving (its mission: supplying the boondocks). The pilot of an F-101 Voodoo, just back from dodging flak over North Vietnam, waggishly waves his fuel probe up and down at you in greeting.

Sitting incongruously in this crowd of military hardware are the familiar Pan Am and Air France 707s, DC-6s of Vietnam Airlines and swing-tail Canadair 44 turboprops of Slick and Flying Tiger Airlines.

On the main strip, a four-engine C-141 cargo plane touches down and rolls quickly to the major unloading area. As it brakes to a stop beside a mountain of supplies, a huge flatbed vehicle trundles up to the back door. The door opens and the palletized load rolls out of the airplane onto the truck to be carted away and stacked, or shifted to another part of the field for transhipment.

As soon as the C-141 is empty, a crew of mechanics climbs into its cavernous belly and sets up stanchions and litters five high, transforming the huge jet into a medevac plane. Right afterward, a fleet of ambulances arrives from the local hospital specializing in preparing the wounded to travel; the C-141 is quickly loaded with wounded men, their nurses and attendants. The C-141 taxis out and leaves for the Philippines.

Minutes later an air alert sounds. All traffic gives way to a squadron of F-102s that race out of their Armcoclad antimortar revetments and scream off, in formation takeoff. The all-clear is called and yet another senator flies in to have cocktails with General Ky, get the complete picture of what's going on in Vietnam, after which he'll hurry on to Bangkok or Hong Kong for R and R.

Premier Ky's famous Coup Squadron of black Skyraiders, with their swish insignia and Vietnamese markings, stand jauntily in a row.

Armed choppers orbit steadily over the field, rotors muttering, doorgunners sitting, black visors down, with their hands on 7.62 mm. machine guns, watching for the first sign of a mortar attack or a VC infiltration, ready with the most hellish firepower ever assembled in so small a machine. These are the Huey gunships, known among the VC as "The Muttering Death," and in this writer's opinion the most savage machines of the Vietnamese war. They patrol Tan Son Nhut and the other American air bases around the clock.

The newcomer to Tan Son Nhut is soon struck by the type of Americans who inhabit the place. A hot shooting war seems to float the take-charge types to the surface. There are very few flabby nearsighted officers or petty by-the-book non-coms. In fact, you might think you had somehow stumbled into the Green Bay Packers' preseason training camp. Everywhere you look there are big guys with clippered heads and deep tans. They wear dark jungle fatigues with huge pockets in the baggy pants, Special Forces canvas boots with deep mud cleats and either turned-up Aussie jungle hats or dark loose-crowned baseball caps.

The Officers' Club bar at the base is jammed, starting at 10 in the morning. The noise level is only slightly less than the chipping bay of a steel mill. At times, in order to hear what your companion is saying, you have to put your ear a few inches from his mouth. He then shouts. The barroom conversation is not wholly dedicated to women, stateside ball scores and how many days, hours and minutes until a hitch is up. They also talk shop. Fighter-bomber pilots argue the merits of low-level lay-down versus high-angle dive bombing. Air Commando guys (they fly the paradrop and short-field supply runs) discuss such matters as going to full power with water augmentation if you get in a bind coming up a canyon and have to pole-vault over the ridge, or how to bounce yourself 30 feet at the last moment, to clear the trees, by dumping full flaps on the C-123.

The Air Force's twin-engine C-123 Providers, some modified by adding GE jets and tail-braking chutes, are designed to be STOL (short takeoff and landing). You could get an argument on it. Some say, ungently, that the only way to get a grossed-out C-123 in the air on a hot day is with a hydraulic jack.

Nonetheless, the C-123 is the best we've got for small-field supply runs. Just about every C-123 ever built is here. Our jocks have shoehorned them out of plenty of back country jungle strips. Some Air Commandos say they've gotten them in and out of 1,200 feet, which is taking your life in your hands. Now, in the middle of 1967, the Air Force is also using Caribous. The payload is only half as big, but the Caribou is more STOL, and a lot thriftier on the old adrenalin supply.

One of the places the Information Office will not encourage you to visit is the mortuary at Tan Son Nhut, where all American dead are prepared for shipment to the States. Such visits are verboten. Nobody is supposed to really get killed in this war, and if they do, let's whisk them out the side door quickly and be about other business. But I had smelled the C-123 death ships on the line at Tan Son Nhut, and I had seen men quicken their pace during the hot Saigon day as they walked by the big mysterious building where the American dead are processed.

With the help of an independent-minded noncom, I was able to get inside the warehouse-like building. I saw the man-sized aluminum containers stacked high against the wall. I saw the ambulances back up tight to the door and unload the bodies of American soldiers. I saw the white-tiled floors, the tilting tables, the grim but necessary tools. I spent an hour there. The dreadful task was being handled as well as is humanly possible.

One of the last things I did at Saigon before going south to Can Tho, and the war in the Mekong Delta, was to visit the Tactical Air Control Center at TACC, which is the major nerve center of the whole air war. TACC in Saigon assigns all missions over South Vietnam. The direction comes out of a grand-style war room, with the usual impressive array of radars, radios, elaborate phone hook-ups, plexiglass grids, flashing lights and battle maps, all manned by skilled operations directors.

The TACC briefing itself, to be honest, was a drag. Important as hell. But alphabet soup. My mind was already on the live action in the Delta, and anyway, I tend to go to sleep in flip-chart briefings where they have these big, meaty titles like OVERALL INPUT TO THE MAGNAFLUXOMETER-MOD 3. Old Hermann Magnaflux himself would have to struggle to keep his lids open. I generally nod politely and murmur, at appropriate intervals, "Really? Why, that's *fantastic.*"

After furious attempts at concentration I can now tell you that the TACC is backed up by the DASC (Direct Air Support Center) and the DASC is backed up by the FAC (Forward Air Controller) and the FAC is backed up by the ALO (Air Liaison Officer) and they are all assisted by the TASS (Tactical Air Support Squadron) and the whole ball of wax is a JAGOS (Joint Air Group Operation System). The TACC is composed of a staff of VNAF (Vietnamese Air Force officers) and their opposite numbers in USAF (U. S. Air Force). So much for alphabet soup.

On one corner of the Tan Son Nhut Airfield were some very beatup-looking twin-engine airplanes, gunked up with a film of something or other, covered with big and little metal patches, and smelling like leaky kerosene drums. They were the C-123 Providers, twin-engine transports built by Fairchild-Hiller, which have been adapted to spray 2-4D to kill plants and trees, which is obvious as you look at the long spray tubes hanging under the wings. The code name for these defoliation planes is "Ranch Hand," and the pilots of these planes are said to be the most shot-at people in the war. They are known by the crude but descriptive name of "magnet-asses." Ranch Hand's motto, placed there over the Ready Room door at Tan Son Nhut is there to remind the pilots of their mission: "Only You Can Prevent Forests."

Maj. Ralph Dresser, USAF, a rugged All-American football player from Texas, was Ranch Hand's commanding officer when I visited their headquarters. He was a very formidable-looking man, the kind you could well imagine coming through the line digging with his cleats on legs like big sinewy pistons, head about three feet from the ground, about as easy to stop as a charging African buffalo. He had a powerful neck, a grim look around the mouth and eyes, and yet he had one of the most charming personalities I encountered in Vietnam. He was intuitive about divining what I wished to know about his operation and most articulate and factual about telling me. He spoke softly, almost gently, and yet I would as soon have offended Maj. Dresser as gone over and tweeked the nose of a Bengal tiger. He gave the impression that if he decided to he could simply grab your arm, tear it off and hand it back to you. He ran a taut, self-contained outfit, had, at that time, flown 278 missions personally and his plane had been hit 78 times.

The Ranch Hand shop was tucked back behind an old hangar that had once housed General Ky's Coup Squadron, and Ky's present headquarters were embedded in great coils of accordion barbed-wire and high piles of sandbags a few hundred feet from Dresser's door. There were a few people around, Dresser said, who might want to eliminate Ky from the scene and he wasn't taking any chances. I noted that there were wicked-looking guys with submachine guns sitting unobtrusively in little niches of the sandbag walls, and also around the small landing area that Ky used to come and go from his fortress in a helicopter.

Dresser showed me around the squadron rooms. It was a Spartan place. The familiar sign, FUCK COMMUNISM, which was painted horizontally in stripes of red, white and blue, was tacked to one wall. Each crew member had been permitted to design and assemble his own idea of a survival kit, and there were some exotic items hanging on the pegs in the Personal Equipment room. Two places on the human body seemed to concern the Ranch Hand troops the most: the head and the testicles. One man had designed a bizarre steel helmet with a steel visor that could be lowered over the eyes, and it looked very much like the jousting headgear used by the knights of old. Steel jock-strap covers were popular. And, of course, the paint jobs on the helmets were exotic, to put it mildly. "The boys are motivated," Dresser said. "They're all volunteers." He smiled slightly. "You wouldn't stay in this business long if you didn't dig it," he said. "It gets a bit hairy."

Ranch Hand operated on a six-day week, two-mission-per-day schedule. A mission lasted from 40 minutes to two hours—depending on the target. The seven-plane squadron had, at that time, earned 27 Purple Hearts and seldom returned from a mission without bullet holes, largely because the defoliant spray must be applied from a height of 150 feet at a speed of 130 knots. Any higher and the spray doesn't get on the foliage in sufficient strength. Any lower and the foliage is overkilled—a waste of expensive chemicals. An average 11,000-pound load costs $5,000, takes four minutes to spread and kills everything green over 300 acres.

Dresser's C-123s operated 10 to 15 knots above stalling speed (the speed at which the plane quits flying with the engines still running smoothly, because the air quits rushing tightly over the wing to give it lift—and breaks up into whorls, eddies and burbles, which give no lift). When this happens, the airplane simply dives uncontrollably into the ground. Ten knots isn't much leeway between life and death. Particularly since the planes must make steep banks, as much as 60 degrees, at 100 feet of altitude—and a banking plane needs much more lift than one flying straight and level. In pilot language, they operate "at all times on the ultimate edge of the airplane's performance envelope."

The 1,000-gallon chemical tank is carried inside the fuselage with tubing out to the spray nozzles. The spray operator sits inside an armor-plated box near the rear cargo door and monitors the pump that forces the spray out of the dispensing tubes. I sat in the box and it seemed to afford pretty fine protection, but Dresser said that was apt to be an illusion because the plane often banked so steeply that the ground gunners were shooting almost straight into the box and had, in fact, hit the occupant in this manner a few times.

The pilot triggered the actual release of the spray from up front because he has a better look at the area and a better knowledge of how to release most effectively. Normally a C-123 would spray an area 14 to 17 kilometers long by 80 meters wide. When the ground fire started to crackle (it sounds like popcorn popping, Dresser said) a crewman hurls out a smoke grenade to mark the spot and the escort planes—Skyraiders or B-57 jets that are "flying shotgun" roar in with guns blazing and bombs tumbling to suppress the fire.

The morning I talked to Dresser, Ranch Hand lost a C-123 to ground fire up near Danang. Rescue helicopters got the crew out but several men were very seriously injured. The VC were attacking both the downed spray plane and the rescue chopper. They detest the mission, which is probably understandable. Dresser said the Mekong Delta missions were the worst. The Delta country is flat, and the Vietcong gunners can see you coming for miles. They have time to get set, draw a bead and let fly. Dresser said he came in about five feet off the deck, his props leaving a white, frothy wake on the water of the rice paddies, then popped up to 150 to spray. "Even so," he added, "we get nicely ventilated very often on those Delta runs."

The areas sprayed most often are those along highways and railroads to make it more difficult for the VC to ambush convoys. It often happened that the VC mined a road, blew up a vehicle—tank, six-by, or antitank vehicle—which blocked the road. Then the guys in the underbrush zeroed in on the men and machines in the rest of the convoy, which were bottled up by the damaged point vehicle. It did not seem to me that the Americans were using our famous Yankee ingenuity in these probing patrols over roads they thought might be mined. Dick Cloy, outside Can Tho, said he sent an M-113 armored personnel carrier over the perimeter road from his village back to town to "blow up any mines they might have buried in the night." And I saw a number of newsreels showing damaged tanks that had been put out of action on roads up north of Saigon. I recalled the old French trick they'd been using when I went through Vietnam in 1954 to protect their railroad locomotives. They'd been chugging around the country with a couple of flatcars up front, so that if the tracks were mined the flats got it and not the engine. It seemed to me that a "mine-detector" tank could have been constructed by a savvy mechanic crew. They could merely have welded a bumper to the front of the tank—say about 10 feet long—with a set of bogie wheels that would press hard on the road, and trigger the mine, before the main treads of the tank arrived.

Dresser's men sprayed the perimeters of Special Forces camps out in the jungles to give the defenders a field of fire. This was also done around the perimeters of large air bases, where thick high stands of swamp grass were often found, and where snipers hid to take potshots at planes that were landing or taking off. When I was at Binh Thuy, for example, a DC-3 cargo plane was hit by a sniper at high noon while taxiing out for a takeoff. The shot came from the tall grass. The sniper was never caught.

Rice and other crops that might provide food for the VC were sprayed and killed. It takes three to five days before the sprayed leaves start turning brown and dying. A tree then dies in five to six weeks. The defoliant kills the plants and trees by overstimulating growth. The plant "grows itself to death."

"This is a very touchy thing," Dresser told me. "A mission to kill crops is particularly serious. We have to take it right up to the American Ambassador himself for approval. It can boomerang badly if it's not handled right."

Peasants who lose their crops are supposed to be paid in full for their losses. Unfortunately, they aren't always paid in full. Greedy province chiefs and sub-chiefs sometimes pocket the money the U. S. earmarks for peasant victims of Ranch Hand.

"The VC tell the peasants that our spray is deadly poison," Dresser said. "I'm going to show you now that it isn't."

He stuck his finger under one of the spigots of a dispenser drum, then licked the oily stuff. "It tastes like kerosene with chemical overtones—not good, but hardly a deadly poison unless you drink it, which nobody is likely to do."

Dresser and I walked around one of the Ranch Hand planes. It was a sorry-looking mess, coated with spray, pock-marked with patches that covered bullet holes, squat, dirty, ugly. It did seem, however, an appropriate machine for the job it had, which was certainly ugly too. "We are the most hated outfit in Vietnam," Dresser said. "Nobody likes to see the trees and the crops killed. But we're in a war, and Ranch Hand is helping to win it. The Ranch Hand mission is effective and necessary."

Dresser is right on all counts. Ranch Hand spray missions to defoliate the main trails, river banks in the Delta and truck routes over which the North Vietnamese infiltrate and resupply the South. Defoliation has also been used with great effectiveness in the Demilitarized Zone between North and South Vietnam to uncover ammo dumps and truck parks there. There has been talk of a massive effort to spray a wide buffer strip across the DMZ—a sort of "Dresser Line" so to speak—but the argument is that the VC would skirt it, just as the Maginot Line was skirted through Holland. The Big Defoliator—tactical atomic bombs—has been suggested, and may eventually be used—but Ranch Hand won't drop them. They'll come out of jets if they come at all. A C-123 couldn't possibly escape its own blast if it tried to deliver A-bombs, unless, of course, they had delayed fuses or floated down with parachutes.

It is good to report that the defoliant used by Ranch Hand does not permanently sterilize the soil. The climate and rainfall in Vietnam is such that trees and plants grow back rapidly, so that no permanent damage will be done by this operation. Ralph Dresser, who went to college in San Antonio to learn how to grow things—not kill them—is glad. He has no quarrel with the trees. Just with the VC.

5   INTO THE DELTA

I flew from Tan Son Nhut to Can Tho, a large Vietnamese city on one of the branches of the Mekong River in the Delta and an important headquarters for Army of the Republic of Vietnam, ARVN, troops. These men are universally referred to as "Arvins." We departed in a Caribou twin-engined transport, a brown-camouflaged plane with a high tail that looked as if the designer changed his mind after the plane was built and bent it upward quite a bit.

There were quite a few passengers, most of them officers, and most of them husky and sunburned, with the hard businesslike manner of combat pros. The pilot gave us a little briefing from the front of the plane before takeoff. He explained that if we were shot down or had to ditch for some reason, he would give several short rings on the alarm bell. We would then tighten our seat belts and put our arms over our faces at the moment of impact. The pilot then put on a flak vest, a heavy garment made of many layers of nylon, which can stop a rifle bullet.

"None of you people have these flak vests," he said, smiling. "Reason I've got one is—*somebody* has to survive to tell what happened." It seemed probable he used this gag before every takeoff with a new group of passengers and it earned a couple of grins.

The Caribou is a beautiful little transport. It was said to be powerful enough to take off from a newly plowed field after a heavy rain, but I don't really know for sure that it could. It rattled over the loose pierced-steel-planking that served as a runway for that section of the field, and without any fussing around the pilot opened his throttles and we tore madly along a short distance and leaped into the air.

The rear cargo door had been left open (things were pretty casual) and I could see out and down. The Vietnamese landscape south of Saigon is a great watery plain crisscrossed with canals and light green with rice and other plantings. It is the breadbasket of Vietnam, and from the high-flying Caribou (we prudently cruised above 4,000 feet to be above small-arms fire), it looked warm, peaceful and productive. There was no sign of the war, flashes, smoke, movement, just an enormous watery expanse delicately cloaked with green under a gentle blue sky.

My first destination was not the city of Can Tho but the U. S. Air Force base about four miles out of town, known as Binh Thuy. It was a large clean base that served among other things as the home of a number of Dragon Ships—old pre-World War II Douglas DC-3s that began carrying passengers in the United States 30 years ago. These ancient planes, which fly at a top speed of around 140 knots, have been fitted with three rapid-firing machine guns known as "miniguns" that stick out of the side windows on the left side of the airplanes.

As first conceived, the old DC-3 carried 13 light machine guns mounted through the windows and the cargo door, but as testing of this configuration progressed, certain drawbacks were noted. Thirteen gunners is a lot of people milling around in the cabin and loss of an airplane would have meant serious casualties. So the 13 machine guns were replaced by three, designed like the old-fashioned Gatling guns, which had rotating barrels cranked by hand. The miniguns are not cranked by hand. They operate electrically and each gun spits out 7.62mm bullets at the rate of 6,000 per minute—*300 per second* out of the three guns.

Aiming and firing are done by the aircraft commander in the front cockpit. He peers through an illuminated ringsight mounted beside his left shoulder. At night he can light up the target, if he cares to, by having the guys in the back throw out flares. They are magnesium and burn with the intense brightness of the sun, giving off 1,000,000 candlepower. The three guns are fed by the "gunners" in the back of the plane (really just reloaders and maintenance men). The guns gobble up 1,500 rounds out of "pods" that are replaced rapidly by the gunners when they run dry. One round in five is a tracer. The tracers give the aircraft its name. During the first missions flown over Vietnam, the outpost defenders compared the stream of tracers coming down from the darkened aircraft to the "fiery breath of a dragon." From this somebody came up with the term "Puff, the Magic Dragon." For several months the squadron used "Puff" as its tactical radio call, but for phonetic reasons this was later changed to "Spooky."

The Dragon Ships operate mainly at night, when they fly to the aid of the many forts spotted around the Delta, some manned by American Green Beret Special Forces teams and some manned by the Regional Forces and Popular Forces (RFs and PFs), known as Rough Puffs. The Rough Puffs are not regular army men and get low pay, but they are said to fight harder, at least at times, than the Arvins. The Vietcong attack these forts frequently, sometimes several forts in the course of an evening, and without the help of Puff, the Magic Dragon, many forts would doubtless have been overrun and all the defenders killed.

I flew over a number of these forts, and they fit a fairly

common pattern. The walls are usually made of mud, but some forts in strategic locations are walled by concrete. Their shape is triangular, several hundred feet or more on a side. Masses of springy accordion wire surround the outer walls. Claymore mines, which are large grenades designed to discharge a hail of fragments in one direction like enormous sawed-off shotguns, are concealed in the wire and can be fired electrically from the fort.

Inside the fort are the living quarters for the Rough Puffs and sometimes for their families. Usually the quarters consist of bunkers or blockhouses that can absorb direct hits from mortars. Some of the forts also had an "inner perimeter" of wire and a last-ditch network of trenches from which the defenders could make a stand if the outer walls were breached. Some of the VC attacks on these forts have been suicidally determined. The raiders have been known to attach high-explosive charges to their bodies and run into the wire to blow holes in it to provide an access path for their buddies racing in behind them. In desperate situations, when the VC had got through the wire and were actually on the walls about to enter the fort, the defenders have called for Dragon fire right into the fort itself.

Isolated forts, deep in the Delta, have to be resupplied by air, and sometimes, when weather has prevented the planes and choppers from arriving, the defenders get pretty short of everything. VC pressure was intense, day and night, and the Rough Puffs got pretty discouraged with their lot: low pay, constant danger and miserable living conditions. I heard that there were times when the resupply choppers had trouble keeping the Rough Puffs off the skids when the time came to take off and leave the place. The reason the Rough Puffs fight so hard is no mystery. If they don't, the VC may overrun them and kill them.

American Green Berets do this same kind of work. They not only man fortified bases in the Delta but they go one step further. They establish smaller and much more vulnerable positions known as forward operating bases, or FOBs, which are some distance from the stronger base. A couple of Green Beret guys go out and lie behind a makeshift mud wall, with a handful of Vietnamese troops to help, and monitor a canal intersection, say, where VC troops may be expected to pass in boats. If they see such a movement, the FOB chaps radio the information to armed helicopters or jet fighters and our guys come in and blast the night-moving VC. Naturally the enemy takes a dim view of FOBs, and inasmuch as these outposts are the least heavily defended, many an attempt is made to overrun them. When an FOB sends in a call for help, American air power gives the call first priority. Even a few minutes delay may be too late.

There was a very large Green Beret headquarters near Binh Thuy, at what was known as the Old Can Tho Airfield, and I went to see them in their compound there. A great deal of high-powered publicity has been disseminated about the Green Berets: how brave, capable, ingenious and versatile they are. Before going to Vietnam I visited Fort Bragg and talked with the 12-man A-Team that had been led by Capt. Roger Donlon when he won his Congressional Medal of Honor in a desperate fire fight. I observed the Green Berets training and it did seem to me that they were about as well trained in as many fighting techniques as it was possible to be. I learned how to make a bomb out of matchheads, bolts, wadded paper and an old piece of pipe. I discovered the secret of the "flour bomb," which, for the safe-and-sane future of the U.S.A. (juvenile delinquents being what they are) I will refrain from describing in detail. Suffice to say that this crude device, made of flour, TNT and common fertilizer, can knock down a very large reinforced building!

I saw Green Beret paratroopers leap from a chopper 8,000 feet in the sky and land in front of the general's box in an area about 200 feet square. They used parachutes with vents in them that can be used to guide the falling man like a rudder. I talked to a jumper who bailed out at 43,000 feet and fell to 1,800 before he pulled the ripcord.

Another fellow demonstrated how they can swim underwater with a "self-contained oxygen breathing" device that does not send up any bubbles to the surface. He explained how a team of Green Beret guys could blow up a huge dam. They'd jump out of a high-flying jet—probably a C-130—at about 40,000 feet, too high to be noticed. They'd "group up" as they fell, by "flying with their arms and legs" in what is known as the "French Cross" position. They would fall in a tight little gaggle until they were precisely over the spot on the dam they had selected as the place to enter the water. Then they'd open their black chutes, land in the water, discard the chutes and swim below the surface with their nobubble breathers to the face of the dam. They would fix the demolition charge of plastic explosive (which had been carefully prefigured in power to do the job) to the base of the dam, using a delay fuse, and then they would swim to shore, peel off their gear, hide it and take off through the night in their peasant costumes (and with enough facility in the local language to pose as natives if accosted).

It seemed a bit fantastic, a sort of James Bond charade, but I guess it really wasn't. The Green Beret guys *are truly elite troops,* even though the publicity they have been getting annoys the ordinary army soldiers who fight their battles without benefit of a green headgear. When I wrote an article about Donlon and his men I got a few bitter letters from combat veterans who said they were just as tough and capable as those overpublicized so-and-so's in the green berets. It wasn't fair, wrote the straightlegs, and they were getting pretty fed up with it.

The Green Berets in the compound at Old Can Tho Airfield were certainly tough. One officer in particular made my blood run cold. He wasn't talking, but I had heard about him from another source in town, and his job was "Counter Terror," which is a branch of the Vietnamese operation few people have heard about. I verified this report unofficially by asking a number of other people. They said the VC had been using terror tactics in the villages for years, swooping down on a place, pulling the village chief out of his hut and killing him brutally in full view of the villagers, which was intended to demonstrate what happened to people who failed to go along with the VC ideas. Counter Terror, I was told, was our way of fighting back. We used the same technique, except that our man killed a VC, not a chief. He did it publically, and presumably it had the same but opposite effect; made the villagers reluctant to give aid and comfort to the Vietcong.

Green Berets are supposed to be, in addition to tough soldiers, specialists in "civic action." That means they know how to build (or supervise the building) of sanitation systems, schools, dispensaries, wells, roads and similar helpful things. Donlon's men did these things. It was probably one reason the Vietcong hit them so fiercely. Donlon's men were making the grade with the people.

I talked at length with Sgt. Chuck Koscinski, who was a medic on Donlon's A-team. He was a young redhead and when I first saw him he was plunging down a long rope off a six-story wooden tower, putting on a demonstration for some visiting brass. He did it with a little steel clip, which the rope was threaded through, abruptly halted at the end of his plunge by another guy with a snub-rope above him on the tower. It looked like a thinly disguised form of suicide and Koscinski was getting brutally jarred on each trip, but he was cheerful enough, although a bit winded, when I met him.

He said he got into the paratroopers at age 20, won his wings at Fort Benning, volunteered for Special Forces and went through the 37-week course given to medical specialists. This included work in an Army hospital at Fort Sam Houston, on-the-job training in a field hospital and advanced work, including surgery, at Fort Bragg. When you finished the 37 weeks, Koscinski said, you were considerably more than an iodine-and-stretcher man. You were called "doctor" in Vietnam, and were looked upon almost like a God by the natives. Koscinski liked it so much he was getting out of the Green Berets and starting to try to work his way through college and med school with the idea of being a real doctor. He said that sick call, in his opinion, was the most effective way to win the war in Vietnam.

"Those poor little people have an average of two diseases all the time—sometimes more. Almost everybody has malaria. It's kind of the lowest common denominator. *Everybody* has stomach worms from babyhood. The skin diseases are awful. There are so many varieties it would take quite a while to list them all. Then there's typhoid, dysentery, pneumonia, flu, cholera, leprosy, and every now and then an outbreak of the plague.

"Everybody seems to be suffering from malnutrition —perhaps because the stomach worms eat up so much of what goes into their stomachs. That means that their resistance to infection and various disease germs is lower to start with. So if you have antibiotics and are able to help them eat a decent diet, and run a sick call every day, you really get to be a big man around there. You have hundreds of daily patients and sometimes you can perform what must seem to them to be a miracle. Have you ever seen a bad case of yaws?"

"No."

"Well, it can turn a person's face into a reasonable facsimile of a piece of ground-up hamburger. Penicillin happens to be a specific for it. A good course of penicillin shots and the hamburger look goes away and the kid starts to look like a human being. It can happen very fast, and it gets their attention."

Sgt. Koscinski gave his own recipe for winning the war and the peace, and from the plans subsequently issued by our high command on the conduct of the pacification of the country, they seem to be doing exactly what Chuck recommended. "Move into a village," he said. "Run a daily Sick Call—real big—all day every day. Stay there. Guard the place so the VC can't come back, ever. Keep doing this in enough places and you'll win the war."

While I was at Binh Thuy I was entertained by the pilots who flew the U-10 psychological warfare (Si-War) planes. The U-10 is an adaptation of the civilian Helio Courier, a monoplane with a high-lift wing fitted with special devices that pop out of the leading edge of the wing and maintain lift as the speed of the plane decreases. This plane can get in and out of tiny fields surrounded by trees and can land in a crosswind (it has "crosswind landing gear," which means the wheels can be swiveled to line up with the runway, while the body of the plane is headed into the wind). There was, however, some difference of opinion among the pilots about the efficiency of this crosswind grear. It was tricky, some of them said, and it could get you in deep trouble in a hurry if you didn't know how to handle it.

The purpose of the Si-War flights was to drop leaflets known as *Chieu Hoi* (Open Arms, in Vietnamese) by the hundreds of millions over VC areas in the hope that the VC will pick them up, read them and "rally" (desert their own troops) to our side. The *Chieu Hoi* leaflets promised a man that if he came in and gave himself up he would be given food, a clean place to live and a chance to learn a useful occupation. He would not be mistreated, tortured or molested. It was a chance for him to start a new life. The program seemed to be quite effective. On December 14, 1966, the Air Force officially announced that 19,073 "ralliers" had answered the *Chieu Hoi* leaflets and given up. When you consider that it takes about $100,000 to kill a VC, you see the efficiency of what the Si-War boys have been doing. Those 19,073 ralliers would cost $1,907,300,000 to kill.

There are various types of messages in the leaflets, in addition to offering amnesty and food: Tips on rice growing, fishing, health, sanitation, building and other helpful ideas for a better life were explained, often by simple drawings, on the leaflets. Near Danang, the Si-War pilots went even further. When a civic action field man asked them to drop small packets of salt, pepper and other condiments along with their leaflets, the boys got permission and complied.

"I guess the people in the village didn't really know what to make of it," pilot Robert Gille said. "Usually we just come sailing over, play our tapes and paper the area with leaflets. When they saw we were dropping packages, they came out in droves, grabbed them off the ground and beat it back to their huts."

At Nha Trang, 2,800,000 leaflets (which the Navy wanted to drop to inform Vietnamese fishermen and sampan dwellers of the dangers of assisting the VC) were obligingly prepared and dropped by the Air Force Si-War pilots. DC-3s are used in addition to the smaller planes to broadcast and drop leaflets. Their slogan was, "Every litterbit helps," and if you watched a DC-3 dumping leaflets you certainly get the idea they are littering; it looks like a snowstorm.

When you are around Si-War pilots you hear them say that they are working "to win the hearts and minds of the people." They sometimes say it casually, in the manner of a man who says, "Guess I'll drop down to the corner for a pack of cigarettes." No doubt many Si-War pilots feel sincerely that they are speaking to hearts and minds in their work. But I met some who did not. On their lips this phrase rang false. It sounded cynical and in fact I do not think that these leaflets and aerial broadcasts really win anybody's heart or his mind. If you are a VC, the leaflets offer you a way out of what must be an increasingly difficult and painful mess, and you are harassed and scared and weary, so you pick up a *Chieu Hoi* amnesty leaflet and bring it in. I doubt very much if your heart or mind has been affected basically. Maybe later, if the Americans and the Arvins really give you good food, clean sheets, teach you a trade and don't patronize you too much, your heart and your mind may change from distrust and hatred to acceptance and regard. I sincerely hope so. However, even if we are not winning hearts or minds, if we are only winning "ralliers" whom we no longer need to kill, and who no longer try to kill us, the Si-War program is definitely one of our best efforts in this unhappy land.

6 THOSE MYSTERIOUS BLACK BOXES

The name of this new game in warfare is Weapons Systems Management. The pilot or his assistant is office manager of the contemporary attack aircraft—fighter-bomber or interceptor. Because of the burden of accurately flying, navigating and attacking at high speeds in all kinds of weather, a large portion of the responsibility has been shifted onto electronic aids—black boxes.

In terms of mass alone, the black boxes add up to a surprisingly large element in first-line aircraft like the A-6 Intruder, F-105 Thunderchief, F-4 Phantom and the upcoming F-111.

For example, in the Intruder, the most sophisticated of the present lineup in action over Vietnam, electronics add over a ton and a half (3,192 pounds) to the fighting weight of the aircraft. This amounts to almost 13 percent of the empty weight of the airplane (25,468 pounds).

The function the black boxes fill on the A-6 is infinitely complex. They provide automatic flight control, communication, navigation, attack maneuvers and electronics countermeasures. About all the pilot has to do is take off and land, and, in between, he and the bombardier select the various navigational or attack alternatives offered by robot boxes.

By automatic flight control is meant something more sophisticated than mere autopilot maneuvering. The system in the A-6 also dampens out movement along all three axes to cut pilot fatigue. It provides a stable flying platform for rocket and missile firing as well as various bomb delivery techniques, and it answers to preprogramed automatic maneuvers for both navigation and attack.

Furthermore, it knows enough to do all of this within the aircraft's speed, altitude, attitude and G limitations.

In the A-6 there is a special network of systems called DIANE (for digital integrated attack navigation equipment). It consists of ballistics computer, guidance control set, autopilot, air data computer, inertial navigation system, search and track read out, vertical display indicator group, radar or electronic altimeter set, integrated electronic central and intercom system, radar navigation set, electronic countermeasures and ground control bombing system.

Add to these an environmental control system to provide air conditioning, cockpit pressurization, exposure suit ventilation, oxygen, defogging, defrosting, rain removal and equipment cooling and pressurization; along with complex engine controls, fuel system, hydraulics and armaments, and you have a fantastically intricate balance of elements tucked into an aerodynamic receptacle.

To keep this black box nightmare operating properly takes a navigator-bombardier systems operator probably more highly trained than the pilot. To keep it working at all takes an extremely ingenious maintenance system.

To this end each piece of black box equipment is designed to be yanked easily and tested quickly. It's interesting to note that the art of testing has, if you would believe the manufacturers, fully kept pace with the increasing sophistication of the gear it is built to test. Hence, self-check mechanisms in the airplane itself catch some of the problems immediately; the others are isolated by automatic test equipment that says, in effect, *such* is the problem, and it's located right *there*.

Thus electronic probing, searching and backtracking are held to a minimum.

Who performs the necessary black box maintenance in the field? White-collar factory representatives tagging along on the fantail of the carrier? Fatigue-uniformed high school grad caliber military personnel?

According to Grumman, fully 99 percent and more is handled by none other than the old-fashioned potato-peeling GI—but one who has been trained to be an effective technician.

Nevertheless, the final test of the effectiveness of the black box philosophy has come about in Vietnam under actual combat conditions with aircraft subjected to intense high-speed low-altitude turbulence, soggy tropical weather conditions, brain-jarring carrier landings—not to mention enemy antiaircraft fire.

This kind of situation is commonly regarded with apathy by nontechnical observers and with rose-tinted glasses by manufacturers. Questions generally are answered by vague references to the "learning curve," which usually means the slow and stumbling adaption of complex equipment to actual conditions.

Therefore, Grumman's report on the super-sophisticated A-6 after just over a year's combat experience came as a bit of a surprise:

"Bugs? We've already got 90 to 95 percent ironed out."

Maybe the black box is here to stay.

7 THE DEATH BRINGERS

The dominating figures in the air war in the Delta (and, in fact, in all of South Vietnam) are the forward air controllers, or FACs as they are called. They fly around looking for signs of guerrilla activity in the little single-engine Cessnas known as O-1 Bird Dogs. (These small airplanes looked and handle much like the Cessna 170, well known to civilian pilots.) The FACs have the authority to call missions only after approval by the province chief whose area is involved, except in emergencies when friendly troops are in contact with the enemy. The FACs have the authority to divert preplanned strikes to targets of opportunity when they deem it necessary. They cruise around over the Delta like a vigilante posse, holding the power of life and death over the Vietnamese villagers living beneath their daily patrols.

Much of the raw intelligence processed by the Tactical Air Control Center back in Saigon comes from the FACs. From the air, all the communities in the Delta look bucolic and peaceful to the unpracticed eye. But to the FAC pilot, ordinary-looking things sometimes read danger. Each FAC is permanently assigned to an area of responsibility so that he gets to know it well enough to be able to see a change in it if one takes place. During the daily visual recon over his particular area a FAC might spot a concentration of men where it shouldn't be, a mass movement of sampans, fresh earthworks; if anything looks suspicious the FAC can radio for an attack (after checking it with the province chief) and bring in jets or artillery or helicopters in a matter of minutes.

The FAC in his small low-powered plane really runs the

war. He has a terrifying fleet of planes and weapons at his beck and call. How many and what kind of weapons he employs depends on the targets in prospect. The daily strike schedule into the Delta is planned the night before at the Tactical Air Control Center in Saigon, based on FAC reports and reconnaissance photos, or on targets the American or Arvin troops have asked to have hit. Both Air Force and Navy planes are allotted their own particular missions. Pilots are briefed on the target location and any dangerous ground fire that might be expected. The best ordnance for the job is then hung on the aircraft, either aboard carriers on Dixie Station or at one of the air bases in South Vietnam, and the jet pilots are given the time and place to rendezvous with the FAC.

The FAC's list of fireworks is long and deadly. Napalm, or jellied gasoline, comes in aluminum tanks with fuses of white phosphorus. When it hits and ignites, the burning napalm splatters around the area, consuming everything burnable that it strikes. Napalm is considered particularly useful for destroying heavily-dug-in gun emplacements since it deluges a large area with rolling fire, and rushes, burning, down into narrow openings. You might spend a long time and a lot of high-powered bombs trying to get a direct hit on a gun pit that, if you were using napalm, you could wipe out in one pass. Napalm also is said to be effective against troops hiding in caves and tunnels since it suddenly pulls all the oxygen out of the tunnel by its enormous gulp of combustion, and suffocating anyone inside.

Napalm is highly respected and feared by the VC. It is hard to stick to your gun and keep on firing at an incoming jet when you believe he is going to drop napalm on you. Some VC gunners did it: When I was airborne out of Can Tho in the backseat of a FAC ship an F-100 was shot down on the outskirts of Can Tho by ground fire. Those who saw it said it was like an air show. The Supersabre was hit as it came in low to drop; it pulled up and began to trail fire. The pilot ejected, got a good chute and floated down into the paddies; almost at once armed helicopters arrived to protect him while another chopper landed and lifted him to safety. It was a bright sunny day. The spectators were highly entertained and all that was lost was the F-100.

Getting shot down in the Delta, provided you weren't actually wounded, is not pleasant, but it isn't too dangerous, really. I visited "Paddy Control," a heavily sandbagged and barbed-wire-protected radar-and-radio center at Old Can Tho Airfield, which bore the sign "The Eyes and Ears of the Delta." I toured this place and watched the controllers monitoring the sky over the Delta on their radar scopes. If a pilot got in trouble, he turned on the IFF (indentification, friend or foe) transmitter in his cockpit. This was instantly received on the radar as a highly visible "triple-bogey" (not the small single matchhead of greenish light that is normally painted by the turning sweep arm). So the pilot in trouble was under surveillance, even before he radioed his plight. The controllers in Paddy Control did not waste time before helping him. They diverted any armed helicopters or jets that were in the area (and which they were also watching on their scopes) to the emergency position (which they could see by the position of the IFF image). It was an efficient, almost routine matter. Hundreds of emergencies took place, of course, and a number of pilots had gone down. Their average time on the ground was 11 minutes. Only a few downed airmen were captured. In one case it happened because they were flying an Air America plane and had neglected to file a flight plan, so nobody knew where they were when they got in trouble. They happened to be outside Paddy Control over near Cambodia.

The Vietcong had made a practice of hiding from recon planes by submerging in the waist-deep water of the rice paddies and breathing through a hollow tube. The ingenious Americans solved that problem by providing an 18- or a 36-inch projection on the nose of a bomb so it would go off *in the water,* before burying itself in the mud. As anybody who has seen fish dynamited well knows, a heavy explosion under water kills or stuns any living thing in the area. These special bombs were known as "daisy cutters," and if the VC were actually there, holding themselves under water and breathing through hollow tubes, a daisy cutter would float their bodies to the surface like corks. But napalm was the favorite weapon of most people I talked to. "One or two napalm attacks can change the fighting spirit of a whole company," a Navy A-4 Skyhawk pilot, Lt. Comdr. Fitch, told me.

White phosphorus bombs were another incendiary that the VC feared greatly. This stuff is even more vicious than napalm. In the civilian hospital in Can Tho, I saw a man who had a piece of white phosphorus in his flesh. It was still burning.

But the deadliest weapon of all, at least against personnel, were CBUs—cluster bomb units. One type of CBU consisted of a long canister filled with metal balls about the size of softballs. Inside each metal ball were numbers of smaller metal balls or "bomblets." The CBUs were expelled over the target by compressed air. The little bomblets covered a wide swathe in a closely spaced pattern. They look like sparklers going off and were lethal to anybody within their range. Some types were fitted with delayed action fuses and went off later when people have come out thinking the area was safe. If a pilot used CBUs properly he could lawnmower for considerable distances, killing or maiming anybody on a path several hundred feet wide and many yards long.

The FACs favored CBUs for "recon by fire" missions. They called in a fighter to cruise along a highway or canal, dropping CBUs. The bomblets made a distinctive noise, which from the distance sounded like rolling thunder and anybody hiding in the undergrowth waiting to ambush a convoy could hear the CBUs coming. If a FAC saw people break out and run in front of the plane, he'd officially flushed some VC and could call in a Huey or two and wipe them out.

The Huey gunships were equipped with enormous fire power for so small a platform. Some types were capable of launching a fuselage of rockets, grenades and machine gun bullets powerful enough, or so I was told, to "back up the chopper a hundred feet." These powerful flying gun platforms were available on short notice to come to the assistance of Arvins or Americans who might be under attack.

A variety of rockets were used: Zunis, five-inch ballistic rockets; 2.75 HVARs, high velocity aircraft rockets with folding fins; Sidewinder heat-seekers that home on the hot tailpipe of an enemy jet; radar-guided Sparrows also used in air-to-air combat; the Shrike, a Navy-developed air-to-surface missile being used against SAM sites in the north; the Bullpup, a large missile launched and then guided remotely into the target by the pilot. Some new missiles were soon to be deployed: the Genie Magnum air-to-surface missile that may carry a number of small bomblet clusters as well as a single large warhead; the Phoenix, a radar-guided missile for use with the new F-111 "switchblade fighter," a new plane whose wings sweep back for supersonic flight and forward for a relatively slow landing.

Many sizes and shapes of bombs were used. The "snake-eye" bomb had an air brake that deployed when it is released, slowing up its fall so that the plane could escape from the resulting blast. The 3,000-pound "swimming-pool maker" is used by the big F-105 fighter-bombers against hard targets in the North. A pilot I talked with said that these powerful bombs sent out a visible ripple of shock "like a small atomic bomb" and dug craters so large that flying over later, you could see them as ponds the size of swimming pools, filled with tropical rainwater. The staple demolition bombs used in Vietnam were 250-, 500-, 750-, 1,000- and 2,000-pounders. They came in the "fat lady" or "Slim Jim" shapes, depending on how much air drag you were trying to eliminate from the airplane that carried them.

The popular coming thing in air delivery of ordnance is the gun pod and rocket pod (which can be bolted under the wing) and the various bomblet dispensing devices such as the CBU container described above. General Electric's Missile and Armament Department has repackaged and improved the 7.62mm minigun used on the Magic Dragon. The improved rapid-firing gun will be used on both fixed and rotary wing aircraft operating in Vietnam. It holds 2,000 rounds and can be depressed 18 degrees for raking targets, and is being tested on a military version of the civilian Cessna Super Skymaster (an odd-looking plane with a pusher and puller propellor behind and in front of the pilot, who sits in a cockpit between twin tail booms). This plane, also being fitted with a rocket pod, is important because it is the replacement for the smaller, more vulnerable, unarmed Bird Dog, long the standby plane used by FACs.

The FAC operates in a fairly routine manner. When he puts in an air strike he makes contact with the oncoming attack planes and talks them in over the target. When they have him in sight, the FAC rolls in on the target and fires a rocket that leaves a telltale little cloud of white smoke when it hits. If the rocket misses, the FAC tells the attack planes how far from the smoke puff and in what direction from it he wants the ordnance to be delivered. The FAC circles the spot, observing the accuracy of the drops and advising the attacking aircraft how to make the proper corrections.

The VC hate the FAC. It is he who fingers for the attackers. After his little plane begins to circle overhead, the fury is usually not far behind. The FAC is in truth a death bringer and if the VC catch him they usually kill him. Near Pleiku, one FAC was said to have been skinned alive by the VC. More FACs have been killed in Vietnam than any other type of pilot.

When you are dawdling around at 70 knots, 1,500 feet in the air over people you intend to barbecue, they tend to want to zap you in the behind. Every now and then they do.

I flew one FAC mission out of Can Tho in the back seat of a Cessna O-1 Bird Dog behind a very capable pilot, Col. F. R. Goldsberry, USAF, the number-one man in the Can Tho DASC (District Air Support Center, remember?).

"You can put this flak vest on, or you can sit on it," Col. Goldsberry said as we stood on the pierced steel planking beside his bird.

"What do *you* do?"

"I sit on it."

"I'll sit on mine," I said.

We took off. It didn't seem as if we were going to war. It was as if we were leaving the Square Deal Flying Service for a little duel over Floral Hills, New Jersey. The sun shone brightly. Down below, the scenery wasn't like New Jersey, but it was just as peaceful. Little clumps of palm trees in the sun. People trudging along paths with stuff on their backs, paddling up canals in their small boats, hoeing the garden plots behind their hootches (a house or hut is known as a hootch in Vietnam). The rice paddies were lush and green. As we flew along, the reflection of the sun kept pace with us, glaring up blindingly from the standing water around the green shoots.

I expected we would fly south for maybe 50 or 60 miles and get over some wild country where VC would be skulking in bunkers and firing at us. I was surprised, therefore, when only about five miles from Can Tho, Col. Goldsberry suddenly threw out a red smoke grenade, which landed in a rice paddy near a line of houses along a canal. A rich cloud of crimson smoke poured out over the greenery. This technique is called "recon by smoke." If any VC were hiding in the paddy, the smoke might scare them into trying to make a break for it. If that happened we would call in an air strike.

But there was no sign of movement in the rice paddy. In fact, by the time we circled back over the houses, moments later, the people who had been standing outside them had vanished. The countryside below us now seemed deserted. Col. Goldsberry stared down, eyes squinting intently, his jaws working tautly on a stick of gum. Finally, when it became apparent that the red smoke wasn't going to flush anybody, we moved off a couple of miles farther south to where the informer had said there was a VC hootch.

When we got there, Goldsberry circled, consulting his map, making sure he had the right house. I had been inside the FAC control center in Can Tho where we had picked up the information that they had received from the informer, and had seen Goldsberry check the positions (there were several) where Vietcong were said to be operating. I had asked who the informer was, and they said in this case it was an old man. He had been most useful. His information, they discovered, was accurate and valuable. The VC had killed a member of his family. But there were many informers, young and old, male and female. Informers, in fact, supplied a great deal of the information that was used in daily strike assignments.

"How do you check them out?" I'd asked. "How do you know the information is valid?"

"We size them up, for one thing," the man in the FAC center said. "You can often tell, by the way a person acts, if he's telling you the truth or is maybe trying to get you to go and wipe out some person he's been feuding with. Also, after working this area for a long time, we have a pretty good idea of where the VC really hang out. If we get a report of activity in such an area we tend to believe it. When you get out there and look down, you'll see what I mean. The paddies and canal banks are full of foxholes and bunkers that the enemy has dug there."

After Goldsberry had circled for some minutes, and had satisfied himself that we had the right place, he radioed a nearby fort to start shooting with long-range artillery.

I could see from the mildness of the explosion and the clean-looking white smoke that the first shells were marker rounds. Goldsberry now was keeping up a running conversation with the gunners on the ground. He flew the Bird Dog with his left hand and made notations of coordinates and code names on the plexiglass windshield with a grease pencil. His jaws worked steadily on the gum. He swiveled his head in alert jerks from side to side, and up and down. Every now and then, when he turned to the left, I could see his eyes and most of his face from the rear seat where I was. He looked like a fighter pilot, which in fact, he had been most of his life; his face was tanned, taut, and his eyes were hot-looking and squinted in the sunglare from the paddies. The gunners weren't doing so good. The first round hit long. Goldsberry radioed the error. The second round hit short. Then they got into the trees along the canal.

Goldsberry made a final correction and called in high-explosive shells. These made heavier bursts of brown smoke. We were at about 1,500 feet but I could see the fragments slashing the trees. Finally, the fifth or sixth HE shell hit the hootch we were aiming at. I couldn't tell if anybody was in it. The other shells had exploded in an area of some hundreds of feet in all directions.

We moved a few miles away to another canal. It was lined on both sides with Vietcong hootches, and Col. Goldsberry began to talk to some F-100s on his radio. He directed them to a position over our heads at about 15,000 feet.

"Do you have me in sight?" he asked the F-100 leader.

"Rodge," said a ghostly voice.

"Rolling in in 15 seconds," Goldsberry radioed.

"Rodge," said the ghostly voice.

I watched the second hand jerk around the dial of my wristwatch.

"Rolling in—now!!" Goldsberry said. He pulled the Bird Dog up into a steep nose-high altitude; then made a violent wingover that turned instantly into a vertical dive and fired one of the rockets on the left wing. It made a loud explosive *honk* as it left us, and hit about 50 feet from a hut, in what appeared to be a vegetable garden.

"Target 50 feet from smoke burst," Goldsberry said laconically. "Hut at edge of garden." He was leaning forward, peering up through the Cessna's windscreen. An F-100 Supersabre was up there knifing across the blue sky on its side in a shallow bank, going like hell. "Drop your left wing, Blue Queen Leader," Goldsberry said. "That's it. A little more. Make your pass up the canal—west to east—"

I lost the F-100 for a moment, then picked him up to the south as he made a sweeping turn to give himself room to get lined up properly. He seemed to be coasting, his jetscream lost in our engine and flight noises. He turned base. We banked to keep him in sight. He was on final, so low he seemed to be skimming the hootches. He flashed along the canal and I saw bright aluminum cigars detach from his belly and tumble, end over end. Two cans of napalm hit without exploding. Then more cans hit and part of the line huts was obliterated in a rolling cloud of flame. Involuntarily, I looked away. When I looked back two of the huts were burning brightly.

"Couple of duds," the F-100 jock said disgustedly over his radio. "The damned igniters must have goofed."

Now the two jets were setting up their strafing pass. They took their time. There was no hurry. Nobody was shooting back. One at a time, they made a deliberate racetrack pattern and a long careful final. Then they flashed over the huts at 400 knots and walked their 20mm shells through the thatched roofs and the dirt street in a flurry of dusty explosions. When they had fired out their ammo, they pulled off the target. I asked Col. Goldsberry if he would please take me home as I felt a little queasy. He was a very considerate man. He said he would indeed.

A FAC must be very sure of what he's doing before he calls in the jets. He can kill a lot of innocent people if he makes a mistake, which sometimes happens.

I met a FAC who had been directing gunfire from Navy destroyers against hootches and VC concentrations for several months. The destroyers were miles off shore in a moving ocean. This young man had been relieved of duty because he had openly declared himself guilty of assisting in killing many civilians because the long-range guns fired wild so often, hitting homes and people in the vicinity of the target coordinates. It was impossible not to feel the agony this boy was suffering. "I just want to go home and forget it forever," he said.

Another FAC, who had just flown his last artillery-directing mission over a nearby village, was in the bar at the Eaton Compound in Can Tho. He said he was going back home to the States the next day. He had been ordered to direct artillery against a village because "three VC were reported there this morning." He got over the village, he said, and looked down and all he could see were men, women and children walking around. He radioed back to the Arvins who were waiting to fire the long-range guns and told them he didn't see anybody who resembled a VC but that there were civilians in the village. Did the province chief really want the place hit? They radioed back that the province chief did, and to send the coordinates. "I sent them" this young FAC said, and drained his drink.

"You must have seen a lot of people killed."

"No," he said. "No people got killed. Nobody was in the paddy where I directed the artillery fire."

8 VILLAGE SICK CALL

The chopper that was taking us out to the small village of Phong Dien, about 10 or 15 miles from Can Tho, is known as a Kaman HH-43 Huskie and is used to carry medical personnel and supplies, to put out fires with a large red fire bottle that it lugs at times under its belly, and for various little emergency jobs that come up. It is a boxy little helicopter with twin tails and two large rotor blades that flail around together but in opposite directions like the beaters of a monster blending machine. These two long blades are tilted at an angle to the ground so that if you happened to approach the machine from any direction but precisely in front of it, your head would be nipped off as neatly as the pod off a milkweed stalk.

It was explained that if you approached from the front you could stand erect—but I didn't stand erect. I approached in a low crouch in case the blades were out of adjustment, and crawled into the open rear of the box that served as the body for the Huskie. With me were some GIs lugging large boxes of medical supplies; a young photographer from the Binh Thuy base who wore an Aussie hat and looked jaunty but, it later developed, had approximately the photographic skill of a six-year-old child; Dr. Wiita, a husky, handsome, capable young flight surgeon; and a Si-War pilot named Carl Hye-Knudsen on a busman's holiday. We rose in the bright sunshine and flew out across the paddies, canals, gardens, palm orchards and hootches. As usual, all was peaceful below.

But I knew that there was always the chance somebody down there was even now taking aim at our Huskie and that a bullet could, at any moment, rip up through the floor. It wasn't likely. But it had happened not long ago to an American civilian observer who was standing up in an Army Caribou behind the two pilots as they made a low pass over a village to drop gifts for some kind of civic-action occasion. The bullet struck him in the testicles and drove parts of the map he had been unfolding between his legs up into his bowels. He died in the hospital.

Those things make you think as you mutter along in a chopper over VC country—and they particularly make you think when you descend from the relative safety of 2,500 feet and pass over the thick palm groves toward the rich plume of crimson smoke that the American Army team in residence at our village unloosed in a little meadow to guide us down to the proper place. I peered down at those shining palm thatches, rising like elevators to meet us, half expecting to see the telltale puff of blue smoke that would mean a sniper was trying for us.

Nothing happened. We settled into a sunlit meadow on the outskirts of the village, and everybody got gingerly out and scurried away from the chopper through the safe avenue directly in front, while its long vanes beat the grass flat for yards around and the American GIs frantically gesticulated at a horde of little kids massed on the edge of the field, lest they rush out and get decapitated in the excitement.

The supplies offloaded, the Huskie beat the air madly and rose into the sky and the horde of little kids rushed toward us in a screaming body—hundreds of tiny bodies grinning like monkeys, grabbing at the supplies, at your clothing, shouting and screaming their welcome. A boy of about six attached himself to me, quite literally. He got hold of my hand and refused to let go. He walked beside me, looking up, from time to time, very seriously, as if he'd discovered some kind of rare Martian animal and was leading it home for the family to observe. And of course, to him, I must have been fairly startling. Considering our relative size, it would have been about the same as if I had run over and seized the hand of a monster nine feet tall, with funny round blue eyes, a flaming red face, scraggly white hair and a pot belly hanging over its belt.

This village was, you should pardon the expression, "pacified." That meant that nobody bothered it in the daytime because there were U. S. Army tanks and U. S. Army M-113 armored personnel carriers parked at intervals on the hard mud streets of the town. They were manned by Arvin troops and the only thing to worry about was stepping on a mine. That was unlikely—but still if you were unlucky, you could do it at any time and almost anywhere. Capt. Dick Cloy, who was in charge of the Army team that stayed in the mud fort at one end of town, said that an American officer, due to rotate back to the States in a few days, had stepped on a VC mine not long ago and had his foot blown off to the ankle bones. The mine had been made out of an American CBU unit that had failed to explode and that the Vietcong had cleverly transformed into a booby trap.

Cloy was impressive. He was a tall easy-going rangy guy who spoke enough Vietnamese to be useful as an interpreter at the Sick Call that we had come here to perform. A couple of Army jeeps appeared, I wrenched my hand free with suitable expressions of sadness and regret, from my newfound friend, climbed into the jeep and we took off up the main street, which was lined on both sides with stores crammed with a goodly assortment of well-made merchandise, most of it American but also domestic products, also well-made as I discovered later when I went window shopping.

The horde of children raced after us up the street, a shrilly excited mob, but the jeep outdistanced them and when we reached the far end of town I saw the mud fort where the Sick Call was being held. It was the sorriest-looking fort I guess I'll ever see, with a hodge-podge roof of rusty torn scraps of metal and walls that appeared to have progressively melted in the rains until they resembled piles of mildewed glue. A large assortment of patients was on hand waiting to be treated and Dr. Wiita handled it under fairly difficult conditions: standing up in the middle of the mud walls in the semidarkness with patients and patients' mamas crowding in on him from all sides trying to thrust Junior into his arms ahead of Mrs. Khan's wailing Nugyen or Mrs. Than's squalling Boa Ho!

Dick Cloy was trying to find out from the mother what ailed the child, and he was doing his best but the general excitement mounted and all the children began screaming in anticipation of being examined. Poor Cloy's small stock of Vietnamese gave out, and Dr. Wiita had to fall back on the time-honored method of getting the mother to point to the spot on the tiny patient where he said it was hurting him. Of course, in some cases, the source of agony was all too evident. One small boy had an ulcer on his ankle that had turned pussy blue-gray as the tissue died and was in almost to the bone and as big as a silver dollar. Dr. Wiita gave the lad a shot of antibiotic and gave his mother a tube of the same stuff to put on the ulcer, but he told me later that it had gone so far it really needed intensive hospital treatment over a period of many weeks if they hoped really to bring it under control. But the hospitals were full and that poor kid was going to have to suffer with his ulcer until it either healed miraculously, or, as was more probable, got worse and turned into gangrene and his foot had to be amputated.

Skin diseases seemed the most prevalent among the tots, and I saw one tiny baby who was covered from head to foot with an angry rash—well, not a rash, but rather thousands of open raw sores, and the body so inflamed that even the flesh between the sores was pink through its coffee color. The child was writhing steadily and making a pitiful hoarse little sound, like an animal in a trap. It occurred to me, looking at the child, that if God really wasn't dead He ought to look in on this case. Here was utter innocence in the most intense unrelenting grip of torment. The Devil himself could have been proud if he'd thought of it.

Dr. Wiita injected the agonized child with antibiotics and gave the woman several bars of germicidal soap, indicating by sign language how to use it on the baby. I had to step outside a minute. There are some kinds of agony that are so hopeless and terrible that there's no use in looking at them if you can't alleviate them. Cloy told me that a great deal of this infant infection was due to the carelessness of mothers in not keeping the baby clean, and not looking after small infections before they grew large.

There were, of course, a few malingerers and hypochondriacs at the Sick Call, mostly old men or old women who complained of pains here and there, and who were difficult to get rid of, once they were under observation, since they kept jabbering, pointing at this or that part of their body, and making gestures indicating they wanted this or that treatment. Wiita was loathe to be stern with them but Cloy wasn't. He let them rant on for awhile, and then, when Wiita indicated he'd done all he could, Cloy lifted the patient and set him or her aside, firmly but gently, so somebody else could take the place.

The village itself, however, was a most active and cheerful

place. When I emerged from Sick Call, guess who was standing just outside the door and who grabbed my hand firmly and stared up at me with the air of having allowed a valuable pet to escape but now was happy to have him safely back! My tiny friend and I made our way down the main street beside the Bassac River and I was careful to walk in the tracks left by the jeep, knowing that any mines buried there would already have gone off. We finally reached the Army fort at the other end of town. My friend wished to accompany me into the fort, but Cloy said it was against their rules, so I gave him some *piastres* (knowing I shouldn't!) and said farewell (Farewell? He was right there with his tiny hand outstretched the instant I left the fort on the way to the midtown "Big Sick Call" later on).

I was secretly mighty glad I didn't have to stay out here at night with Capt. Cloy and his fellow officer, Capt. Lucky (a recent West Point graduate). There was a large hole in the wall over Lucky's cot. It came from a round of .57mm recoilless rifle fire. It hadn't exploded on impact as they are supposed to do, or Lucky and Cloy would have been pushing up daisies. Lucky said he couldn't understand why the VC quit with one round. They'd fired it from over there across the river and it was black as your hat and there wasn't a thing to prevent them from blowing the Army bivouac to hell and gone.

But that was good old Charlie. You never could tell what the little sonofabitch would do next because, as Lucky said, he probably didn't know himself. It did get pretty dark out here at night, Lucky said, and their morale hadn't been too good lately since they missed the Arvin sentry who was supposed to be on the front gate of the compound, and found him a couple of blocks down the street handing over some ammo to the VC. A thing like that could shake you up, Lucky said, particularly when the main force the Arvins left there was just him and Cloy and a couple of American sergeants out here 15 miles from anywhere and the VC knew it. Why they were still alive, Lucky said, was sometimes a mystery to him.

Lucky, Cloy and Maj. John Rogers, who was the civic action officer for the Air Force contingent at Binh Thuy and I took noon chow with the local Vietnamese headman whose name I didn't catch. He was most polite and cooperative and set forth an authentic Vietnamese meal of semiraw pork (this scared me almost as much as the VC, since trichinosis is not one of the milder forms of parasite infections and it wasn't unknown here); *Nunc Malm,* the famous sauce made of rotten fish and smelling precisely like rotten fish; marvelous domestic beer in large bottles and served in huge glasses with ice!; and tiny little shrimps fried crisp with their shells on which you are supposed to eat shell and all, and which I did with relish.

It isn't so bad at a meal like this if you aren't afraid to eat and drink *something.* It's when you are scared for your life and health about eating *anything* that the social pressure gets high. Bill Lederer in his book, *The Ugly American,* makes a big thing of us Americans turning to and gobbling up all kinds of native food. If we don't, Lederer says, they won't like us. I once rode in a car pool with Bill when I was a Navy lieutenant in Quonset Point and I feel this gives me the right to reply plaintively to his stern admonition: "If we *do* eat their food, Bill, we're likely to be shipped home in a box!"

I ate the little shrimps like mad and guzzled the iced beer and pushed the raw pork under a lettuce leaf and it was a most happy occasion, full of flowery compliments, fervent wishes for each other's health, and so on. I am sure the chief heaved a sigh of relief when all the windy Americans left. *His* job, by the way, was not one for the growing boys. It takes guts to stay out there the way he was doing with the VC all around. Any night they felt like putting on enough pressure, the Dawi's head could be found on the end of a pointed stick in the town plaza the next morning; many such heads have!

In the afternoon (with my buddy attached to one hand) I observed the Big Sick Call in the town's main square under an open-shed type of structure. The patients were there en masse, hundreds of them, and the spectators were present in even larger numbers to see the fun. It became necessary to rope off the area and even then the villagers, curious about how a needle looks going into the arm of a screaming neighbor, had to be held back by the American GIs doubling as policemen. Capt. Carl Hye-Knudsen proved most versatile. He held the patients while Dr. Wiita jabbed them with the hypo, and then, when business got too frantic for one man, Carl administered the shots himself. I noticed him, later, off in the middle of the plaza throwing *piastre* coins and candy up in the air by the fistful; the activity around him was spectacular.

I knew Carl from having enjoyed his hospitality in his room back at the base (Carl was the spark plug of the Si-War team there and flew the U-10 Courier throwing out leaflets and broadcasting *Chieu Hoi* messages to the VC). At night the Si-War gang gathered in Carl's room, played the latest hit records on his hi-fi, drank his scotch and traded the latest lies about gung-ho missions over toward the Cambodian border. It was a delightful place. Carl presented me with my very own FUCK COMMUNISM sign, which was several feet long and a foot wide and done in delightful vivid red-white-and-blue bands (Dr. Frank Camp later admired it so much I gave it to him before I left Can Tho). Carl had the personality and the temperament for his job, which was dangerous (one day later he came back with the back end of his Helioplane all shot to hell), and he worked in fine at the village Sick Call.

We treated 450 people that afternoon and the overall effect of the mission was undoubtedly good. VD was prevalent in that village, as it was in many others, and the team administered lots of anti-VD shots; maybe five pounds of aspirin and 50 pounds of soap were handed out; hundreds of antibiotic shots were given; salves and iodine were dispensed; and so it went. It was better than nothing, certainly, but it wasn't the answer. A lot of those people needed far more than a cake of soap, a packet of aspirin or a shot of penicillin. They needed a careful program of diet, medication and professional care to recover from the troubles they were showing Dr. Wiita. He knew it and deplored it. But as he said to me, "What can I do? There are so many villages, so few doctors and so many ailments."

"Do the best you can," I said.

"Yeah," Wiita said. "That's about it."

My tiny Vietnamese friend and I walked down the main drag together holding hands after the Sick Call and when the helicopter arrived I gave him all the spare *piastres* I had in my pockets and bid him a relieved farewell (not too sure, however, when the chopper settled onto the field at Binh Thuy 20 minutes later, that he wouldn't somehow be standing there waiting for me, with his tiny little hand outstretched!). He wasn't there. That lad was a real bird dog, but he wasn't *that* good.

9 NIGHT OF THE DRAGON

I went on a Dragon Ship flight from Binh Thuy with Maj. Walter Craig and his crew. Our mission was a general night patrol around Vinh Long, a town on the Mekong River about 20 miles from Can Tho. We were to cruise around and wait for a call for help from whatever boondock fort the Vietcong might choose to attack.

We took off while it was still light and climbed to 3,500 feet to get above the small arms fire. The Dragons carry 40 or 50 flares for night work and a direct hit by a tracer from the ground could set them all off. I was told they burn at 22,000 degrees F.

We flew up the Bassac River, as this branch of the Mekong is called. A big cumulous buildup, lit occasionally by lightning, towered nearby. From time to time we could see the Rough Puffs firing tracers from their forts along the river. They get nervous as darkness falls and want to show Charlie they're ready. It was the first time I'd seen tracers at night. They look like glowing coals of fire and they spew out like roman candle balls, often just about as erratically.

When the darkness got total we began to see flares here and there around the obscured land, shot up by the forts. They drifted down, casting a white glare on the paddies, and abruptly went out. Then it somehow seemed darker than before. Dull orange flashes of artillery could be seen at times in the distance.

We got an emergency call for help from a fort farther south in the Delta about an hour after takeoff. The VC were mortaring the place, and it looked as if an attempt would be made to overrun it.

Forty minutes later we got to the fort. We saw inside the walls a large wooden arrow lighted by coffee cans of sand soaked in jet fuel, burning smokily, pointing the direction of the VC attack. The defenders fired tracers to give us the range. The Vietcong had stopped firing when they heard us coming so as not to give away their position by the muzzle flashes of their guns. Maj. Craig's men threw out some flares. I saw now that the fort was located at one end of a small village beside a canal.

Our tiny Vietnamese interpreter, Nguyen Phu Qui, who was along to speak to the Rough Puffs in Vietnamese, was jabbering with them interminably on the radio. The rules of the Delta war were that all strikes near outlying forts require a formal request from the Rough Puff commander in the fort. Interpreters sometimes yak so long that by the time they transmit the order to fire the VC have left the area.

There really didn't seem to be much to talk about. The lighted arrow was pointed at the VC, and the tracers had given us the range. Finally, in exasperation, one of the crew shouted, "Let's start shooting. That little son-of-a-bitch will be talking all night."

But Maj. Craig abided scrupulously by the rules and waited for Nguyen to give him the official go-ahead, which he finally did. Craig laid Spooky on one wing and banked around the fort. He peered intently through an illuminated sight mounted beside his left shoulder, scrutinizing the area where the fort's pointing fire had landed. Then we commenced firing and the world seemed to blow up. The Dragon Ship was enveloped in yellow fire. A shower of lovely pink lights raced out of the yellow muzzle blast but seemed to strike the earth almost lazily. There was a deafening wail that sounded like a monster air horn. It seemed pretty certain that we had gotten the VC's attention.

Then word came through the interpreter that the fort was reporting fire coming from the village. Craig widened his turn a little. When he came over the village, we fired a sustained burst. The whole village was drenched in crimson hail. There was a pause. As our flares went out, the guys in back kept throwing out more. Two or three were usually burning at once. As we circled, the scene assumed a kind of hellish aspect: the fierce blinding suns, drifting down, leaving white smoke trails in the flare light, and above that the pit of night; below, the blinding reflection of the flares in the canal, the dark mass of the earth, brightened into patterns of hutlines, trees and paddies as the flares dropped close to the earth; then suddenly going black again as the flare fell into the water and went out, or sank into a dark patch of trees and was lost. The cockpit was dark except for the red glow of the instrument lights, to cut down our visibility to the ground gunners, but each time we cut through our flare light in our great circle, we must have stood out clearly.

The cockpit door burst open and a young gunner named Dave Davanay yelled to me to come and watch the firing close up. I rose and went aft. The ship held its left-hand bank, filling the cabin with rushing air currents from open gun ports and the open rear door, where a gunner stood nonchalantly in the dim red battle lights beside the safety strap. He was smoking a cigarette.

Then all three miniguns let go again. The sound was brain-addling. The muzzle flames lit everyone's face in a weird yellow glow. Dave Davanay was grinning with excitement. The glowing tracers seemed to curve as they left the plane because of our forward motion.

We circled the village firing in short bursts for nearly an hour, until we ran out of ammo. The VC must have been waiting for that, because a moment later little Nguyen shouted shrilly, "Let's go! The VC are shooting at Spooky!"

But we stayed in orbit over the fort at the request of the Rough Puffs, dropping more flares so they could see the VC if they rushed the wire. Out of ammo, we were unable to return the VC fire. Craig radioed for another Dragon Ship to relieve us, but none came. I sat tensely, waiting for the ship to be hit, hoping it wouldn't be the goddam flares. A 22,000-degree fire would melt the plane in midair.

Finally, after a delay while headquarters decided whether to send another Dragon Ship or some F-100 fighters, we were officially released to go home. "I'm glad they didn't send the jets," Craig said on the way back.

"Why?"

"We'd have had to stay there and FAC for them. They tool around at about 435 knots, and they're concentrating on the target. In the dark it's easy to have a midair." (It isn't impossible in daylight. I saw an F-4 Phantom jet that hit its own FAC plane near Danang. The jet got home with wing damage. The Bird Dog was smashed to a pulp.)

When we got back to the Dragon's home base, Binh Thuy, the tower radioed not to land. Some VC were out in the swamp under the final approach lane waiting to pot at incoming planes. I had seen the area in daylight. It was solid with high grass, which stood in shin-deep water, making it hard for the K-9 dogs to move with their masters, and I'd heard the base commander wanted it defoliated by the Ranch Hand spray planes. VC could infiltrate it without being detected and now apparently they had.

We stayed aloft for about an hour, circling at 4,000 feet, while the perimeter guards presumably searched for the VC in the high grass. Then since our fuel was getting critical, we asked for permission to land and got it. We came in very low and fast, skimming the tall grass (it's much harder to hit a plane that's just overhead, due to the short time it's over you). We had no lights, not even the red cabin battle lights, and as I looked out the window and saw the lights of the base ahead, almost level with my eyes, and knew we were now passing the VC, if any, I felt the familiar sensation most GIs will recall, when you expect to be shot at: your whole body tries to draw in and make itself just as small as it can, and you tuck your feet under you and hunch your shoulders and feel very little and babyish, somehow. The low final approach finally ended with a brush of wheels on concrete in the total darkness, and a fast long rollout, with Craig braking hard.

We taxied back and I thanked the boys for the ride and went to my barracks to bed, completely pooped. Craig and the crew, however, were only half through with their night's work. I left them drinking coffee while the ordnance gang loaded a fresh batch of ammo aboard to feed the hungry miniguns: 18,000 rounds—to replace the 18,000 we'd fired down in the Delta an hour ago.

10 —MEANWHILE, ON THE GROUND

The civilian hospital in Can Tho was a disorganized jumble of old concrete buildings built by the French many years ago, jammed into a mud compound with open sewers, a row of barred cells full of VC prisoners, a Buddhist pagoda presided over by a monk in an orange robe, a snack bar known as "Howard Johnson's," a kitchen that consisted of several vats full of stew simmering over charcoal fires, a laundry where the work is largely done by hand with the assistance of four little Maytags (the bloody sheets and dirty towels and gowns were usually stacked in a chest-high heap the length of the long room) and three operating rooms that ran from dawn until dark seven days a week, and often through the night. It was one of the largest in the Delta. Patients arrived here from distant points by sampan, cyclo, buffalo cart, on foot or on somebody's back. Many people never arrived at all. They died on the way.

There were usually two persons to a bed. And, the laundry problem being what it was, they lay on straw mats that can be hosed off to remove pus, blood, vomit, feces, urine and paddy mud and that do not have to be put through the little Maytags or be hung up in the saturated monsoon air to stay wet indefinitely because of the humidity.

Dr. Frank Camp, the U.S. Air Force major who was head of the military surgical team in the hospital, was the spark plug of the place. He supervised the American civilian doctors who came over under Project Vietnam (they received a free round-trip ticket and $10 a day to cover their expenses and stayed usually for two months). Camp also "advised" the Vietnamese doctors who were associated with the hospital and took a hand with the nurses, cooks, laundresses, truck drivers who supplied the hospital, electricians, mechanics and odd-job people. I met him one afternoon in his office at the Can Tho hospital without any prior knowledge of him, expecting to spend maybe half an hour in talk and another half hour touring the wards. It went this way:

"I'm a reporter," I said, "over here writing up the air war."

"You won't find any air war here," Camp said. "This is a hospital."

"Some of the patients are here as a result of the air war, aren't they?"

"They are here because they got wounded or have some disease."

"Well, would you mind if I walked around the wards?"

"It depends on how you intend to write it up."

I felt my hackles rising. Here was one of those coverup boys who wanted a sanitized report of his doings. *Well, be damned to you,* I thought.

"I won't waste time with you," Dr. Camp said, "if you're over here to pretty up this war. If that's your pitch, let's forget it. I've got to operate in about 20 minutes."

I realized I'd been wrong about this man, and a feeling of excitement welled up.

"You mean you *don't* want a pretty story?"

"It's not a pretty story," Camp said. "This hospital needs a new laundry—big commercial washers and big commercial dryers. There aren't many Vietnamese doctors to help us—and some of those we've got aren't worth much. We're supposed to handle about 400 patients. We've got nearer 900. Red tape is handicapping our whole program at various levels. Neil Sheehan of the *New York Times* was here a while ago and I told it to him and he published it. I got a letter of reprimand out of it."

"But won't you get in trouble if I publish what you're saying?"

"I'm not worried," Camp said. "All I ask you is to tell the truth."

"You've got my promise," I said. "When do we start?"

"Right now," Camp said, "I'm about to make my rounds. You can come with me if you like."

I came to the Can Tho hospital to talk a few minutes and walk through the place for half an hour. Half-way through the rounds with Camp, I decided to stay with him for at least a week if he would have me. We went rapidly from bed to bed and Camp examined patients, checked their charts, made recommendations to the Vietnamese female nurse and male attendant who accompanied us. Communication was made through a tall Vietnamese civilian girl interpreter who wore high-heeled sandals, black silk pajamas, a butter-yellow *au dai* and dark glasses in frames studded with rhinestones.

Camp told me later they called her the Dragon Lady, and that she was very thin-skinned about any sort of criticism. She wasn't a bad interpreter, he said, but she was apt to tell him the things she thought he would want to hear—not the true facts as she got them from the patients and the attendants. That was a dangerous thing in his place, where many patients were hovering close to death, but it was a universal habit in Vietnam, and, in fact, in many backward countries.

"How does he feel?" Camp would ask about a patient. The Dragon Lady would speak to the man in Vietnamese at length. She seemed to be eliciting his entire medical history, and I expected a detailed report on his symptoms, state of mind and specific complaints. "He says he feels pretty good," was what the Dragon Lady would say. Camp would nod. Perhaps he'd knead the belly of a man with an incision from rib cage to genitals in a probing pressure that made me wince to watch it. If the man's face contorted in pain, Camp got the answer that the interpreter might not have given him. I really didn't know. It seemed to me that Camp was working largely from his experience. There was definitely a communications gap.

I made rounds with Dr. Frank Camp for many days and I saw hundreds of cases. Here are a few of them. A man lying on the cement porch outside the emergency room with a punji stake in his heel. I was, by this time, wearing the pale-green cotton surgeon's pajamas, face mask and cloth skull cap that the doctors and operating room people all wore. This man quite naturally mistook me for a doctor. He raised a face that was a taut grimace of agony and pointed to his foot. I knelt down and looked at it. The stake was a big one, about as thick as a clothespin, and it had gone in very deeply. The flesh around the stake was swollen and purple in color and it was obvious that it must hurt like hell. I smiled encouragingly at the man and told him, in English, that I'd try to get somebody out to help him.

But when I stepped into the emergency receiving room I found all three tables occupied by bloody naked bodies, also in pain, and on the floor of the room were four or five other terribly wounded people. There was so much blood on the floor that when I left by the other door, looking for Dr. Camp, I tracked blood smudges out onto the other porch. By that time, of course, I realized why the man with the punji stake in his foot was lying, unattended, on the porch. Bad off as he was, others were worse. And the staff of this place was limited. The male nurse, Capt. Bob Feeny, did minor surgery in the emergency room with local anesthetic. When I asked what minor surgery was, Camp said, "Anything up to and including amputations."

An hour later, when I chanced to walk out on the porch, the man with the punji stake was still there. His foot was now very swollen and growing blackish purple. His eyes were glazed and he seemed to be semiconscious.

There is a certain incision that I saw more of than any other in the Can Tho hospital. I saw it on men, women and children by the dozen—it was, I finally came to feel, a sort of badge of initiation into the Vietnamese fraternity of pain. It was an exploratory incision used on all cases of gunshots or mortar fragment wounds of the abdomen, from the solar plexus down to the lower belly, sewed up with big stitches that looked like the lacing of an old-fashioned football.

Camp explained that they did not have the time for the more sophisticated procedures they knew and used in America. You had to do it quickly because others were waiting, and oddly enough, he said, this type of closure seemed to heal faster and be just as strong as the more complicated closures where the layers of tissue were closed individually with smaller stitches. "I do a major operation in 25 minutes," Camp said. "My new doctors, when they first come here, want to do it the way they used to do it—make observations, tests, check medical histories and all that. They soon see, however, that there's no time for that."

"Do you lose many patients?"

"Of course. But not as many as you'd expect, to look at them when they come in. These people are tough—and they're stoic. Have you noticed anything as we've been walking through the wards?"

"What do you mean?"

"How quiet it is. Nobody is screaming or moaning. And yet dozens of them are in intense pain."

Dr. Camp said that one of the great problems in Vietnam, even without war, was lack of qualified doctors. The training was done after the manner of the old methods when the French were here. They took seven years of lectures. No textbooks, no lab work, no attendance taken. It tended to turn out doctors without the skills of hand, eye and experience—doctors who remembered it, if they'd been in attendance that day, from their notebooks. And there were only a few of these. Out of about 1,000 doctors in the country, Camp estimated that 700 were in the military, 60 were female, 100 were old and ineffective. That left 140 to take care of 15,000,000 civilians—and if you wanted the services of any of these you had to pay for it. The net result is that there isn't really *any* Vietnamese medical care available to the masses of the Vietnamese people and never has been.

There are Chinese doctors, so-called, and I saw the results of one of their treatments in the emergency receiving rooms. The man was in for advanced TB—but his chest (I have a color photo of him) was covered with brown scars where the doctor had burned him to drive the devils out of his body.

A tiny elf of a baby was lying quietly on a bed and its

mother was beside it. I thought it was convalescing and wanted to take a picture. Camp lifted the sterile covering off its chest. There was no chest—just a gaping gluey hole covered with green pus under which we could see the lungs rising and falling. "Gas gangrene," Camp said. "It's attacking the ribs. We'll have to remove them, and if we do I don't know what will support this poor kid's chest."

"Gas gangrene?"

Camp smiled. "Oh, no—not from war gas. It occurs—as in this case—when there's been an untreated skin infection and the gas-producing gangrenous organism gets in deep. There are two kinds of gangrene, wet and dry. The dry type causes the tissue to shrivel. The wet type—as this child has—is much worse. You have to perform extensive debridement—remove all dead and infected tissue from a wide area—as if you were dealing with a cancer, and be sure to leave a healthy base. If the stuff gets in the bone you have to take the bone."

Dr. Camp laid the sterile cloth back over the hideous wound and the child again looked like a little elf or pixie. His mother smiled at us. I don't think she knew how serious it was. She (and all of the hundreds of other patients) had great hope and faith in Dr. Camp. To them he was obviously a kind of superman.

Not everybody was a fan of Camp's, however. He was impatient and very blunt with anybody he thought wasn't doing his job. He was arrogant, and he was obviously driven by an enormous ego. He was, it seemed to me, the kind of man who'd *rather* blow up when the red-tape boys got in his hair (as they, and many others, were bound to do) than patiently sort it out and try to use diplomacy to get his way. One thing was sure. If you did something Dr. Camp did not approve of, you were not left long in doubt. He told you. But in his behalf I must say that he told people matter-of-factly, clearly, and he gave his reasons and he listened carefully to the rebuttal. If it made sense, even though it proved him wrong, he accepted it. And another thing was pretty sure too. A less aggressive man than Camp, who let people fuss around and get away with things, couldn't have handled this big job.

One example: an American surgeon, newly arrived under the Project Vietnam program, had been goofing off. He'd order an operating room to be assigned to him to handle a patient, the patient would be prepped and then this surgeon wouldn't show up. I was at the hospital one morning when he had reserved an operating room to do a skin graft on an area of a boy's arm where the tissue had been destroyed. The boy had been scrubbed up and sedated. The room was ready. No doctor. Dr. Camp scrubbed up and went in to do the job himself.

I went in with him, wearing the green pajamas, mask and cap that had been my uniform for days. I had never seen a skin graft operation and it was interesting. There is a device that shaves off the top layer of living skin (in this case from the boy's thigh) in a patch the size needed to cover the debrided area that waits to receive it. It's a bit gruesome to watch—like a razor skinning a guy alive over part of his body—leaving a bright crimson patch where the skin was.

Camp took the new patch and was sewing it neatly into the debrided area on the arm when the lights suddenly went out over the operating table. It was daylight but rather shadowy in the room, and Camp said to one of the assistants, "Go get a flashlight," as calmly as if this happened all the time. It didn't happen all the time but it did happen frequently, and when the operation was over I asked Camp why he didn't have an emergency lighting system to use when the city power failed.

"We do," he said with a grin, "but it was on the fritz this morning. It often is."

I had recently visited the nearby Binh Thuy Air Base, where I had been entertained by the base commander, Col. Warren D. Craig, and I suggested to Camp that he get in touch with Craig. Perhaps there was a spare motor-generator kit in one of those huge warehouses out there that wasn't being used. Camp reacted in typical Camp manner. He stepped into his office at once, called the air base, got hold of Col. Craig and put it to him. The next morning Craig appeared with one of his maintenance specialists, Lt. Baron, and to make a long story short, Craig *did* provide a motor-generator to Camp. It proved to be a little too big, so Camp traded it off to the Navy for one suited to his needs. Now they don't have to use the flashlights.

What happened to Wandering Boy? I do not know, but I did hear Camp say to his assistant, young Dr. Jerry Baugh, "If you see him, tell him I want to talk to him." My guess is that the surgeon in question either shaped up fast or departed. It would have had to be one or the other, knowing Dr. Camp.

Jerry Baugh, from Tulane Medical School, was one of those guys who stood in line everytime anything worthwhile was being handed out in this life, and then made the most of what they gave him. He was a tall guy, built like an oarsman with long powerful arms and strong shoulders. He cut his light-blond hair skull-close. He was up at dawn, up in the middle of the night, up anytime he was needed, and he never griped or groused, at least in my hearing. He had a smile that wouldn't quit. He was, most importantly, a skillful surgeon and he learned fast and remembered what he learned.

"I wouldn't want you to go around saying this," Camp told me, "but I couldn't make it here without Jerry. He's learning a lot too. He's had the equivalent of three years' surgical experience already. He's been here about six months."

One day I couldn't resist. I wandered into Jerry's room when he was reading a paperback, and spoke to this living improvement on Dr. Kildare at his best, and said, with a serious face, "If you've got problems, Jerry, I'm an older guy and I've been around. If you're worried about your appearance, can't get a date or feel insecure in your work, I'll be happy to analyze your problems and set you straight. I hate to see a poor wizened little fella like you hiding in your room like this."

Jerry hefted his six-foot frame off the bed and tossed the paperback aside with one of his oarsman's arms and smiled his won't-quit smile. "You're cracking up, Mr. Harvey," he said gently. "Why don't you go over and lie down in your room until it gets a little cooler? A man your age shouldn't be up and around like this in the heat of the day."

The surgical team—doctors, anesthetists, nurses (male and female), supervisors, scrub techs and others—all ate together in the large Day Room on the top floor of the old bank. It was, hands down, the best food I tasted anywhere in Vietnam and there was lots of it. The secret of it all was the cook. He had been hired by Camp and he was one of those resourceful characters that books are written around. For example, on top of this old French bank was a weird arrangement of parapets, sundecks, walkways, overhangs—like the set on a TV thriller where the bad guys chase the good guys and shoot it out behind this ledge and that. The cook, whose name I lost from my notebook, more's the pity, had a flourishing garden. He'd carried rich soil from home and packed it in along the walkways and ledges. You could go up and pick a juicy ripe tomato, or a crisp cucumber or a pot of snap beans, plus a lot of exciting Vietnamese vegetables I'd never seen before, but which tasted wonderful the way the cook fixed them.

The cook had relatives in town, of course, lots of them, and some of them were in the fresh-food business. So we got fish straight out of the Mekong, tasty pork chops and steaks and, of course, exotic Vietnamese tidbits that nobody knew the name of but everybody ate like mad. The food was brought out by a little Vietnamese girl with lovely gleaming gold teeth, a fluffy permanent and one aim in life: to outdo herself, day by day, minute by minute, in the quality of service to the surgical team. When I took a color picture of her with my Nikon, I thought she was going to collapse completely from sheer excitement.

Dr. Camp put me up on a couch in his bedroom, there being nothing else available, and he and Charlie and I slept there at night. Charlie was an otter who was having himself (or herself—I never knew) a ball. I assume it was a male with that name. Charlie lived the life of Riley up on the roof during the day, crawling through the drains, twittering happily (an otter sounds just like a bird), but alas, at night, Charlie still had plenty of energy left.

Mostly he slept at the foot of Camp's bed, but when he got restless he came over to visit me. The only way to escape him was to wrap the covers around my head and put my nose tight against the back cushions of the sofa. But even then Charlie made it. A tiny whiskery wet nose would eventually touch the tip of mine, as the loving little bastard wormed his way between the covers and the cushions, and would quiver ecstatically at the contact. I'd rear up and whisper, so as not to wake Camp, who needed his sleep, "Goddamit, Charlie—*get outa here!*"

Charlie also had a keen interest in my two green cloth bags and one morning early I was awakened by the sound of Charlie emptying the bags of my gear. He had the light meter when I caught him, dragging it, presumably, toward his favorite drain.

As I said, all was not sweetness and light in the surgical team. Dr. John Bogard, who did not live with the team but was a Special Forces surgeon and lived at the Compound at the Old Can Tho Airfield, was one of those who, I felt, was less than enchanted with Camp. Or perhaps Bogard was just a reserved type. At any rate, it was like pulling rusty spikes out of an oak plank for Camp to pull a response to a remark out of Capt. Bogard. Bogard wouldn't answer at all, usually, or if he did, it would be in such a low sparing manner that you didn't hear it or understand it. If Bogard reads this I hope he'll forgive me, but I think he'll agree with me. I'm sure, John, that you'd like to know what Frank Camp said about you behind your back.

"He's hard to handle," Camp said, "doesn't like to take direction very much. But he works as hard as I do, he never lets me down when he says he'll do something. I don't care if he likes me or not. We need him here and he's sure as hell pulling his weight."

Camp did, however, really tangle with a female "supervisor type" who arrived at Can Tho and set up shop "to advise, plan, coordinate, write reports and stuff like that." What he needed most, Camp said, wasn't coordinating and planning, but somebody to get out in the wards and nurse the wounded (this female type was a nurse, among other things). But when this course of action was suggested to her, the lady in question countered by telling Camp that her "job description" did not include actual nursing. She was not prepared to waste her experience in such activity. I saw the "job description" she wrote to Camp. It was several pages of closely-spaced polysyllables, and I couldn't make much real meaning in it—and I asked Camp how he reacted. He grinned. "I gave her a great big smile," he said, "and then I told her I had a new job description to suggest to her if she wanted to stick around here."

"What was that?"

"Get your ass out in the ward and nurse," Camp said.

(The supervisor type wasn't there when I arrived.)

After many days and nights in the operating room I got a crude basic idea of what goes on in a civilian Vietnam hospital in wartime. I do not pose as an expert because I'm not. But certain things were done so often and so routinely that they seemed typical. When a person is hit in the abdomen (a very high percentage of wounds are here, probably due to the fact that the abdomen is the largest target of the body) a thorough examination of the various organs in the abdomen is mandatory. It is necessary to remove the intestines in a pile on the man's belly and go over them, carefully, inch by inch, to be sure there is no hole caused by a fragment. A missed perforation means peritonitis (infection of the belly cavity) and another operation at the least, and possibly death. I have seen so many exposed bowels being examined that I could tell, just by looking at the intestine, if it came from a young or old person, and the general physical condition of the owner. Children have firm pink intestines in their bellies. Old sick people have dirty flaccid coils of guts.

I saw, of course, a number of operations involving infections of the abdomen so severe that, when the scalpel cut the stomach wall, pus welled out by the quart, as if an enormous boil had been lanced. For this purpose they have a vacuum bottle to suck the pus into under reduced air pressure. It's run by electricity, and Camp said that the vacuum bottles, as well as proper illumination, were the reason he was glad Col. Craig was supplying him with an emergency generator. You can let the pus gush out and wipe it up as best you can, but it isn't the ideal way to handle an operation.

One very interesting case involved worms (which are always present in the bowels; you can see them moving in great masses under the walls of the bowel during an operation for some other reason). But in this case, a worm had been killing its host. It was in the main bile duct between the liver and the small bowel completely filling and choking this relatively small tube and making the man sick. Jerry Baugh found the worm and called me in to look at it. There it was, a long, white, wriggling thing, trying to crawl out of the opening Jerry had made in the tube. He helped it out, tossed it aside with his tweezers, and sewed the man up neatly and quickly. A small incident in a day's work.

I saw and photographed, in color, cases so terrible that when I brought my films back home a lot of people could not stand to look at them. I mention this for two reasons: (1) I can prove with pictures what I say in this chapter, and (2) it's not so easy to say, if you haven't been there: "I'm sorry it's necessary to fight this kind of war, where civilians are bound to get hurt, but there's no way out of it. Civilians have always been hurt in wars and they probably always will be."

When you see a woman recovering from some kind of attack, a grotesque, scarred nightmare creature except for the smooth untouched breast the child is sucking at, you get an idea of it. When a lovely young girl of 20 holds up the raw stump of her leg for you to photograph and smiles at you gratefully because you care enough to want to take her picture, you get an idea of it. When you see a rice farmer who stepped on a VC mine and his hoe sliced his face wide open from his chin up through his nose into his forehead, so it is lying open like a butcher's side of meat, you have an insight. Or the man dying of napalm, his face black with third-degree burns, bandages over his whole body, but the festering that follows the death of tissue and the agony that will go on until he dies yet to come, because he is still in shock, and somebody speaks to him and he smiles with his doomed black face. Or the child dying of tetanus with the soles of his feet and the palms of his hands green and a rigid smile of agony, known as *risus sardonicus,* on his face. Or the girl with a perforated typhoid ulcer who you can smell three beds away, as you approach, and who, when Dr. Camp presses gently on her abdomen, grimaces in such high intense pain that you shut your eyes and then open them and see a curtain of pus has welled out of the incision and has bathed her side and is wetting the straw mat she is lying on.

Or the casual remark Camp made one evening during his rounds, to the little Vietnamese nurse who was attending us. "Now you're letting the floor get bloody again. You know I told you not to do that." Or the flies that buzz from wound to wound in a ward, despite the best efforts of the doctors to keep them out. Or the VC in their cells like a pack of wolves, staring at you through the bars with black hating eyes, and the smell of their urine and feces strong in the heat. Or the man who tried to commit suicide and is resisting, violently, the efforts to save him in the emergency room one night. Or the girl who somehow had been shot from the side, and had both her eyes torn out, but no other injury, and how you crushed an empty film can in your hand without realizing it while you looked.

Or the little boy who'd been mortared in his bed and who Dr. Chuck Beychok and Mr. Ba, the deft, inscrutable Vietnamese assistant, were working over, amputating the three middle fingers of one hand, which were hopelessly torn, and trying to save the thumb and the little finger, to give the boy a "claw grip" as Dr. Beychok explained to me in his quiet matter-of-fact voice as they cut and sewed on the tiny crimson hand.

I could go on and on, giving specific instance after specific instance that I photographed in the Can Tho hospital during those days and nights. But these things finally cease to have any impact. After you have seen enough of them you become used to them and you take them as facts of life the way the surgeons of Camp's team do. But I will admit that when I focused my camera on that boy's shattered little bloody hand between those two careful steady hands wearing rubber gloves and trying to save a thumb and finger for a claw grip, the focusing window blurred before my eyes. All my life, when I see flowers, crushed in a roaring street, I'll think of Can Tho.

One evening when we were having supper at the team's headquarters in the old bank building, Dr. Camp told the story of the frog and the scorpion, an old Vietnamese fable I had not heard. It seems that a frog and a scorpion were sitting on the bank of a stream and the scorpion wanted to get to the other side and asked the frog to carry him over on his back. The frog was reluctant, saying that the scorpion might sting him and kill him. The scorpion argued that if he stung the frog he too would die, since he couldn't swim. So finally the frog agreed to carry him over. In midstream the scorpion stung the frog, and the frog, sinking to his death, looked over his shoulder and said, "Why?"

"Xin Loi," said the scorpion.

Camp explained that *Xin Loi,* in Vietnamese, had a translation that meant simply, "I'm sorry." But in this fable, Camp said, the phrase was understood by the Vietnamese to have a more far-reaching meaning. To them, in this context, *Xin Loi* meant: "I'm sorry, but in this country nothing really makes sense." Camp was suggesting that there was really no solution to the trouble these poor people were undergoing because of the essential senselessness of so much of what went on. I do not agree. I think that it is too easy to make this kind of blanket appraisal of the fury, death, destruction and misery that is going on in Vietnam now. Certainly it makes sense. Anyone who had read *Lord of the Flies* knows that. There is a thin veneer of restraint covering everybody. A minor scratch is enough to let out the savage beast that lurks underneath. The war in Vietnam, and the many other big and little wars raging around the globe now, and which will no doubt continue to rage as long as the combatants have the energy and the means to wage them, are not a senseless thing. They make sense, all right. The nature of man is basically combative and it probably always will be. The strong kill and maim the weak. They always have, using whatever excuses seemed plausible at the moment, and they no doubt always will. A man—or a nation—allows itself to grow weak at its peril; horrors, injustices and tragedies notwithstanding.

I do, however, feel a little sorry for myself and the rest of us human beings who are trapped by our basic nature—the urge to violence, particularly toward strangers who can be imagined as "foreign devils," particularly when there's a war going on. "Killing a man is murder," said Voltaire, "unless you do it to the sound of trumpets."

There's been some speculation going around that God is dead. I don't think God is dead. I do sometimes wish, however, that He hadn't set up the rules in such an even-handed fashion between Him and the Devil. The Old Boy from Down Below seems to win an inordinate number of them, as our world population grows larger, and frankly I don't see much hope for improvement in the short run.

11 PATROL WITH THE RIVER JETS

There are two kinds of jets in Vietnam—those that fly in the sky and those that whine through the yellow rivers on long frothy rooster tails (made by high-powered plumes of water from the pumps that propelled these craft). These are called "patrol boats, river" or PBRs. Since these two kinds of jets work hand in glove, it seemed to me that a coverage of the air war in Vietnam would not be complete without a look at the river jets.

When I got to Can Tho, in the Delta, the Navy was just beginning to operate PBR patrols out of a new base they'd set up on the riverbank in the center of town. It was a pretty impressive sight. They had these big gray fiberglass hulls neatly nosed in, side by side, with guns sprouting out of them, looking very efficient against the tawny yellow surface of the Bassac River. Downstream a couple of hundred feet was the Navy Can Tho Operational Headquarters complete with a ceiling-high detailed map of the Mekong river system with its various mouths, cross canals, islands, inlets, hamlets and so on, so that the patrol boats could be vectored from home base with great accuracy, once the coordinates of the target were established. Since I am an old Navy man, air-craft-carrier type, the Navy guys at Can Tho took me right back in the Club and were happy to welcome me aboard for a night patrol on the Bassac. My PBR was commanded by a big aggressive boatswain's mate second class, William Pollard, dressed in dark coveralls and hung about with personal weapons, a steel helmet, everything but a dagger in his teeth. Pollard so impressed me that for a long time (he wore no insignia of identification) I thought he was a full commander: I guess because he was introduced to me as the commander of the boat. He had a scary manner about him, as if he not only patrolled but brought back scalps and things like that when he knocked off anybody. He said they'd been under heavy fire last night and he expected more tonight (which surprised and scared me: I'm not a bit gung-ho and like to go on patrols that are exciting but safe). But I had more or less committed myself and shame drove me aboard the PBR against my better judgment. Pollard fitted me with a steel helmet and a heavy nylon flak vest and they also broke out an M-16 automatic weapon for me to use if things got really hot and they needed another gun. By this time, believe me, I was wishing I'd left the PBRs alone! In the first place I don't believe in correspondents killing people. I think it's a crummy thing for them to do. If they want to kill people they ought to jolly well join up, get a uniform and become a GI. Of course, if it was kill or be killed, I would no doubt be in there firing the best I could, and I suppose this was what Pollard had in mind.

The crew of our boat was made up of Kyle Wakker, engineer and aftergunner; Mike Reboulet, radio and radar operator, and second in command; and Jon Wisth, forward machine gunner. The PBR is 31 feet long, made of fiberglass, and mounts a twin .50-caliber machine gun on the bow, a single .50 on the stern, an M-79 grenade launcher, a hand-held M-60 machine gun with a small tripod fastened to the muzzle for steadier firing; three automatic M-16 rifles and a 12-gauge shotgun. The armor, however, was pretty skimpy. A

PBR has two thin sheets of steel armor plate erected parallel to each other on the afterdeck, which a man can crouch down between, and two thin sheets on either side of the control cockpit. These are said to turn ordinary rifle bullets but a .50-caliber would go through them like paper. They are really for moral support, according to PBR men I talked to in the Delta. "When you duck down behind these plates you can't see the muzzle flashes from the shore," they said. "It's kind of like the ostrich sticking his head in the sand—but it's better than looking at the flashes."

I was told that the fiberglass hulls were given added buoyancy by filling up the various voids with plastic foam—a kind of internal life-preserver, in case the VC ventilated the fiberglass hull extensively. Chief Ed Canby, USN, who was the most celebrated Vietcong fighter in the river war at the time, wasn't quite as optimistic about the PBRs as the Navy Public Information Service. "Ever see the hole a fifty-seven recoilless makes?" he asked me.

"No."

"Well, some dark night Charlie may decide to ambush one of our PBRs in a narrow cut. They can do it any time they want to. They practice in the daytime by setting up the weapon in the tall grass and then running a boat up and down the channel, figuring the range and the approach angles and so forth, so they've got the place zeroed in. They could put a .57 round through us at the waterline, and if they do, I don't know if we'd stay afloat or not."

"But if they missed," I said, remembering the publicity, "you could pour on the coal and get out of there. Those boats go like hell wide open."

"They go 25 knots wide open," Canby said drily. "Ever try to outrun a cannon shell at 25 knots?"

So when our night patrol eased out from the Navy dock in Can Tho, I had all these little facts and figures in mind and they weren't particularly soothing. We were taking two boats. Lt. (jg) John Smith, USN, was in the lead boat (we were the backup). They had been ambushed last night, Pollard said, and they were going back tonight to get revenge. The ambush had come from a VC-controlled island, 10 or 15 miles down the river. But Pollard advised me to put on my steel helmet and flak vest because you never could tell when a VC might be taking aim at you from the dark shore. Chief Canby had mentioned this too. He had spoken of sitting chatting with a pirate-type friend in a junk (Canby was one of those fire-breathers who fought in junks before they gave him PBRs) when suddenly the friend's face blew up like a ripe tomato. "Sniper hit him," Canby said. "Must have been a mile to shore. Damndest thing."

"Kill him?" I asked.

"Dead," Canby said.

The night I went on patrol, we left the dock at 1900 in full darkness and it was spooky out there on the black river, with dim lights glowing behind the tropical vegetation on the shores and the thought that gun muzzles might be seeking my head as we followed Smith's PBR down river. I have never been a cop at heart, and this was what we were, river cops. Our mission was to stop any sampan or small boat of any kind that was moving after darkness (enforcing the curfew American and Arvin forces had placed on the Mekong Delta). Somehow I kind of hated it when Smith's PBR, looking huge and somehow bullying, moved in on a man and wife in what appeared to be a rowboat with a little blob of palm fronds for a roof. The lead boat turned a high-powered searchlight on the rowboat. It was illuminated vividly. We, in turn, trained our heavy machine guns on the man and his wife (in case they tried to shoot Smith's boys). The PBR eased in. I could see the man bowing his head in what seemed to be a plea to let him go, but they didn't let him go. They took him and his wife on board and both boats turned back to Can Tho and carried them to the local jail where they were booked and held.

After we'd locked up the rowboat people we made a short trip across the Bassac to a local fort manned by Vietnamese police. Our PBR docked. The shore was lined with shacks full of people and I could see people moving in the dim light through the undergrowth. I didn't really want to do it (because if you got zapped here, there wouldn't be much you could do about it), but I took off my flak vest and steel helmet and climbed off the deck of the PBR onto a wooden ladder that let up to the jungle bank. Here, illuminated by the lights of the houses, a man was really a prime target. The ladder was rickety, and if you fell off, you would fall into a spooky pit of darkness (mud or the river, I couldn't tell), but I went up that thing like a monkey after a coconut and crossed the local alley in what could only be described as a panicky canter and followed Smith past the armed guards into the fort.

It was worth it to see the inside of a Vietnamese fort at night. The place had stone walls maybe three feet thick. There was no glass in the windows, which were heavily barred. The walls were pockmarked with bullets that had come in through the windows. It was inhabited by little Vietnamese policemen and little Vietnamese women, presumably their wives, and little Vietnamese kids of all ages. They were all overjoyed to see us and smiled broadly with their gold teeth and demanded cigarettes or anything else we might have handy. Laundry hung on lines in the dim light of candles and there were plates of partly eaten food on a rough table in the middle of the room. The place smelled of cooking.

Smith spoke slowly to the commanding officer, using his small store of Vietnamese as best he could, but the conversation did not seem to be getting anywhere. Then somebody brought out a gasoline lantern and explained in sign language that it wouldn't work. Smith pumped it up and fiddled with it and lit matches and I was sure it was going to blow up, but it didn't. Pretty soon it glared in that vicious, hissing, blinding way lanterns have, and from the way the Vietnamese took on you'd have thought Smith had just invented electricity. Everybody cried out and smiled gold-glittery smiles and one man got carried away and seized my hand and shook it warmly. I must say that in addition to not being a cop I am also foolishly sentimental. I have, in my life, seen so much complaining and self-pity by people who had everything but a gold-plated kitchen sink that I felt sympathy and liking for these people who had almost nothing and were so damned grateful for the light of a gasoline lantern.

And yet, when you think of it, this is probably the way most humans react. When you don't have much, little things mean a lot: a fellow who's *really* hungry goes for simple bread and butter like it was going out of style. I'm not one of those who downgrades Americans and upgrades other people just because they are poor. There are rich slobs and there are also poor slobs, in America, anywhere. The do-gooders don't seem to take this into account sometimes.

We left our Vietnamese friends sitting in their bullet-

16 pages of drawings by noted illustrator **Keith Ferris**

★★★★★★★★★★★★★★★★★★★★★★★★★★★★★★★★★★★★★★

PRINCIPAL OPERATIONAL AIRCRAFT
in use in the Vietnam Air War

★★★

Grumman E-2A Hawkeye

DH/Canada U-6A Beaver

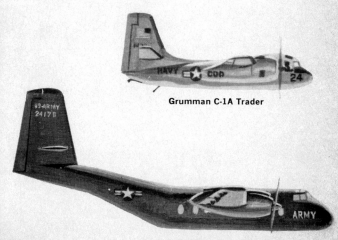

Grumman C-1A Trader

DH/Canada CV-2B Caribou

Bell UH-1 Huey Army utility and transport helicopter gives high mobility to allied troops. Heavily armed "Huey Hog" gunship version performs fire support and search and destroy missions.

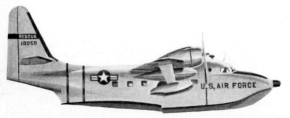

Grumman HU-16 Albatross rescues downed aircrew off Vietnam coast.

North American T-39 Sabreliner

Boeing B-52F Stratofortress can carry 30 tons of bombs from Guam to Vietcong concentrations in the south. Enemy is forced to keep moving and dispersed, denying him permanent bases.

Kaman HH-43 Huskie is used in crash rescue fire fighting. Delivers fire-fighters and equipment to crash site; hovers overhead suppressing flames with rotor blades.

Fairchild C-123 Provider defoliates trees to deny cover to Vietcong. Airlifts troops and supplies; evacuates casualties; drops flares.

Republic F-105 Thunderchief USAF fighter bomber. Vulcan cannon armed; workhorse of operations against the north from Thailand; typical load: two 450 gallon fuel tanks and six 750 pound bombs.

DH/Canada U-1A Otter

Douglas AC-47 Dragon Ship is familiar old "Gooney Bird" armed with three Gatling-type Miniguns firing from gunports in the cabin. Can put 300 rounds per second on one spot in night attack missions.

Douglas A-1 Skyraider continues to serve Navy and USAF Air Commando units for attack and close support missions. A-1 is also the principal aircraft of the South Vietnamese Air Force.

Sikorsky CH-37 Mojave

Convair F-102 Delta Dagger

Grumman A-6 Intruder all weather strike aircraft flying from carriers offshore. Only aircraft capable of attacking targets at night; excellent radar and nav system; up to 15,000 pound load.

Douglas A-4 Skyhawk is used by Navy and Marines from carriers and ashore in the daylight attack role.

Boeing KC-135 Stratotanker

Cessna U-3A Blue Canoe used by USAF
for utility transport between bases.

Boeing/Vertol CH-46 Sea Knight

Helio U-10A Courier

Lockheed EC-121 Constellation

McDonnell F-4 Phantom serves Navy, Marines and USAF over north and south. Performs strike, reconnaissance, escort and high cover missions with air to air missiles and up to 6 tons of bombs.

Lockheed C-130 Hercules heavily used in logistic pipeline. Airlifts troops and material in-country; performs low level supply drops; evacuates wounded; rescue version makes airborne pickup of downed airmen.

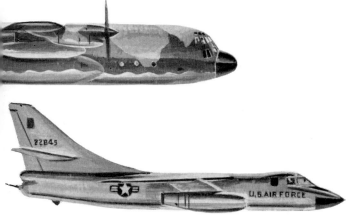

Douglas B-66 Destroyer

North American T-28D Trojan

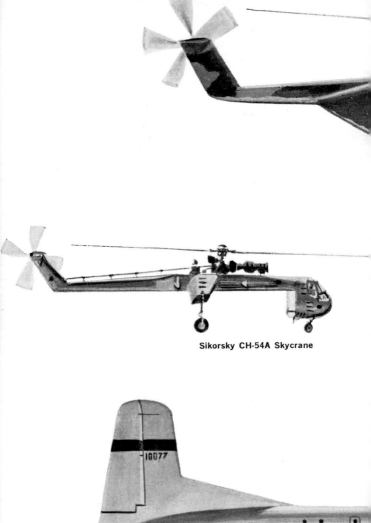

Sikorsky CH-54A Skycrane

-10077

Sikorsky HH-3C Jolly Green Giant of Air Rescue units flies some of war's most dangerous missions deep into North Vietnam to retrieve downed U. S. airmen.

Kaman HH-2 SeaSprite

I1-28 Beagle

Douglas C-124 Globemaster 2

North American RA-5C Vigilante

MiG-17 Fresco is aging Russian-built fighter armed with cannon and air to air missiles. Is still a threat to heavily laden fighter bombers.

North American F-100 Supersabre is used mostly in the south for FAC directed close support with cannon, rockets, napalm and bombs.

Lockheed C-141 Starlifter

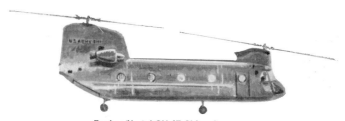

Boeing/Vertol CH-47 Chinook

Lockheed F-104 Starfighter is used as a MiG cap for fighter bomber strikes. Has Mach 2 performance; Vulcan cannon; Sidewinder missiles.

Ling Temco Vought F-8 Crusader carrier based fighter is armed with cannon and rockets. Used air to ground; also good air to air weapon capable of handling MiG-21; recon version available.

McDonnell RF-101 Voodoo unarmed photo reconnaissance aircraft covers targets in the north before and after fighter bomber strikes.

MAC
91415

Cessna O-1E Bird Dog is principal Forward Air Controller aircraft in South Vietnam. Spots targets and directs fighter bomber strikes.

Yak-25 Flashlight

Tu-16 Badger

Martin B-57 Canberra

Douglas C-133 Cargomaster

Douglas A-3 Skywarrior

Northrop F-5 Skoshi Tiger

Grumman OV-1C Monawk

Sikorsky CH-34 Choctaw

MiG-21 Fishbed Mach 2 interceptor is used by both North Vietnam and China. Our most potent adversary in north; cannon and missile armed; pilots being trained in Russia.

spattered fort jabbering madly around their glaring gasoline lantern, and I did a panicky canter back to the PBR.

The Bassac River (one of the mouths of the Mekong) gets very wild and lonely at night when you leave Can Tho. The banks are black and forbidding. This was not the best night for patrolling, because there was a moon and our boats must have stood out blackly to the VC watching from the shore. The old saying, "the night belongs to Charlie" isn't a romantic bit of meaningless chatter. You might have survived if you had walked out of Can Tho along some road after dark, but then again you might not have. I can say this: Nobody in his right mind was doing it.

Some gung-ho guys took off their flak vests and steel helmets and relaxed in the balmy night air as the boats moved at modest speed in the middle of the channel. At times, Smith's boat, in the lead, would throw a searchlight beam over to illuminate a sampan or to look at a suspicious object on the bank. Several times, both PBRs moved right up to the bank to investigate something and when this happened, I noticed that the guys who had taken off their steel helmets and flak vests put them on. The truth was, there was a certain amount of danger from sniper fire when the boats got close to shore. The enemy, if he was there, could certainly have shot and killed any one of us. But he had a strong deterrent. If a muzzle flash bloomed in the night from the shore, the man who pulled that trigger (unless he happened to be shooting from a slit in a dugout or tunnel) would have been instantly killed by a fusillade from the guns of both our boats. So anybody who killed one of us must be willing to trade his life for the privilege and this made it a bit safer.

At one time, an airman told me about a Navy commander who'd been very severely wounded by sniper fire while on patrol. The bullet had come in from the side and taken him in the arm and torn him up pretty badly. He'd lived but it was necessary for him to go home to the United States to recover. It wasn't unusual, after a patrol, to find bullet holes in the PBR that hadn't been there when you started out. He told me these things with obvious relish. I asked him if he dreaded a fire fight and he said he did not. He said he welcomed them. The truth of it is, most front-line GIs who volunteer for their duty (the PBRs were manned at that time by volunteers) *do* enjoy shooting and killing. There's a great deal of high-flown theory going around that Americans aren't bad old killers like the vicious ratty little VC are. If Americans kill, the story goes, it's only out of reluctant necessity and we are very sorry about that. Bull shit. Americans like to kill as well as the next man and they do it more effectively than most. It happens to be a built-in factor in the basic nature of all men, like sex, food and alcohol.

We followed the river downstream for a long time. There were no longer any lights to be seen. It appeared that we had entered an area of solid jungle (not so: in the daytime you find that the river banks are lined with huts in most areas; at night they keep them dark so they won't attract anybody's attention).

"See that island up ahead?" Bill Pollard said.

I looked at a dark promontory on the palely moonlit water and said I did.

"That's a rough place," Pollard said. "The VC control it. We've never been able to drive them out and keep them out."

"It looks deserted to me."

"It looked deserted to us last night," Pollard said, "until the tracers started coming out of it."

"You think they're in there now?" I said, feeling my scalp shrinking minutely under the helmet and experiencing that involuntary drawing in of the body that everybody gets when he realizes that bullets soon may be coming his way.

"I dunno," Pollard said, "but we are gonna see."

As we drew near the island, Pollard radioed Smith, who was in command of the two boats, asking if permission had come through from Can Tho Base to fire on the VC island. Smith radioed that he was working on it. I monitored the talk and it seemed that the base was reluctant, for some reason, to let us fire unless we were fired on or thought we had a real target. Whether they were saving ammo or what, I don't know. But Smith kept insisting that we fire and presently we got the green light to do it.

Now, for me, was the only really scary part of the mission. We didn't actually get too close to shore, but we did slow down almost to a stop, and it seemed to me that if the VC were really there and had some .50-caliber guns, Harvey might be just on the point of meeting his maker. Then suddenly, a few feet from my head, Mike Reboulet fired the M-79 grenade-launcher. The sound seemed to punch a hole in my right ear and out my left and I quickly jammed my fingers in both ears—which was just as well, because Kyle Wakker, in the stern, was firing steadily with his .50-caliber machine gun. Tracers at night certainly do look erratic. Wakker's seemed to be flailing around like a firehose gone mad. But Mike Reboulet was putting those M-79 grenades into the nearby treeline and I could hear them explode viciously and I realized why a lot of soldiers say the M-79 is such a bitch of a weapon. It sure is! If there were any VC in that treeline without protection, Mike was certainly killing them.

Now Smith's boat, 100 yards away, began firing at the island. It was a spectacular and *very loud* business—at least to me. The gunners later told me that they never heard their guns at all when they got into a fire fight. Too much else was riding on it, I guess, to be bothered by a few little concussions. At any rate, we fired quite a lot of ammo into that island and then started out of there, and now, for the first time, we had a problem. Smith's boat wouldn't go faster than 10 knots. Something had gone wrong with one of its underwater jets. That meant that our boat wouldn't be doing much over 10 miles an hour. And there we were, in the bright moonlight, having just assaulted this supposed hornet's nest of Vietcong, a couple of limpy cripples.

War, luckily, is not operated on logic. Logically, about this time, we should have been under heavy fire from the bank—but nary a tracer flamed from the dark trees as we crept pass them, going upriver against the current now, on our way back to Can Tho. It seemed to me that we drove by that miserable island, within range of even small arms, for an hour. Actually, it was about 10 minutes.

There were only 10 PBRs in Vietnam when I went on that patrol. Now there are 150. Lt. Jerry Flynn, USN, operations officer at Can Tho when I was there, told me that the PBR program has gone very well. There are bases at Can Tho, Nha Be, Cat Lo, My Tho and in the South China Sea, seven or eight miles off the mouths of the Mekong River. An LSD (landing ship dock), the *Tortuga,* had served as a mobile sea base for PBRs in the beginning. Ten patrol boats based off the *Tortuga,* refueling from her and tying up to her when not in the river channels. The *Tortuga* has been replaced by the *Comstock,* an LST (landing ship tank), which is somewhat smaller but serves the same purpose. Three LSTs in all were based off the mouths of the Mekong, each one with 10 PBRs and two armed helicopters (which land and take off from platforms aboard the LSDs).

Chief Canby and I spent an afternoon together in the Chief Petty Officers' Club at Can Tho, drinking beer and talking about the war. Canby had *Sat Cong* tattooed on him. That means "Kill Vietcong" and the old junk fighters sometimes had this tattoo. But not everybody had the guts to get it. If the VC capture you and see it, they kill you—often slowly and painfully. We sat on a high balcony behind the anti-hand-grenade netting that screens the fronts of all American billets and felt the Delta heat press down on us soddenly, making the beer heavy and gassy in my stomach, making my head throb. A leaden lassitude settled over me so that even moving to get out of the pattern of the shifting sun was an effort almost too much to make, even though I was already sunburned and getting worse.

Canby had killed lots of men and I asked him how he felt about the Vietcong. He said they were rough, tricky, brave and they could stand living conditions Americans couldn't. He didn't particularly hate them. He intended to kill them every time he met them, but they were better soldiers by far than the Arvins; their discipline was better, their fighting spirit was better.

I asked him why this was. He said he wasn't a strategist, he just drove boats. But Canby had figured out some pretty good strategy as it turned out. He said the only way to use the PBRs effectively was to block off the river—seal it up tight by stretching heavy steel cables across it on pilings, leaving a couple of "gates" in it where the PBRs could stand by and check cargoes as the traffic came up or down the river. It wasn't his intention to stop a boat and search it minutely, Canby said. With the heavy traffic on the river that would create too great a bottleneck. Just go aboard and take a quick look for really big and dangerous arms shipments. It could be done and it would really make a dent in the ammo supply lower down where the VC have their strongholds in the U Minh Forest and other remote areas.

Canby's idea is a good one. The Navy did not implement it, perhaps for political reasons. This checking of river traffic wouldn't be popular with the Vietnamese civilians, since it would be very inconvenient and would slow up their daily work considerably. The truth is, of course, that if you make things too miserable for too many people, you get them so upset that they wish you'd go away and forget it, Communists or no Communists. Many of them feel that way already, for a lot of reasons, and the less we push them the better.

Now a variation of Canby's idea is in use: Navy PBRs hang around the narrow passages between extensive installations of river fishing nets, which force the river traffic to converge automatically at certain choke points, and our guys go aboard suspicious rivercraft for spot-checks. This makes it more difficult for the VC because they can never be sure if an arms-carrying boat will be stopped and searched or not. These spot-checks, incidentally, are carried out anywhere, at any time, and make it harder for the VC to prosecute the war.

The PBRs work in close cooperation with Army and Navy helicopters and with Air Force jets. These glass-hulled boats, powered by two 220-horsepower diesels and pushed along by jets of water spurting backward from two Jacuzzi water-injection pumps, can work in nine inches of water, carry Ratheon radars that can cover the river at night for a distance of three or four miles and can pick up the blips of anything moving in that area. At night there is a curfew. Anything that's moving at all is likely to be a VC boat—particularly if it's moving across from one shore to the other. The PBR radar pick up these telltale bogies, radio the information to home base and home base calls in a strike by armed choppers, jets or Dragon Ships as the case may be. The PBRs race to the scene and join in the melee. One of the most outstanding actions where the PBRs and the helicopters ganged up on the VC occurred on October 31, 1966, and is known in the Delta as "The Halloween Massacre." A couple of PBRs on patrol were fired at by some guys in small boats. The small boats ducked back into a slew. The PBRs followed them in, discovered a whole armada of boats making ready to cross the river with supplies, ammo and troops. The PBRs called in other PBRs and helicopters from nearby Vinh Long, and a monstrous VC-shoot ensued that the official Navy release describes as follows:

"Forty-three enemy sampans and seven junks were sunk by U.S. Navy crews of armed Seawolf helicopters and river patrol boats (PBR) during a running battle between six and nine p.m., October 31st. The PBRs sprang the trap on a major Vietcong troop-crossing attempt on the My Tho River. In excess of 75 sampans and junks, many carrying enemy green-uniformed troops, were sighted by Navy crews in one of the largest Operation Game Warden battles of the Vietnamese war. The action took place midway between Vinh Long and My Tho on the My Tho River of the Mekong Delta, approximately 47 miles southwest of Saigon. There were two Vietcong confirmed killed. There were no American casualties and only light damage to the PBRs. The two enemy killed were wearing uniforms. Two of the seven junks sunk were believed to be carrying explosives. One junk, when hit by U. S. fire, exploded in a huge secondary explosion sending debris and water 300 feet in the air. Another craft also disappeared in a secondary explosion. The VC made repeated attempts to sink these large junks to prevent their capture. Three enemy junks and three sampans were captured and towed to My Tho."

12   VINH LONG

Vinh Long is a good-sized town on the Bassac River about 20 miles from Can Tho. I spent several days there, certainly not enough to know much about the place, but enough to provide a few details that may be interesting. The most impressive structure in Vinh Long—in fact one of the most impressive structures in all Vietnam—was the enormous unfinished Catholic cathedral that stood there. It must have cost several hundred thousand dollars, perhaps more, but it was only a shell—nothing had been done inside since the death of Premier Diem, in whose honor it had been erected. There it stood—tall, massive, lonely—rising like a shining white palace out of the rat's nest of grimy hovels that surrounded it. I asked what it would be used for and nobody knew. It was just there. Maybe someday, when the war was over, they'd get around to finishing it. Maybe not.

The second most impressive building in Vinh Long was a large, modern, trade school—more like a college than a shop—fitted with the latest types of machinery of all sorts, classrooms with new blackboards, American-type student chairs with flaring arms for taking notes on, laboratories, just about everything you'd need to turn out technicians and skilled people in quantity. There was only one trouble with this trade school. It was empty.

"Where are the students?" I asked the little Vietnamese who was showing us around, and who was, in fact, the superintendent in charge of the place.

He looked at me with what appeared to be dislike, and remarked that it was summer and the students were on vacation.

"How long is their vacation?"

"Three months," he said.

I had just come through a town full of decrepit vehicles and other items in need of some kind of repair, and I was tempted to say that in wartime, under emergency conditions like these, wasn't it odd that vitally needed skills were put off for three months while everybody went on vacation. I didn't say it, but it occurred to me that the Americans who were out in the paddies fighting were not on vacation, and that these machines I was looking at certainly hadn't been made in Vietnam. They'd been made in the United States and delivered here free, and the building itself looked as if it had been at least designed, if not built, by Americans.

"Do the students like the school?" I asked.

The superintendent shrugged—a small shifting of the shoulders, a small raising of the eyebrows, as if to say, *Yeah, I guess they like it all right——*.

I did not say what I felt like saying because, to be truthful, I might just have had a surly guy, and you can't judge a program by one foul ball; but I did leave that big, well-equipped, empty trade school with certain misgivings. How, I wondered, can you help people if they go on vacation in the middle of a war and leave all your fine expensive machines gathering dust in the big expensive building you designed and paid for when their skills are so urgently needed?

I was ashamed of myself just half an hour later when we drove by what appeared to be the largest mudhole I'd ever seen in my life. It was near the river and covered about four or five acres and it was full of little naked boys and girls who were wallowing and wading around in it up to their thighs and seemed to be groping in the mud for something. The sergeant from the helicopter base who was driving the jeep explained that they were after mud-fish, which they found by feeling around in the slime, and which they then pulled out and took home for food. The mud-fish, the sergeant said, made mighty good eating—if you were a Vietnamese. Personally, he wouldn't touch one unless he was starving.

There was an orphanage near the mud-fish bog, and the sergeant took me there to talk to the Mother Superior about the war. The Mother Superior was ill but Sister Mary, her stout right hand, was not. Sister Mary was tall, ruddy of face, keen of eye, stern of jaw, and with a smile warm enough to light up an arctic igloo. She was, in fact, one of the outstanding people I met in Vietnam and she certainly had the courage of her convictions and the Catholic church can be proud of her. She took me around the orphanage and showed me the various activities the orphans—many of them grown teen-age girls—were taking part in. No make-work operation this! The girls were busily washing and ironing the uniforms for the helicopter base nearby, for which the orphanage received a generous remuneration from the officers and men involved, which was used to help pay the bills. There were classes in sewing, cooking, English, religion and the general studies that American youngsters receive in school—but tailored to fit the needs of the Vietnamese. The Sisters teaching the classes were serious and so were the students. You can't really fake this kind of thing. Either it's a good show or it isn't. Sister Mary was showing me a very good show indeed.

I happen to disagree violently with the Catholic faith on their birth control policies, and when Sister Mary and I had sat ourselves down with some fine hot tea that one of the orphans brought, smiling and writhing with shyness, we forthwith got into a knock-down-drag-out argument over birth control. Neither of us, of course, managed to change the other's mind a hairsbreadth, and then the little orphan girl came in with some cakes and we called a truce while we ate them. Then we got into another argument over Diem. From most of the books I'd read, I gathered that Diem had become, over the course of his years in power, an inflexible dictator whose repressive measures (many of them suggested by his brother-in-law, Nhu, and Nhu's wife, the Dragon Lady) had finally become so intolerable that the people couldn't stand it. They'd been bullied, tossed in jail, even killed after getting a mockery of a trial in one of Diem's sudden-justice courts. They saw only one recourse, to form a guerrilla anti-Diem organization, and that's what they did. They called it the National Liberation Front. We called it the Vietcong.

Sister Mary, of course, was Catholic, and so was Diem, so

I expected her to defend him, and she did. She pointed out some things I hadn't taken into account, and perhaps there are two sides to all issues, even Diem. She pointed out the obvious truth that the intrigue in Saigon, the constant pulling and hauling among the various individuals and groups of individuals who wanted to seize control of the government, made it very difficult for any one person to stay in power unless he was strong, and, at times, ruthless. If I didn't believe that, Sister Mary said, I should count the coups since Diem was killed. There'd been eight or nine of them as she recalled. Some leaders hadn't managed to stay in power more than a day or two. Diem had stayed in power eight years, which, no matter what else you said about it, was the record. Sister Mary flashed her beguiling Irish grin, and I grinned back. It was, indeed, a record.

Then Sister Mary pointed out that Diem had been hounded in the jungles by Ho Chi Minh for months, had nearly died of the fevers he contracted there, had had one of his brothers killed and had barely escaped death himself. And when he finally came to power nobody gave him a hand for months; what he did he had to do alone. Any advice he got he had to get from Madame Nhu and his brother. If he took advice from his so-called "advisers" in Saigon, Sister Mary pointed out with a twinkle, he might have jolly well found himself out of a job—or worse. The Buddhists, the intellectuals, the generals and other miscellaneous power-hungry plotters were all waiting around like hungry tigers for Diem to make a slip. It was enough, begorry, to make a man suspicious and wary, yes, even a bit ruthless—or didn't I think so?

I said if you looked at it that way, maybe she had something.

"I'm not saying Diem was perfect," Sister Mary said. "But then, when you think about it, who is? Would you be carin' for another cookie?"

I said I'd love another cookie, they were delicious, and Sister Mary said the orphans made them in the cooking class and those lovely boys from the helicopter base brought in nice things like sugar and nuts and stuff whenever they had anything to spare. Sister Mary was very friendly with the Huey drivers and they liked her just as much.

But Sister Mary didn't feel so friendly toward the local Vietnamese doctors in Vinh Long—at least certain among them—who, she said, took over the American shipments of medicines, particularly the high-prized antibiotics that are specifics for so many of the terrible ailments in this country, and injected them only if they got a nice fat fee! Sister Mary's ruddy Irish face grew noticeably pinker when she said this, and her normally warm Irish eyes got bleak. She said she'd marched right in and made a big fuss about it, after a number of sick people had come to her to complain, but nothing had been done. Those Vietnamese doctors! Somebody sure ought to be takin' a stout stick to um, and that was the truth!

Nor did Sister Mary have unalloyed praise for the province chief of Vinh Long Province. She did say that he was a strong and capable man, that he kept order beautifully, and that they could certainly have had a lot worse. But she told me I ought to go take a look at his house—and at his guest house—and maybe I'd understand how she felt.

Later on, I did. The province chief's house was the third most impressive building in Vinh Long, right behind the big school and the Diem memorial. It was a gorgeous white mansion with pillars, ornamental railings, porticos and all the trimmings: the guest house, across a small private park from it, was only slightly less pretentious. And, of course, across the street was the usual rat's nest of hovels. I suppose a province chief can't conduct his business in a thatched hootch—but I heard that Ho Chi Minh, when he was coming up, did it—and Ho Chi Minh happened to be still popular in South Vietnam. This bit of information was transmitted to the pilots aboard the aircraft carrier *Constellation* when we were on Dixie Station, by the escape-and-evasion briefing officer from Saigon, Maj. Young. "If you are shot down in South Vietnam, boys," Maj. Young said. "Don't badmouth Uncle Ho. He's the boy who threw out the French—and they still love him down here."

Dr. Neil Taylor, a quiet self-effacing surgeon who lived in the MACV compound at Vinh Long and operated daily in the Vinh Long hospital, was another one of the top people I met in Vietnam. Before I met Taylor I saw some black-and-white photographs tacked up on the bulletin board in the lobby of the MACV main building. I stopped and stared at them. They were pictures taken before and after an operation for harelip. The results were dramatic. Before the operation the child might look like a savage beast, the teeth jutting out like fangs through the cleft in the horribly disfigured mouth.

The picture taken after the operation showed the teeth repositioned back in the mouth, quite normal, and the disfiguring cleft closed neatly so that over a period of time the patient might look almost as normal as you or I. But what struck me in these pictures were the eyes of the patients, which I was able to examine because the photos were clear and good. The eyes in the "before" pictures looked so sad and despairing it was hard to look. The eyes in the "after" pictures were different. They were almost gay.

Those Si-War pilots who kept saying they were out to win the hearts and minds of the people, with pamphlets and loudspeakers from 2,500 feet in the air, ought to have come down and taken a look at those photos. They might have got a glimmer of how it's *really* done.

13 "THE MUTTERING DEATH"

Our combat flyers in Vietnam are distinctly different from those in past American wars, because they are career pros, almost to a man. The average age of our pilots there is 33, 10 years older than American flyers in the Second World War. They're precisely trained and they know it. And they're absolutely hard-nosed. You'll never find these qualities better exemplified than in the Huey gunship 13th Aviation Battalion, which headquarters at Can Tho.

The skipper of the 13th, Col. William Maddox, has the look of a gladiator. His eyes glow fiercely in his red-tanned face. He speaks quietly. He grudges the time spent at his desk. He would rather be out in a gunship leading a strike but he still finds time to run a taut ground operation. His men, who respect him for his aggressive leadership, were afraid his luck wouldn't last.

"Col. Maddox is the first man to the landing zone," they told me. "If there's any VC fire, he's going to draw it."

"The other night the old man went out by himself in a gunship," one of them said. "You're not supposed to do that. But he gets bored sitting around the club, I guess."

Maddox had me in his office and briefed me on an upcoming mission. They were going south to Camau, near the U Minh Forest, in a few days, to put in a big force of Arvins with the slicks (lightly armed choppers used to ferry troops are called slicks). He would be leading. If I wanted to ride along, I was welcome. This was the heart of VC country—there would almost certainly be a fire fight.

At this point I was fresh from the night mission in the Dragon Ship, not to mention a six-hour night patrol on the Bassac River in a Navy patrol boat. My ears were still ringing from the sound of the M-79 grenade launcher that had been fired two feet from my head and from the sustained firing of the boat's 50's. I thanked the Colonel but declined. He then offered to send me to Vinh Long, 25 miles north, to spend some time with his Huey fighters there, and this I gladly accepted.

The American Huey troops at Vinh Long are without doubt the most savage guys I met in Vietnam (and the jolliest!). I was impressed by them. But they scared me. They didn't hurl impersonal thunderbolts from the heights in supersonic jets. They came muttering down to the paddies and hootch lines, fired at close range and saw their opponents disintegrate to bloody rags 40 feet away. They took hits through their plastic windshields and through their rotor blades. They wore flak vests and after a fire fight was won they landed on the battlefield, got out and counted their VC dead. Each man had his own personal sidearm he carried along for mopping up. A Swedish K automatic pistol seemed to be the favorite.

Capt. George O'Grady wears a steel helmet modeled after the old Roman battle helmets. His door gunners were enlisted people and as savage as the drivers. I saw a door gunner who affected deerskin gloves with long gauntlets. One man I met had been mustered out and had gone home to civilian work. He couldn't stand it at home. He reenlisted and went back to Vietnam for another tour.

It used to be that Charlie could hide in the tall grass beside a road and blast a convoy moving across country to flaming bits with his recoilless rifles and mortars. Maj. Dresser and his Ranch Hands have made this tougher by killing the foliage on both sides of main highways. This sets things up for the Bell Hueys, which now fly shotgun on the convoys. These planes are equipped (the "Hogs" at least) as follows: four fixed 7.62mm machine guns, two more 7.62mm on flexible mounts wielded by the door gunners, pods of 2.75 HVAR rockets on either side of the door and a device called the M-5 that hurls many 40mm grenades a minute and is automatically aimed when the gunner-pilot moves his hand-held illuminating sight. When a Huey Hog lets loose with all its armament, you feel as if you were inside an exploding ammo factory.

I spent most of my time at Vinh Long with Maj. Dick Leister's "Outlaws" squadron. Dick's job as squadron commander is crucial. He rides in the control ship during a strike and monitors four different radio channels at once. All of them are filled with excited chatter. Dick has to sort it out like lightning and direct the action. "The first time I went up and listened to it," Dick said, "I said 'I can't do this. I can't understand a word that's being said.' But after awhile I got so I could blot out the useless babble and begin to hear only the key transmissions. Then I could run the show okay."

Leister, in his spare time, was editor of *The Branding Iron,* a one-page mimeographed publication intended to improve the morale of the Huey squadrons at Vinh Long. It certainly improved my morale to read in it a grand old chestnut about the life of a pilot. Dick claims it was sent to him by a fifth-grader back in the States:

"I want to be a pilot when I grow up, because it's a fun job and easy to do. That's why there are so many pilots today. Pilots don't need much school, they just have to learn numbers so they can read instruments. I guess they should be able to read maps so they can find their way if they are lost. Pilots should be brave so they won't be scared if it's foggy and they can't see or if a wing or a motor falls off they should stay calm so they'll know what to do. Pilots have to have good eyes so they can see through clouds and they can't be afraid of lightning or thunder because they are closer to them than we are. The salary pilots make is another thing I like. They make more money than they can spend. This is because most people think airplane flying is dangerous except pilots don't because they know how easy it is. There isn't much I don't like, except girls like pilots and all the stewardesses want to marry them so they always have to chase them away so they won't bother them. I hope I don't get airsick because if I get airsick I couldn't be a pilot and would have to go to work."

The shop talk of the Huey pilots was grim, colorful and to

the point. "I shot up a Charlie in the paddies today," one of them said. "I ran that little mother all over the place hosing him with guns but somehow or other we just didn't hit him. Finally he turned on us and stood there facing us with his rifle. We really busted his ass then. Blew him up like a toy balloon."

Another pilot commented on this. "You got to hand it to those little mothers. They got the guts. If we had them on our side, we'd wrap up this war in about a month."

The Outlaws finally shamed me into going on a night mission in one of their Huey gunships. They carefully explained that the chopper would stay over the base; in 20 minutes we would land; there would be no danger. That sounded about right to me, so I agreed to go along.

We took off in a dark overcast, Tail-End Charlie in a formation of three armed choppers, and, to my surprise, instead of hovering safely over the field, we headed straight toward VC country. We snaked along in big S-turns, our red beacon lights blazing.

After we crossed the Bassac River, the boundary of the hard-core VC country, the lead chopper turned on his searchlights. He was trying to draw VC small arms fire so we could pick up the muzzle flashes on the ground and zap them. This game is known as "lightning bug" and they play it every night. But no muzzle flashes.

"Charles baby is a little timid this evening," Maj. Hube Merritt, our pilot-gunner, suggested over the intercom. We stayed in trail over the river for awhile, probing around with our searchlights. Nobody down there wanted to fight. Then we went out to the "free firing zone." Hube explained what that meant: "It's a place where we practice up trying to kill VC," he said, "and they practice up trying to shoot down choppers."

Suddenly in the darkness ahead, the lead ship began shooting. Tracers flew from the door guns, followed by bigger flashes—rockets. Then the first Huey broke off and the number-two ship in front of us began firing. Suddenly, unexpectedly, a fire-ball billowed up from the ground. It was what is known as a "secondary explosion." By luck the second Huey had blown up a cache of powder or ammo.

Then we arrived over the firing point in our number-three ship and opened up with all our guns and rockets. The fire-flashes leaped out ahead of us and converged in the pitch darkness on a distant point. This noise was worse than it had been in the Dragon Ship, worse than the PBR boat on the Bassac River. (I must have reacted rather strongly, because it was relayed to me later that the door gunner had said to his buddy, "That poor old white-headed son-of-a-bitch from *Flying* damned near jumped out of his skin.") We made several passes, emptying a full load of ammo into the silent darkness and went back to Vinh Long; nobody will ever know if we hit anything but we certainly did a lot of shooting.

The missions I have described exemplify the fact that it isn't much of a problem, with our overwhelming aerial fire power, to shoot up Charlie pretty bad once we engage him. It isn't easy to lose with a modern air force when all you're up against is small arms fire. But to destroy the enemy you first have to find him—the classical problem against irregulars, the goal of all our reconnaissance activity.

The essence of successful guerrilla warfare is sneak attack. The hit-and-run can still be a great equalizer when one force has superior arms and equipment but is frozen in a defensive posture. The Vietcong had depended almost exclusively on this strategy. They counted on being able to strike hard without warning and then vanish, before pursuit arrived, into the almost impenetrable jungle that they know so well. But things were changing. Our airborne surveillance was of such a high order that it was increasingly difficult to find a place to hide. The impenetrable cover of the jungle was being pierced.

Charlie used to feel safe in his jungle redoubts. He could light up a cooking fire at night and eat his supper with serenity. But now we fly over him in RF-4C Phantoms with infrared cameras and take pictures ("red haze photos") in which his fire shows up as a white dot with a tail. We turn these pictures over to the Arvin gunners; the coordinates of the campfires are established; and suddenly, out of the peaceful sky, a large explosive shell falls in the middle of Charlie's meal.

If Charlie tries to cross a river in boats on a pitch-black night, even in rain or under a solid overcast, the RF-4Cs still find him—this time with a radar camera that takes pictures in darkness almost like your new Nikon takes them of Aunt Susie at high noon. The recon planes give the word to the fighter bombers or to the artillery, and suddenly Charlie's piece of the river blows sky high. Charlie never knew what hit him or why.

Infrared cameras can sometimes pick up his truck exhaust as Charlie moves along a jungle road at night. His speed can be calculated and therefore the spot where he will be 15 minutes later can be estimated. The coordinates of this spot and the time for attack are relayed to the artillery or infantry. Result: Charlie gets zapped again.

Even more advanced night-vision equipment was moving in. Unbelievably clear pictures can be picked up on some of our latest radar scopes. These images are then photographed and the film becomes a permanent record.

Image intensifiers resembling large telescopes have been issued on a selective basis to Army infantry battalions. They have been used in combat and the Vietcong already have captured some. Army leaders in the field believe a military victory is impossible unless they can take the night away from the VC.

When I was at Tan Son Nhut field they were testing a C-123 Provider that mounted a powerful battery of high-intensity lights under its belly. When the lamps are turned on, they illuminate the whole countryside like a stadium during a night baseball game. The plane flies its missions at 3,500 feet, above the reach of small arms fire, which is a good thing, because this is one bird that's *got* to be visible to ground gunners!

In the daytime, the Air Force keeps the surveillance pressure on with long-range Lockheed Connie C-121 radar-picket planes called Big Eyes. They were formerly used off American shores to guard against surprise bomber attacks. They orbit on their stations watching for bogies that might be trying to sneak in and bomb one of our bases. They also watch friendly blips and warn them if a bogie appears on screen coming at them from behind. The Navy's Super Fudd E-2As, of course, perform this same mission in the Tonkin Gulf. "Nobody moves without we see it." We have backups for our backups.

We know how to use this superb surveillance to optimum advantage. If word comes that the VC are trying to get a little rest in some forest retreat like the Iron Triangle 35 miles north of Saigon, the Strategic Air Command loads a flotilla of B-52 bombers from Guam or Thailand with fifty-one 750-pounders per plane, flies over and wipes out a whole valley. They do it from 40,000—too high for anybody to see them or hear them. The drop is fingered by a Bird Dog or a chopper hovering in the area, so the load lands exactly where it was intended to. When I was sleeping in Saigon one night the house trembled. I woke up thinking it was an earthquake. It wasn't. It was a B-52 saturation drop or "carpet raid" into the Iron Triangle.

Once the VC in the Delta are located, and they have to stand up and fight, they have about as much chance against American air power as our planes would have against fleets of spaceships with death rays. So Charlie has to run, and increasingly, he has only one refuge remaining, the U Minh Forest, at the southernmost tip of Vietnam. The French used to call it *"le forêt de la nuit";* it is a typical tropical rain-forest, a dark labyrinth of mangrove, covertopped with high jungle trees. Charlie still owns the "forest of darkness," even during the day. But all else has slipped away from him, except at night. And although Charlie still owns the night almost everywhere, we are making it tougher for him with each passing day.

A big chopper mission carrying Arvins south to the edge of the U Minh Forest took place just before I left Vinh Long. It was the operation Col. Maddox had invited me to go along on a few days before. Every slick (troop-carrying) and hog (gunship) chopper that was not needed for home defense took off full of ammo and Arvins in the early morning. I remained on base with Dick Leister and Hube Merritt, who stayed behind to hold the fort. The day passed slowly.

As night fell, nobody had returned or been heard from. We walked over to the Control Center, which was under Hube's direction, and asked Twinkle Toes and Tinker Bell (the two tough sergeants on duty there) if any word had come in. None had.

We went over to Dick's room, and opened up a bottle of Haig Pinch and sloshed in half a tumbler full for each man present (the Huey pilots don't drink it by the shot at a time like this). We waited around, slapping mosquitoes and making meaningless conversation. Finally Hube said, "Would you believe we lost anybody today?" Nobody said nothing.

Half an hour later we heard the characteristic heavy muttering sound, and the air over our barracks was beaten by the choppers coming back. A few minutes later the screen door at the back of the room opened and Maj. Jerry Hileman stepped in out of the dark. He wore the dark fatigues and the crushed baseball cap. He was pale and obviously very tired, but his eyes glinted in the lamplight.

"Big day," he said, with a fierce little smile. "Had to extract the Arvins after dark. Charles baby was on the rampage. He'd have wiped our little buddies out if we'd left them there."

"You kill anybody?" Dick asked.

"Yeah—30. Maybe 40." Hileman shifted his shoulders the way a man does when he has been sitting in a fixed position and feels stiff. "Those little mothers were shooting back today, though. I took one through the windshield between me and the gunner and a couple up through the floor."

His face was now white and still, and as he shifted away from the lamplight, the glints were gone from his eyes. Under the crushed cap his face suddenly looked like a skull. Then he said, "Well, you guys, aren't you gonna offer your buddy a drink?"

14   NORTH OF SAIGON

The war north of Saigon is almost 100 percent an American war. Its essential feature is the large-scale use of all types of aircraft in close support of ground troops. The "American war" is being fought in the northern part of South Vietnam—that part of the country extending from the Central Highlands around our base at Pleiku, northward through Danang and Hue, to the Demilitarized Zone (DMZ) that separates North and South Vietnam.

The American war is different from either the Delta war, where the ground fighting was done largely by Arvin troops supported by our Special Forces teams (the Green Berets), or the "Out-Country war," which consists of U. S. air strikes into North Vietnam. The American war is being fought almost exclusively by Army and Marine Corps ground troops supported by Army, Navy, Marine Corps and Air Force air power, and Americans do most of the dying—both on the ground and in the air.

Here is where the bulk of our fighting men now committed to Vietnam operate. Here is where Marine units pursue their bloody "Search and Destroy" missions, supported by F-100, A-4 and F-4 close support strikes. Here is where the Army's vaunted First Cav Airmobile—the first military unit in the world with total airlift capability—fights.

But here the enemy is not just the Vietcong. Regular North Vietnamese Army units in company, battalion, regiment and even division strength infiltrate from the north, either through the DMZ or down the Ho Chi Minh trail, through Cambodia and Laos. And here the enemy is armed not just with rifles and light automatic weapons, as in the Delta, but with heavy machine guns, artillery and, lately, with a steadily increasing number of triple-A guns.

The thick jungles of northern South Vietnam are difficult to penetrate, and search-and-destroy missions are very hazardous. There are many booby traps and buried mines. A Marine sergeant told me the Arvins had abandoned 1,500 of our "Bouncing Betty" mines on Marble Mountain, about five miles south of Danang, when Premier Ky suddenly called them in to quell another Buddhist riot. The Bouncing Bettys, when stepped on, leap almost face high into the air and then explode, scattering a hail of fragments in all directions. The VC buried the mines along paths on the perimeter of Danang where Marines must patrol. The casualties have been sickening.

I flew up to Danang from Saigon one evening in a C-130 shuttle plane.

Danang is located on the coast, up in the northeast corner of South Vietnam, toward the DMZ, and the countryside around it is charming. With a 7,000-foot-high range of mountains just to the west, it reminds one of the Southern California coast. The beaches around Danang are as fine as any I've seen, and they extend south for hundreds of miles. If this war-torn country ever knows peace again, and a stable government dedicated to the whole population of Vietnam is set up, it will be hard to find a finer resort area anywhere in the world.

The airfield at Danang is the second busiest in Vietnam—not quite so busy as Tan Son Nhut at Saigon, but still among the busiest in the world. It is operated by the Air Force, but also used by the Marine Corps, the Navy and the Army. (The coordination of Air Force, Marine Corps and

Navy planes by the Air Force tower operators is remarkable.) Many Air Force F-100s are based at Danang as are several squadrons of Marine Corps F-4 Phantoms. The Air Force also keeps a number of B-57 Canberra medium jet bombers at Danang. Air Force and civilian transport planes continuously shuttle in and out. Army liaison planes—Beavers, Caribous and the ever-present Cessna Bird Dogs—and helicopters are all over the place. The Navy uses the Danang strip as a divert base for its carriers, and a number of Navy Phantoms, Crusaders or Skyhawks are usually in evidence. The Danang-based aircraft are the planes that fly the bulk of the support sorties for Marine and Army search-and-destroy operations in the area around Danang and in the mountains to the west and south.

Personnel accommodations at the base are spartan. A Marine Corps lieutenant from an F-4 squadron told me he'd been living in a tent for the five months he'd been there.

The primary mission of the Marine Corps F-4 squadrons operating out of Danang is close support for Marine troops operating throughout the northern half of South Vietnam. The F-4s work in flights of two to eight planes. They are armed with combinations of rockets, bombs and napalm. Ordnance is mixed from plane to plane within a flight. On a typical four-plane flight, one F-4 might carry only napalm, another napalm and bombs, a third rockets and bombs, and a fourth all rockets. This way the forward air controller can call in exactly the kind of firepower he wants considering the situation.

The F-4s are under the control of FACs at all times. The FACs may be either ground-based or in Bird Dog spotter planes. As in the Delta, a strike can be diverted at any time to another target by an airborne FAC. Ground troops under fire always receive the highest priority.

A ground-based FAC might be a Marine Corps captain operating with a forward ground element. When the situation dictates support fire, he will either radio for "Artie" (artillery) or call in an F-4 strike. The F-4s are given coordinates, and as they vector in toward the target, the ground troops mortar in a few rounds of "Willie Peter" (white phosphorous) to pinpoint the target. The F-4s then hit with whatever combination of ordnance the FAC requests.

"Nothing is more challenging than close air support," the Marine lieutenant said. "Accuracy is extremely important.

This is the kind of a war where a ground element can be moved into an area by helicopter, and in ten minutes be surrounded. Then they need you bad, and—real quick—you're right in there with them. But, as I said, you've got to be very accurate."

The full meaning of the lieutenant's statement hit shortly after I returned from Vietnam. A detachment of troops, surrounded and under heavy fire, called for a napalm strike against enemy positions. The F-4 flight delivering the strike was off by just 50 yards, and the napalm hit our men instead, killing and wounding more than 60. But the commanding officer of the regiment involved stated such things had to be expected; that without the close air support his men would have probably been lost anyway; that we are fighting so close in to the enemy that sometimes less than 25 yards separates the combatants; that he'd call for napalm again in a minute.

I asked the Marine lieutenant in Danang what he thought of the F-4. "It's the outstanding airplane for the job," he told me. "When you're faced with a situation where you need both air-to-air and air-to-ground capability, the F-4 is the finest airplane in the free world today—far superior to the F-105."

"You mean you're worried about MiGs coming down from North Vietnam?" I asked him.

"That's the point. With this airplane, you don't worry. You've got the firepower to support the ground troops and the superior air-to-air performance to outfight the MiGs."

"Do you worry about MiGs hitting the airfield?"

"We don't even think about it. They've got Hot Pad Alert and Hawk missiles here. No problem."

The town of Danang was off-limits to military personnel when I was there, but not to civilian newsmen. I stayed most of the time in the Press Center, a small compound on the river front. It is surrounded by high, barbed-wire barricades, with a Vietnamese on the gate. The quarters are large, with big mosquito-net-covered beds, and are fitted with old-fashioned airplane-propeller ceiling fans. The water came on and off erratically, and seemed to be off more than it was on.

The Press Center in Danang is operated by some of the savviest public relations people in the Marine Corps. Particularly outstanding was young Sgt. Greg Pearson, a big, friendly combat reporter. Pearson was currently being publicized in absentia for high public office in his home state. (If people at home like Greg as much as people in Danang do, maybe he'll be Senator Pearson before he's through.)

One day the Secretary of the Navy, Mr. Nitze, came to visit the Center and held a brief press conference. He was asked if there was a bomb shortage, and Mr. Nitze said there was not. "In certain types of bombs, perhaps, but not an overall shortage." After Nitze left, one reporter remarked he'd seen F-100s taking off from Bien Hoa with a single bomb on one wing and a concrete weight on the other. Later, I talked with a couple of nearly apoplectic F-4 pilots at Danang who told me they had recently gone out on a four-plane mission carrying a very small bomb load. "We risked eight guys," one pilot said to me, gritting his teeth in anger, "when we could have hung the whole load on one plane—risking only two people—and done the job better."

"Then why send out four planes?" I asked.

"Damned if I know, unless it's just to keep our sortie rate high," the pilot said disgustedly. "But I'll tell you this: It's a goddam crime."

I had heard about this sortie business out on *Constellation*. Navy pilots had told me they could do a better job with a few A-6s, operating in the safety of darkness, than with all those Skyhawks skimming around with light loads in daylight.

So while it didn't seem possible, it appeared that the Navy was trying to out-sortie the Air Force, and the Air Force was trying to out-sortie the Navy. The guys who were flying the sorties took a dim view of it. "If McNamara can't send us bombs," one pilot remarked with typical American irreverence toward high-echelon brass, "he ought to at least send us some of his baloney. We have to drop *some*thing." (Note: The bomb shortage was later alleviated.)

I spent an afternoon at Danang with the Air Force's 480th Tactical Fighter Squadron, listening to two of its F-4 pilots, Maj. Paul Gilmore and Lt. Bill Smith, describe in detail how they shot down a MiG 21.

Gilmore and Smith took off at 1:30 on the afternoon of April 26, 1966, as part of an F-4 flight assigned to fly MiG CAP (combat air patrol against MiGs) for F-105 Thunderchiefs out of Thailand. The 105s were hitting the Bac Giang railroad bridge near the big North Vietnamese MiG base at Kep.

The F-4s plugged into a jet tanker near the target area and topped off with 15,000 pounds of fuel. Gilmore and Smith then set up an orbit pattern at 30,000 feet, which permitted them to keep an eye on the F-105s and be ready if they were called on for help. They were indicating 450 knots TAS (true air speed), which is slow for this bird.

At 2:45 p.m., Gilmore, in the front seat, was looking out the left side of the plane toward the strike area when Smith, in the back, picked up two bogies coming in at one-thirty high. Smith recognized them immediately as the dreaded MiG-21s, known by the code name of Fishbed, which were supposed to be able to whip any fighter in the sky—including the F-4 Phantom. The MiGs passed overhead, in a shallow diving turn toward the rear of the American plane.

Smith alerted Gilmore, who reacted instantly by pushing the Phantom's nose straight down and belting it into full burners. The F-4 plummeted from 30,000 to 15,000 feet, quickly picking up speed to 1.5 Mach. At 15,000, Gilmore made a steep pull-up. The MiGs, meanwhile, had continued their shallow, diving turn.

Gilmore shot up like a rocket beneath the MiGs at terrific overtake speed, sighted one at short range and let go a Sidewinder from 2,500 feet out and below. The missile hit one of the MiGs (the other vanished) but Gilmore's Phantom was traveling so fast he quickly overran the target and thought he had missed. He rolled his F-4 in a desperate attempt to give the MiG time to get ahead of him again, hurriedly fired a second Sidewinder without giving his sight time to settle down, and missed.

Gilmore then fired a third missile and watched it leave the plane, wiggle around and fly right up the MiG's tailpipe. The MIG blew up immediately in "great big chunks of fuselage and aft section," as Gilmore described it to me at Danang. "The remains of the plane pitched straight up, and it seemed to be starting a loop. As I went by, it stalled in a hammerhead and went straight down. I split-S'ed to go after it when I heard Bill Smith yell, "We have a MiG on our tail. No! No! It's our wingman!"

But behind the wingman was another MiG and Gilmore said he quickly lost interest in the one going down. He pulled the F-4's nose up, hit the afterburners and started a vertical climb, intending to head in what he thought was the direction of home at high altitude.

He did not trust his inertial navigation system at this point because the F-4's violent maneuvers had probably tumbled the gyros. Turned out Gilmore was heading south and west instead of south and east, and the first time he got his bearings was when Smith looked down and saw the confluence of the Red and Black rivers.

"When we finally got over South Vietnam," Gilmore related, "I started yelling for a tanker in a voice about four octaves higher than usual. I don't really know how I got plugged in, but I did. Then I got to shaking so bad I had to ask Bill to take over from the back seat. I didn't know whether to laugh or cry. I landed at Danang, and 15 minutes later here comes my wingman. He'd had a partial radio failure—he could receive up there but couldn't transmit. We knew something had gone wrong, as we'd been trying to call him on our way out. Now we asked him if he had seen the kill. 'You got him with your first missile,' he said. 'The MiG pilot ejected immediately. He popped a red and white chute. We saw you make two more firing passes and thought you'd gone out of your mind.'"

That night the biggest party *ever* was held at the Danang Officers' Club bar to celebrate the first MiG-21 kill in history. $400 worth of drinks at 15 cents each were consumed. Gilmore and Smith were carried around on the shoulders of the crowd. Gilmore himself was nearly decapitated when they carried him almost into the huge rotating fan hanging from the ceiling. It missed him by inches.

The morning after I talked to him, Bill Smith was flying an F-4 when another F-4 in his squadron was hit by 37mm ground fire. The right engine caught fire. The stricken F-4's pilot, Frank Lennon, stopcocked the engine and the fire went out. But when he and his rear-seat copilot tried to get the big fighter out of a steep right bank, the controls would not respond. The plane went over on its back and started an upside-down corkscrew toward the sea. Both pilots punched out inverted. Smith, in the other F-4, got off an immediate position report, which brought in an HU-16 (twin-engine Grumman amphibian) from its offshore standby station. Navy jets off a carrier arrived almost at once and began making firing passes up and down the beach, since VC shore gunners were trying to hit the two pilots bobbing in the sea. The rescue mission was successful: 16 minutes after they punched out, Lennon and his copilot were safely aboard the HU-16 on their way to the base hospital at Danang.

I was there when they landed. Lennon's back had been broken by the force of the ejection, and his copilot's back had been severely strained. I then learned that people who punch out of F-4s very often receive severe back injuries. Evidently the primary ejection handle is lower than the top of your head, so you have to duck your head and bend your spine to reach it. When you finally pull it, you are not sitting stiffly erect—as you should be to avoid spinal injury. Worse still (and this is what happened to Lennon and his copilot) you may not be able to use the primary ejection system, which means you have to reach down between your legs and pull the secondary. This makes it even harder to keep your spine stiff and rigid, for you tend to bend forward quickly, particularly when you are excited—like when going out inverted in an uncontrollable spin. This ejection seat is hurting a lot of backs, but a fix is in the works.

My visit to the town of Danang itself left me with many impressions. Streets crammed with jeeps, six-bys, troop carriers and a madhouse of cycles. Hordes of people carrying great baskets on opposite ends of a pole across their shoulders. Cocky young Arvins, natty in berets, with stubby machine guns slung over their shoulders. The bustling marketplace full of goods. The home of the local province chief, looking like a palace or an embassy building—in contrast with the miserable native hootches. The harbor front alive with people fishing, paddling, loading and unloading.

All during my trip I asked our troops how they felt about the war. Ninety percent gave me roughly the same answer: "We have to stop Communism and we'd rather do it here in Vietnam than on the coast of California." One F-4 fighter-bomber pilot in Danang told me he thought we should start at the DMZ and kill every man, woman and child in North Vietnam. His squadron-mate took instant exception, stating we should limit the killing to the Vietcong and the North Vietnamese regulars.

I did not meet anybody who thought the VC were yellow. In fact, their courage and tenacity were universally acknowledged. It was the murders and terror bombings carried on by the VC that were universally condemned.

Many thought the VC were getting younger. Some were 15 years old and others as young as 12. Nobody seemed to understand what kept them fighting in the face of such superior weapons and communications. "Up north here they've at least got trees to hide under," one pilot told me. "Down in the Delta it's like a rabbit shoot."

I left Danang on the C-130 shuttle and flew over the mountains to Pleiku, in Vietnam's Central Highlands. These mountains look much like those of West Virginia—low, but steep, with twisting narrow valleys cut by little streams, and a thick forest canopy. As a forced landing area—forget it. If you get hit, or lose your engine, and you can't make it to the coast—punch out.

The mountain area was occupied by Vietcong. The combination of rugged terrain and heavy forest growth makes it very difficult to find them and kill them.

Pleiku, located on a 2,400-foot-high plateau about 30 miles from the Cambodian border, is the great U.S. central power base. It is gloriously cool after the tropical lowlands; there is an autumn tang in the air and at night you need blankets.

The Pleiku strip is only about 7,000 feet long, but the approaches are so good that even the enormous C-141 jet transports can use it. Military installations of all types sprawl over the rolling meadows around the strip, and giant radars jut up. The Knudsen construction consortium has an army of its own here, building all sorts of things—barracks, storage facilities, radar housing units, etc. As in Danang, it is obvious we are not doing things on a temporary basis; we are at Pleiku for the long pull. Billions of dollars are being invested in permanent facilities such as Pleiku, Danang and Cam Ranh Bay.

In the hills around Pleiku, elements of the Army's First Cavalry Division (Airmobile) are deployed. The First Cav Airmobile is truly unique, being the first military ground unit in the world with complete air mobility. It was organized early in 1965 at Fort Benning, Georgia, out of elements of the Army's 2nd Infantry Division and the experimental 11th Air Assault Division. (The original First Cavalry Division, then stationed in Korea, was redesignated the 2nd Infantry Division.)

The First Cav Airmobile consisted of 15,787 men equipped with 434 aircraft (most of them helicopters) and 1,600 land vehicles. (By contrast, a regular Army infantry division is made up of 15,900 men, 101 aircraft and 3,200 ground vehicles.)

First Cav's aircraft breakdown is as follows: 111 Bell turbine-powered UH-1B "Huey" helicopters (two crew and seven passengers or two litters) with heavy armament (these are usually the "Hogs" or "Gunships"); 176 Bell UH-1D Hueys (same as the UH-1B except it carries just one crew and either 11 passengers or six litters); 48 Vertol CH-47 "Chinook" twin-engine, tandem-rotor, passenger-cargo, all-weather helicopters (three crew, dual controls, 33 passengers, rear loading ramp); 93 Hughes LOHs (light observation helicopters); and six Grumman OV-1 Mohawk twin-engine, STOL surveillance aircraft (two crew). The OV-1s are used for both visual and photo reconnaissance and some of the later models have both infrared detection equipment and side-looking radar.

According to U.S. Secretary of Defense McNamara, the formation and deployment of the First Cav Airmobile "marks the beginning of a new era in land warfare." And while the First Cav does have fixed quarters—about 78 square kilometers near An Khe—it is only rarely found there.

For the First Cav fights the land war from the air. Helicopters have replaced trucks and jeeps as the transportation vehicles for men and equipment. And wherever—within a radius of more than 200 kilometers—American or Arvin troops fall into a Red trap, or a fast-developing search-and-destroy mission evolves, the Skyraiders move in. Where regular infantry soldiers might take days or even weeks to move through the impenetrable jungle, or over the hills and mountains, the air cavalry moves men, weapons, ammunition and supplies rapidly and repeatedly to the battle scene in a few hours.

Special light equipment has been developed for the First Cav Airmobile. Ammunition, for example, is so lightweight that every First Cav trooper can carry 29 magazines of 20 cartridges each for his M-16 carbine.

The Vietcong have always been noted for their great mobility. First Cav troops are infinitely more mobile. "The VC need ten days to transfer three battalions," U.S. Maj. Gen. William E. DePuy explains. "We manage five battalions in a day."

Nowhere was this new mobility better demonstrated than during the battle of Plei Me at the end of 1965. First Cav elements chased a Vietcong unit for an entire month, packing up and being airlifted to new positions no less than 40 times, skimming over the treetops in helicopters while the Vietcong slogged through the jungle. During the engagement, 13,257 tons of supplies were brought in by air. Wherever the Vietcong turned, fresh new units of First Cav troopers appeared with plenty of ammunition and supplies. The remnants of the VC unit finally fled into Cambodia.

The First Cav Division has been so successful in Vietnam that a second Airmobile Division is being formed.

C-141 jet transports bring First Cav Airmobile Division replacements into Pleiku direct from the States and take back troopers who've been there a year. I saw a gang of these "one-year-olds," as they are called, marching toward a C-141 to load up for home. They maintained their military posture, but still gave you the feeling that any minute they might throw their M-16s in the air and start capering like school kids. To a soldier who has just been through the sheer hell of 12 months of search-and-destroy, the yawning rear cargo door of a transocean jet C-141 must be a lovely sight.

Our reconnaissance eye over Vietnam is the 13th Reconnaissance Wing based at Tan Son Nhut. A fleet of modern but subsonic RB-57s and RB-66s, supersonic RF-101 Voodoos and doublesonic RF-4C Phantoms is fueled and ready to go day and night. Nowhere is aerial reconnaissance more helpful and more efficient than in the close support war south of the DMZ.

The 13th Reconnaissance Wing flew recon missions for all four services on the basis of priority. A top-priority mission is indicated when, for example, the enemy is engaging our ground troops with heavy fire, and our commanders need information on the reinforcements the enemy is bringing in and where he is positioning his guns. The 13th flew this mission immediately, and rushed the freshly obtained pictures back to the lab at Tan Son Nhut, where they are developed and interpreted. The results are reported to the field commanders by radio if possible, and the prints are flown back to the field at once. If the plane can't land, the photos are paradropped.

You have to tailor the scale of your photos to the situation. A high-altitude photo scale of 1/250,000 would be totally useless to a Special Forces outfit wanting to find trails to get through a forest valley. They need a close-in look—a scale of 1/5,000 or less. Recon photos have picked up such details as a single strand of copper wire between a pair of jungle trees—an aerial—and a tiny pile of firewood tucked in the corner of a clearing (the interpretation: guerrilla base).

For high-altitude, large-area photos, we use the RB-57, the Martin version of the old British Canberra. It has a wide wing with enormous lift, and one version can fly as high or higher than a U-2. The RB-57's high-altitude photos are carefully controlled as to field of coverage so a number of them can be joined into a mosaic that becomes a master map of an entire region. Subsequent photos taken of the same area are compared with the master. If there are any discrepancies, they are carefully scanned for signs of enemy buildup, and more detailed photos are then taken at lower altitudes.

The RF-4C Phantoms are our night eyes. Their main job is to go deep into North Vietnam every night and shoot infrared pictures. These are actually heat pictures; everything is shown in terms of temperature difference. These pictures can pick out anything that gives off a measurable amount of heat—roads, campfires, trucks and other heavy equipment and concentrations of troops. The Phantoms can also photograph in black-and-white. Finally and very important, they can photograph with radar—a technique that has been so amazingly developed that nighttime radar pictures are almost as detailed as full-daylight black-and-whites. In fact, radar pictures sometimes show up details that are invisible in black-and-white because of camouflage. Night missions over North Vietnam are considerably safer than day missions, but the Phantoms are still fired at by radar-controlled guns on virtually every trip.

The RB-66 also does some night work, equipped with a giant electronic-flash unit of 4,500,000 candlepower mounted under its belly. The automatic cameras of the RB-66 are triggered by light from the flash unit bouncing back from the ground. As a result, the reconnaissance planes often return with unintentional photographs; the camera responded to enemy shell bursts.

Supplementing the night-flying Phantoms and RB-66s are the day-flying RF-101 Voodoos, which take pictures in both black-and-white and color. Color is particularly valuable because it enables the photo interpreters to detect camouflaged targets that wouldn't show up in black-and-white. The VC cover all sorts of potential targets with fresh-cut foliage. But when a branch is cut, its leaves lose chlorophyll, and on special color film the foliage looks yellow or brown and is easily recognized.

All the three types of pictures—radar, black-and-white and color—are used in conjunction. Comparison of the three may reveal camouflaged objects when any one would not have been conclusive.

The use of recon to alert our troops to a big enemy infiltration, such as the move by North Vietnamese Regulars in the summer of 1966 through the Demilitarized Zone, can mean the difference between being caught in a deadly surprise attack or nipping the infiltration in the bud. In this case, recon caught the PAVN (People's Army of North Vietnam) 324th Division coming through the DMZ, and our B-52s took a terrible toll of them. Heavy reinforcements of American troops were rushed north, and what could have been a catastrophe for us turned into a crushing defeat for the North.

To guard against a suicide bombing attack against U.S. air bases, our supersonic seeing eyes inspect the airfields in North Vietnam day and night. If they detect a buildup of MiGs and Badgers, we can get on the horn to Washington posthaste and get a go-ahead to smash the fields.

BDA (bomb damage assessment) is a day-to-day assignment for the RB-57s and RF-101s, and it is one of the most thankless and dangerous jobs the war has to offer. The enemy knows our boys will be over to photograph the results soon after one of our strikes, and they are set up and waiting to shoot them down. BDA is the key to whether you strike the place again. If you find you have destroyed most of it, you get on about other business. No use getting shot down for the last 10 percent when you have targets with 100 percent.

The interpretation of BDA photos involves a battle of wits between our photo interpreters and the North Vietnamese, who have become masters of camouflage. Sometimes they use bombed-out areas for POL stores, which they hide under the debris, figuring the last place we'll hit again is an abandoned ruin.

Capt. John Irwin, one of our film analysts, gave this description of a typical duel: "A connecting road ended at the banks of a river. We had destroyed the ferryboat. But was there a new ferry, and where was it? We studied the photos of the riverbank and discovered a bush that wasn't there a week before. Bushes just don't grow that rapidly." He requested a new strike.

The photo lab at Tan Son Nhut is a mass-production operation handling 3,000,000 feet of film and prints a month. Every day a ton of processed material is shipped around the war theatre in the Blue Canoes (Cessna 310s). The results of important bombings and pictures of politically sensitive targets under consideration for new raids are flown back to Washington for the President and the Joint Chiefs to evaluate. In addition, over 1,600 routine photos go back to the U.S. every day.

All our recon information is filed and cross-indexed in Tan Son Nhut, and any authorized commander who wants to check it out can do so. "Target folders" containing the latest dope on AAA, SAMs, small arms concentrations and so on are given to pilots before they go on a strike. These target folders are constantly updated as new recon is processed. Some 2,000 target folders are now in use in Vietnam.

Recon also keeps a running check of where our own troops and the Arvins are at any given moment (it is considered bad for morale to drop bombs on your own guys). The men in the read-out rooms at Tan Son Nhut look like space-laboratory technicians. They wear white skull caps and long-gauntleted white gloves to keep dandruff and sweat marks off delicate material. Be a shame to call a bomb strike on a bit of dandruff, or interpret a sweat mark as a VC trench.

A number of big battles, involving large numbers of troops, have been fought in the Central Highlands. Typical among them were the battles of Ia Drang Valley, Plei Me and A Shau. Each of these engagements was a bitter, complex, yet highly interesting exercise in the use of air power to save, or at least take the pressure off, desperately pressed ground soldiers. Without air support, U.S. troops in each of these three battles would have been overrun and very probably wiped out to the last man.

In fact, A Shau *was* overrun, but the survivors were taken out by air. A Shau was a Special Forces camp located in a narrow valley on the Laos–South Vietnam border, about 375 miles northeast of Saigon. The VC were massed around the isolated camp. The weather was so miserable that the clouds got down over the surrounding hills and put a thick, zero-

zero lid over the whole valley. Beneath the lid was a layer of murky, rainy "clear" air with half-a-mile visibility.

Letting down through the soup into the "clear" layer in the valley was dangerous enough because the whole place was walled in by hills and you couldn't tell where they were until you saw a black wall rushing at you through the murk. And once a pilot got down, the weathered-in little valley was so massed with VC automatic weapons that every plane immediately came under heavy fire at close range.

In short, the battle at A Shau was as desperate an air-ground fire fight as could be imagined.

One of the heroes of A Shau was Air Force Maj. Bernard Fisher, who let down through the clouds many times in his A-1 Skyraider. For hours Fisher attacked, led other planes in, directed, encouraged, went back to Pleiku to refuel and returned to attack again. He was hit time and again. During one of his firing passes, Fisher spotted squadron-mate Maj. Dafford Myers hiding in a ditch alongside the short air strip at the besieged camp. Myers had been shot down earlier and had crash-landed his Skyraider on the runway. Fisher landed on the strip, which by then was pockmarked with shell and bomb craters, taxied under heavy automatic weapons fire to where the wounded Myers was crouching, picked him up and somehow got off again. When he landed back at Pleiku for the last time, his ground crew counted 19 holes in the Skyraider.

Another A Shau hero was 1st Lt. Delbert R. Peterson, copilot of a Dragon Ship that got down through the cloud cover and made its characteristic slow, banked pass over the VC encircling the camp, all the while pouring out thousands of rounds of deadly 7.62mm cannon fire from its three side-mounted miniguns. The VC gunners cut loose at the Dragon Ship as it swung slowly around, and on its second pass, at about 1,000 feet, .50-cal. slugs tore the right engine from its mount and, seconds later, also knocked out the left engine.

The Dragon Ship's pilot, Air Force Capt. W. M. Collins, crash-landed the plane on the slope of the mountain about seven miles north of the camp. The plane slid to a stop at the base of the mountain. One of its five crewmen, S/Sgt. R. E. Foster, suffered two broken legs. But the others were relatively unhurt, and since Foster couldn't be moved, they decided to throw up a defensive perimeter around the downed plane. One of the crew got on the radio in an attempt to call in air strikes and a rescue helicopter.

Fifteen minutes later, VC troops attacked the tiny perimeter, but the crew repulsed them with automatic rifle fire. The VC then brought up a .50-cal. machine gun and attacked again, killing Capt. Collins and Sgt. Foster and seriously wounding the navigator, Lt. J. L. Meek.

By this time, the rescue helicopter was overhead, but the hail of VC bullets was so heavy it looked as though the chopper wouldn't be able to land. Realizing there was little chance of rescue unless the MG was knocked out, Lt. Peterson went after it alone, armed only with his AR-15 and a .38 revolver. He silenced the MG, permitting the chopper to land and pick up the other two surviving crew members. But VC fire again became so intense that the helicopter could not wait to pick up Peterson. He and the bodies of the two dead crewmen were left behind.

15 INTERCONTINENTAL BOMBERS VS. JUNGLE HIDEOUTS

The Boeing B-52 eight-jet intercontinental bomber being used so continuously against jungle hideouts in South Vietnam, was originally built to deter Communist attack on the United States. This airplane is enormous. It has the range to fly to Russia and back from the United States and deliver an H-bomb. It can fly very high—around 50,000 feet, and can cover the ground at 520 knots. The normal crew is six men: aircraft commander, pilot, observer (he drops the bomb), navigator, electronics countermeasures operator and gunner. Extra range is made possible by enormous teardrop tanks that carry many hundreds of gallons of extra fuel. Several ferocious innovations have been added since the B-52 was first deployed in the Strategic Air Command over 20 years ago. The *Hound Dog* missile, which can be carried under the massive wing of the B-52, can be launched (it's really a small radar-guided jet plane) hundreds of miles out from a target and can deliver a nuclear warhead in advance of the arrival of the bomber (which carries a much larger warhead in its belly). The electronics countermeasures equipment carried by the B-52 is there to confuse and hopefully to render impotent any fighters or missiles that the enemy may send to knock down the approaching bomber. There are various kinds of ECM: devices that make the bomber appear as a whole fleet of planes when, in fact, there is only one; devices that make the enemy radar scopes turn into crazy jumbles of spokes, squiggles and whorls, thus obscuring the actual position of the planes. There is also a decoy known as the Green Quail, a small jet plane that carries its own ECM gear, and, when launched from the B-52 appears to the radars on the ground as a large raid of B-52s. The Green Quail's purpose is to draw missile and fighter attack in one sector, while the actual bombers sneak in on the target from a different angle.

The B-52 is subsonic. That, of course, makes it highly vulnerable to attack from supersonic interceptors and missiles. Some years ago, therefore, a new technique for delivering H-bombs was devised and was practiced intensively over Maine, for example. It was quite simple. The B-52s did not try to run in on the target at high altitude where they could be picked up on radar. They came in "on the deck" as the saying is, skimming the treetops, and thus were hidden from enemy radar until they were very close to the target (radar is a line-of-sight detection weapon; anything below the horizon is invisible to a radar scope). Then they "popped up" to 5,000 feet and dropped their theoretical H-bomb. The reason they popped up was to avoid the resulting multimegaton blast, which would have destroyed the B-52 itself, traveling at high speed trying to escape. As a matter of fact, some H-bomb blasts are so enormous that a B-52 would have to drop a bomb with a parachute to delay its fall, or with a delay-action fuse, even from 5,000 feet—or be destroyed by its own blast.

At any rate, the B-52, like all Boeing bombers, was a very soundly designed and durably built airplane. The basic airframes went on and on. Newer, more powerful jet engines were hung on them to give them more range and more carrying capacity; the various decoys and air-to-ground missiles just described were hung under the wings; the wings themselves were beefed up. Finally, after 20 years, even the tremendous integrity built into these bombers by the world's leading big bomber builder (which Boeing was, and some people, including myself, think still is) began to grow weary. The wings and tail sections began to show telltale signs of fatigue.

Boeing was equal to the problem. They modified test B-52s, fitted with myriads of strain gauges, and other gadgetry that would record signs of danger in the aging planes—and they went out daily and rammed those test planes through the most severe turbulence they could find and examined the test data. When weaknesses were found, the whole B-52 fleet was checked and beefed up, at the weak points. One of these planes hit a gust over the Rockies and lost most of its tail. The pilot, a cool head if there ever was one, stayed with the plane and brought it in on a wing and a prayer.

So it can probably be said, without exaggeration, that the B-52 gave the American taxpayers more solid value for their defense dollars than almost any other piece of military hardware they ever paid for. It can also be said that the men who flew these bombers, and those who stayed on the ground and manned the bases for them, were earning their pay. They were the Big Stick that Gen. Curtis LeMay was ready to pick up and start slamming with at the drop of a hat, and the Russians knew it. A good example was the Cuban crisis. The B-52 bombers of the Strategic Air Command were deployed, armed, briefed and ready to attack if the showdown over Cuba had gone into World War III. Tanker planes were ready to refuel them on their way in and out. The training (and SAC training is the best there is for large bombers) had been drilled into these veterans for many, many years. They had gray heads, and bald heads, but they were deadly and they would have pressed home their attacks to the bitter end and Khrushchev knew it. I do not say that SAC alone caused the Russians to pull their missiles out of Cuba. There were many other American deterrent weapons by that time, and some of them were as fearsome as SAC—or more fearsome. But anybody who fails to give our Strategic Air Command, and its leader, Gen. LeMay, full credit for the job they did during the years of the 1950s and '60s is not being fair to them. They were on the job, night and day, all over the world, and it wasn't much fun, as any SAC pilot who's pulled temporary duty after temporary duty far from home can tell you.

SAC has been, for some time, flying missions out of Guam

against South Vietnam. The standard bomb load was fifty-one 750-pound bombs per plane if you were using high explosive. Many more bombs if you were using incendiaries. The bombers have been striking at remote jungle hideouts (and also strikes on roads, fields and suspected VC buildings) in the Iron Triangle and in War Zones C and D (north of Saigon)—also in the Demilitarized Zone between North and South Vietnam when it became known that there was a step-up in infiltration through this zone. The raids from Guam have been frequent, often several a day, and a number of planes have been used in a raid to "carpet bomb" a dense jungle area with fire bombs or high explosives.

The main purpose of these raids was to destroy the hard-to-reach jungle sanctuaries to which the VC retired for rest, medical attention and fresh supplies. The jungles were honeycombed with tunnels and these carpet raids caved them in when they found them through the treetops. The Vietcong could not rest. They could not enjoy any peace of mind because they never knew when the whole jungle might go on fire or be blasted to matchwood around them. The B-52s attacked from very high altitude—30,000 to 40,000 feet—too high to be seen or heard. The attack came by complete surprise, and it was usually directed by a low-flying helicopter or FAC Bird Dog plane that was close to the target area.

The technique for making the drop was already at hand. For many years the Strategic Air Command has been running off what they called "The World's Series of Bombing." Select crews from SAC would compete in a mock bombing raid over a preestablished course. On the ground, at the target sites were RBSs—radar bomb scoring systems—which could tell, with very good accuracy, how close the theoretical bombs would have been to the bull's-eye. So it was a natural thing to transplant the RBS equipment to Vietnam—carry it in a small plane—and use it to actually trigger the drops on the jungles, not just to measure a theoretical score in a mock competition.

So this is how the B-52s operate out of Guam, which is 2,530 miles from the drop zone, and are also operating out of the new air base at Sattihip, on the Gulf of Thailand, very much closer to the targets. The B-52s are not molested by missiles, ground fire or enemy fighters in their missions over South Vietnam. Only one B-52 was lost due to colliding with another plane. The raids have been criticized by the fighter-bomber pilots because there really hasn't been any danger compared to the danger of going in low into a furious flak storm as one must do in a fighter-bomber over North Vietnam on nearly every mission. The raids were also criticized at the time of the bomb shortage (now over) when pilots of smaller planes were bitter about the "matchwood missions" of the B-52s over what might be empty jungle—when the single-engine jocks risked their lives going in on dangerous targets with less than full loads of bombs.

The B-52 crews are old pros. They took on the mission of defending the United States when they could, at any moment, have been ordered to fly deep into Russia against deadly defense of missiles and fighters—a mission from which many of them would not have returned. Now they have a quite different set of orders. To blast or burn large areas of jungle (also roads, buildings and fields) containing living things, animals and men, some innocent and unaware, without warning. It's not a mission of their choosing. It's just the way the ball happened to bounce. But one can't help but wonder what a man thinks about, after he'd set fire to 50 square miles of jungle from high altitude with a rain of fire bombs, and wakes up in his room in the darkness—and lies awake watching the shadows on the ceiling. . . .

16 JUST AROUND THE CORNER

While manned aircraft will continue to play the major role in U.S. military strategy, it is unlikely that the next few years will bring dramatic changes in the presently planned aircraft inventory—although there are a number of planes now in various stages of development and test.

Just around the corner are the highly advanced General Dynamics F-111 and the C-5A, and several Stol and V/TOL aircraft. There will also be special-purpose aircraft —generally modifications of airplanes already operational or under development. And there are continuing studies of future aircraft requirements.

The F-111 and the C-5A, when operational, will

provide—for the first time—a real breakthrough both in air-lift and tactical operations: The Department of Defense classified the F-111 as "superior in its class to any other tactical weapons system in the world." First deliveries to combat forces will be made this year. Marked by its variable sweep wing, which operates through a 16- to 72.5-degree wing angle change, the airplane can be flown at slow "loiter" speeds or, with the wings swept back, as a supersonic fighter.

The two-place F-111 will land at about 110-112 knots, take off using less than 3,000 feet of runway and, in addition to its loiter capability, fly supersonic at sea level and Mach 2.5 at altitude. It can fly nonstop to most overseas bases without refueling.

First of four versions to become operational is the Tactical Air Command's F-111A. This fighter will include new attack radar, digital computers for navigation and weapon delivery, air-to-air missiles compatible with the Mark II avionics system and IFF (identification, friend or foe) capabilities. The Navy version, the F-111B built by Grumman Aircraft Engineering Co. under contract, will operate from carriers with fleet defense its primary mission. Two other Air Force versions are under development: the RF-111A, tailored to reconnaissance, and the FB-111A dual-purpose bomber, which will replace certain of the B-52 series and will fly with the Strategic Air Command. All are powered by two Pratt & Whitney TF-30 afterburning fanjets of about 19,000 pounds thrust each.

The giant military cargo aircraft Lockheed-Georgia C-54, termed "the breakthrough in meeting strategic mobility need," is twice the size of the largest existing U.S. airplane. It has a wing span of more than 222 feet and length of 236 feet. It will weigh in excess of 350 tons and can carry more than 100 tons over 3,000 miles and fly at 435 knots powered by four General Electric TF 39 turbofans of 40,000 pounds thrust each.

The Coin—or counterinsurgency aircraft—is the airborne equivalent of the jeep. It is a combination of doctor-lawyer-Indian-chief. As such, it must be capable of performing a variety of missions, from reconnaissance through helicopter escort and attack, and support of ground troops. It also must be able to operate from rough clearings and primitive roads.

This year the Air Force is procuring several new tactical

aircraft designed from scratch or modified to Coin operations. Each should add greater close-air support capability to
the forces in Vietnam.

The A-7A turbojet (Ling-Temco-Vought A-7A Corsair II) is a modified version of the single-place Corsair II
developed for the Navy as a carrier-borne attack fighter. The
heavily armored, subsonic (Mach 8) attack aircraft can carry
a maximum load of more than 15,000 pounds of ordnance. It
is armed with two 20mm guns in pods on wing stations. Its
combat radius with external fuel tanks is 800 miles with
6,000 pounds of bombs, plus a half-hour loiter on station. It
is powered by a single Pratt & Whitney TF30-P-6 turbofan of
11,350 pounds of thrust.

The North American OV-10A Lara, a propeller-
driven aircraft designed specifically for Coin operations, is
capable of performing strike and visual reconnaissance
missions and will eventually replace the 0-1 forward-
air-controller (FAC) aircraft now operating in Vietnam. The
twin-turboprop Lara (light armed reconnaissance aircraft),
in varied configurations, may be utilized as a small six-place
troop or cargo (3,000 pounds) transport.

The North American concept features twin booms with the
horizontal tail mounted high between twin vertical tails. Pilot
and observer are seated in tandem. Armament includes two
7.62mm Gatling guns plus up to 3,600 pounds of external
stores. The airplane can deliver conventional fragmentation,
chemical and demolition bombs, rockets "Eye" series weapons and Sidewinder missiles. Low speed, for helicopter escort,
is 60 knots. With a maximum sea-level speed of 260 knots,
the OV-10A also can withstand eight Gs and 460-knot speed
in dive or attack attitudes. Power is supplied by two Garrett-
AiResearch T76-G 6/8 engines of 660 shp each.

The Cessna AT-37D is a modification of the T-37B
"Tweety Bird," the Air Force two-place (side-by-side)
primary trainer. The AT-37D is fitted with two General Electric J85-J2 turbojets of 2,400 pounds thrust each (as against
the trainer's two 1,025-pound thrust engines). Gross weight is
increased from 6,000 pounds to 12,000 pounds. Armor plat-
ing and shatterproof glass have been added. Thus the little
trainer modification, with a span of 35.8 feet and length of
29.3 feet, includes provisions for all conventional weapons
used in Coin missions. At full gross weight it will take off

over 50 feet in 2,650 feet, climb at 6,500 feet per minute and fly up to 415 knots.

Of no less import to close-support operations is the Army combat helicopter. The newest of the breed, which may become operational in 1968, is the two-place Advanced Aerial Fire Support System (AAFSS), the Lockheed rigid-rotor compound helicopter conceived and designed exclusively as a weapons platform. This 200-knot-plus whirlybird combines its rotary wing (four blades) with a pusher propeller, and antitorque rotor, and the stubby wings of the compound aircraft.

The rigid-rotor helicopter has its blades attached rigidly to the mast (not "hinged" or "teetering"). The resultant stability and maneuverability, coupled to the short wings, give the AAFSS fighter-like capabilities. It is 50 percent faster than current operational helicopters now in Vietnam.

Surrounded by more secrecy than any other operational aircraft is the Lockheed-California Mach 3-plus advanced interceptor, the YF-12A, of which another version, flying strategic reconnaissance, is dubbed the SR-71.

As the world's fastest and highest-flying airplane, the YF-12A (SR-71) has had more airframe-engine experience at the Mach 3 level than any other aircraft now flying. In May, 1965, it set nine world's speed and altitude records, including flight at Mach 3.12 and flight at a sustained altitude of 80,000 feet.

17   R AND R

When I was in Danang I was taken over to see the Vietnamese Air Force's private whorehouse, which was a medium-sized building with many open windows and doors, a patio, lounge chairs, lines for washing and a few minor shrubs to decorate the patch of lawn that separated the place from the main highway. It was not necessary to go in. The girls were all clearly in view, sitting in the sun, skylarking around inside, hanging up clothes on the line; no business would be transacted there until night. But I did get a good look at the girls. They looked young, cheerful, and they certainly did not look the part of the pitiful prostitute who stares out at the world from a diseased body, hating everything in sight. They looked (and they couldn't have been putting it on, because they didn't know me from Adam and wouldn't have cared a fig if they had) like a bunch of giggly young girls having a ball in the sun.

I later saw the other VNAF whorehouse alongside the road to the "VC Beach" north of Danang, where I went swimming one afternoon, and it was a replica of the first—airy, cheery and populated with healthy-looking young girls who, while they weren't raving beauties, were certainly pretty enough to stimulate any normally sexy young Skyraider pilot.

It was explained to me that the Americans had had their own whorehouse too, and the girls were just as happy and cute as these I was looking at—and the VD rate was low, and everybody was sexually defused and happy—until a VIP American (senator, clergyman, diplomat, God knows) arrived and got a look at this depraved state of affairs. The VIP, I was told, laid down the law. He demanded in the Name of Decency, that this disgraceful situation be rectified at once, because if it wasn't, the VIP declared, "some high-ranking heads around here will roll."

Well, nobody likes his head to roll, particularly if he's worked his way up through years of bucking the GI system to a full colonel or reasonable facsimile thereof, and the "disgraceful situation" was jolly well rectified and fast. The girls were sent packing and the GIs were sternly warned to avoid prostitutes on the streets as these unfortunate girls might be expected to be infected with VD.

Well, as anybody but a VIP bent on rectifying disgraceful situations in the Name of Decency well knows, you can't keep GIs and prostitutes apart on the streets at night after the GIs have a few drinks, and they weren't able to do it at Danang. The VD rate rose like a rocket; mayhem in bars went back to its usual frantic bedlam; and God knows how much misery and pain was caused for the girls and the GIs involved. That was the situation that prevailed—for *our* guys—when I was in Danang. The VNAF pilots, on the other hand, were doing just fine.

However, in behalf of the VIP who was reported to have closed down the Americans' official brothel in Danang, prostitution is really not the light-hearted business I have just described. It's brutal, very often, even if you've got your own government-sanctioned place, and it degrades the girls too, even if they do seem happy enough out in the yard hanging up the washing. It would appear that the GIs are going to get sexually satisfied somehow, as all healthy soldiers do when their animal spirits are stimulated by easy access and the natural atmosphere of violence, license, lust and urgency that wartime always brings with it anywhere in the world. American officials have, of course, recognized this as one of the facts of life and have made an effort to deal with it in the now familiar time-off period from combat known as R and R. Rest and recuperation, rest and relaxation, rest and rehabilitation—I've heard R and R described in all those ways.

Both officers and men go on R and R periodically, and where you go depends on your tastes, how much money and time you've got and the availability of free airlift. An R and R traveler usually goes with a group of buddies from his outfit and they ride an Air Force Hercules propjet, or have their way paid on a commercial airplane of one of the many airways serving Saigon, or if they are in a flying unit of some kind, they may hitch a ride with one of their own pilots in whatever is going. Hong Kong, Bangkok, Kuala Lumpur, Japan, Hawaii are the favorite R and R spots outside the Vietnam theatre. Vung Tau (the old French coastal resort they used to call Cap-Saint-Jacques) is the most popular R and R facility inside Vietnam.

TV newsreels showing GIs walking the streets of Vung Tau, girl-watching on the white beach and playing with urchins to whom they give candy while the cameras grind have been seen periodically on American TV screens. The TV reporter usually picks a clean-cut young GI who's just arrived and asks him what he intends to do with his time now that he's out of combat and has a few days to spend in these lovely surroundings. The GI responds predictably. He expects to sit on the beach and look at the lovely sea and at night he expects to catch up on the sleep he's been missing while in combat, and at this point a photogenic little tyke wanders up and the clean-cut young GI pats its head and gives it a lollypop or similar goodie and the little kid, who may or may not have been briefed for the occasion, smiles widely and cries. "Okay Number One!"

It is not that this kind of thing doesn't happen. It does, all the time. American GIs really do like kids, really do give them candy and really do look at the sea and catch up on their sleep. But R and R isn't really like that in a whole lot of cases. I think most GIs would agree if you described the most important features of R and R as booze, girls and fighting, in that order. Booze, of course, triggers off the rest. I would like to quote, now, the most famous story that came out of Korea, which illustrates the happy facade that American public relations seeks to raise between the GI and the public back home. It is known as the "What The Lieutenant Means" story and the characters are: (1) Lt. Zilch, a jet pilot just back from combat; (2) a magazine writer who is interviewing him; and (3) a public information officer (PIO officer, in Air Force language) who is there to help with the interview. It went like this:

Magazine Writer: "Lt. Zilch, now that you're back in the States, I'm sure you just can't wait to hurry home and sit down in the kitchen and have a great big piece of the kind of apple pie that only a mother can bake."

Zilch (picking nose): "The hell I will. I'm gonna get a jug and hunt up some hot little flight nurse and shack——"

PIO (breaking in sharply): "What the lieutenant means is, he feels the need of some relaxation and wants to go to a dance or two before he returns to his family."

Magazine Writer: "All combat pilots are quick to give full credit to the great debt of gratitude they owe their crew chief for keeing their plane in top condition in combat. Do you too feel this way, Lt. Zilch?"

Zilch (shouts): "Top condition, hey? Debt of gratitude, hey? Listen, that two-headed crew chief of mine couldn't get his thumb up his rear end with both hands and furthermore——"

PIO (with authority): "What the lieutenant means is, his crew chief was trying hard, but due to improper working conditions, it was very difficult to service the lieutenant's plane."

Magazine Writer: "One final question, Lieutenant. Would you mind telling me what you did personally in combat against the MiGs?"

Zilch: "Now you finally asked me one, buster. Now you finally proved you got half a brain behind them big glasses. What did I do against the MiGs? I'll never forget that day I was up there all alone at fifty thousand. All of a sudden I looked out and there's MiGs at four o'clock, MiGs at ten o'clock, MIGs all over the place. I'm boxed in, see, but that's exactly how Zilch likes it. I make a feint to the left and then I break hard right and get my guns going and—bingo! Bingo! BINGO! BINGO!"

Shouting voice of PIO: "WHAT THE LIEUTENANT MEANS IS. . . ." (Blackout).

Now it should be made clear that R and R is a personal matter. It is up to the individual GI. He can spend his time in a bar getting smashed and fondling some cutie, or he can explore the cultural assets of the community of which there are often very many indeed. Or he can do both, if he puts his mind to it, and he's really missing the chance of his lifetime if he settles for just the bars and the girls. There'll be bars and girls back in the States as long as he lives. But when he's mustered out and returns home he very probably never again will get a chance to look at the floating markets of Bangkok, the massive reclining Buddha, the Temple of the Dawn, all of which he can preserve in beautiful color on his new Nikon camera, which would cost him around $650 with all the gadgets if he bought it at home—but which he got for $160 in the PX.

GIs who have taste (you can bring back a footlocker full of junk if you don't) can pick up really lovely things if they bother to shop down the alleys for the authentic hand-made things and don't grab up the gaudy mass-produced curios from sidewalk vendors in front of big hotels. There is Thai silk: heavy, rich, almost luminous in its color—the kind of silk old Genghis Khan used to make off with when he came to town. There are chess sets carved painstakingly out of ivory, by unknown artists, which must have taken years to complete and would cost many hundreds of dollars in an exclusive shop on Fifth Avenue. Here you may pick them up for less than a hundred. There are the famous Thai silver and aquamarines, unique knife-fork-and-spoon sets made of beautiful yellow metal with bone handles.

Personally I found Hong Kong, which is touted as the greatest shopping center in the Orient, to be a disappointment. The Chinese shopkeepers, for one thing, are often so aggressive that you hate to go in to browse around. They attach themselves to your elbow and any time you look at an item they give you a loud and detailed sales talk on it.

The sellers of suits (they take your measurements one day

and have the suit ready for fitting on the next) are the most determined and skillful salesmen in town. They pick you up in the lobby of the GI hotel where you are staying, and you'd think you'd happened on some kind of high-level diplomat. Everything is suave, charming, urbane and on a non-monetary plane. They have this large showroom a few blocks away that they would like you to visit, no obligation at all, and if you go they have beautiful young girls to serve you tea and little cakes while you sit in a richly upholstered chair and gorgeous suits of clothing are brought out and displayed dramatically against a damask backdrop under flattering spotlights, etc. After a good session of this, your average American has begun to feel obligated to the suave salesman, nervous about just walking out, and if he has any intention at all of buying a suit and has the money to do so, he usually winds up being measured.

There are places in Hong Kong where you can get a beautiful suit, beautifully tailored, for a reasonable price. But there are places where the workmanship is poor (but hidden from a naïve buyer) and the cloth, which looks so rich and fine, is substandard in number of threads per inch, and where the highly touted low prices aren't really much lower, for what you get, than they are back home. GIs usually go to the suit salesman they've been told to go to by other GIs who've been there before, and sometimes this works out well. But then again it doesn't. The fact that a suitmaker makes a lot of suits for GIs doesn't necessarily mean they are worth what he charges. Americans, alas, are a bit like sheep in these matters. If old Sgt. So-and-So in the good old C-130 outfit from good old Saigon bought one of Mr. Wu's suits, nobody feels the need to check any more. Just find Mr. Wu's address and give that nice man an order. (Wu's suits may be zilch—but his tea and his girls may be magnificent.)

The one rule of thumb that smart GIs who aren't sure of themselves use is to buy the things they want in their own PX. The PX buyer is a pro, and when he brings something in out of the economy it's usually well worth the price tag. The native vendor who sells an American PX is too smart to try to put over any shoddy merchandise because if it's discovered he'll never sell that big PX anything again.

The war, as might have been expected, has involved Thailand to a certain extent. Huge new air bases are being built there and the influx of American airmen has been growing steadily. Bangkok is without doubt one of the finest R and R towns in the Orient. But not as wild as it used to be before they outlawed the opium dens, which were as thick as bars on New York's Third Avenue. I was passing through Bangkok some years ago when the French were still in Saigon, and I had never been to an opium den. I had hired a young pedicab driver for a day's peddling around town and we had gotten quite friendly. At one point I put him in back in the cab and I peddled him around; what the hell, it was a free-and-easy country in those days. He liked it. We bought some fresh pineapples and he and I sat down under a banyan tree by one of the klongs (canals) and ate it with my Swiss Army knife. Then he took me to a place he knew about where they sold good Thai silver and I bought a lovely pin that my wife still wears and finally took me home.

When I got into the lobby of the Princess Hotel, where I was staying, I found I'd lost my wallet. Nobody who hasn't been half-way around the world from his home, and has all but a few *tickels* of his money in his wallet can quite grasp the sudden panic-stricken lurch in the guts a thing like that can give you. I actually got weak in the knees. I was searching all my pockets for the fourth time, convinced that it really was gone, and mentally wondering how in hell I could cable for money without any money to cable with, when in walked my pedicab buddy. He had my wallet in his hand. It had slipped down behind the seat. There was enough money in that wallet for this kid to have retired on for a couple of years at the prices he got for peddling people around Bangkok. People wonder why I get so hot when they refer to the Thais as "gooks" in the years since then.

When the idea of going to an opium den (which has scared me before) now came back to my mind, I asked my Thai friend if he thought it was safe. He said it was pretty safe if he went along, which he said he'd be glad to do, but don't tell his father, because his father had said he would kill him if he ever found him in an opium den. I said I wouldn't tell his father. So one night we walked in off one of the main streets, through a dark alley and into a den my friend knew to be safe.

It was a "family place," he said. By that he meant that middle-class people came here regularly, just as folks come to their favorite bars back in America. The customers were all known and an atmosphere of normal cheeriness pervaded the

Chinese folks who were operating the place. A little girl of about 10 or 12, with cute pigtails, was running around with the pipes and the pills of opium and the coconut oil lamps used to soften the pills and to light the pipes. A nice old lady with gold teeth was running the abacus at the front desk to total up the bills in American money, and it took anywhere from two to four pills (two to four pipefuls) to get you off and running. (Well, not exactly off and running; a man, as he goes deeper and deeper into his opium dream, becomes progressively more corpselike.)

The pill is softened and placed in the bowl of the pipe—a very long-stemmed affair with the bowl about the middle and an extension beyond it which the smoker grips at the moment of inhaling, which is a quite strenuous matter. You really have to drag on that pipe to get the full effects of the drug. The sound of this heavy sucking could be heard from time to time as we wandered through the cribs, as they were called.

I asked if I could get into one of the cribs with a smoker and photograph him from his normal bright-eyed self to the comatose corpse state, as he continued to smoke. My Thai friend asked the management. They said of course, and they produced a young guy who looked about 20 years old who said he would like to be the subject of the test if I would buy him the opium. Through my friend I asked him if he were a steady user of opium and he said he was. Then I asked if he had come here tonight to smoke. He said he had. I asked how many pills he intended to use, and he said three. That was usually about right for him. So I felt I wasn't debauching this citizen and I did want the pictures, so we hopped into the crib—a wooden sink-like perch about waist high and maybe six feet square with a square concrete block that was, they explained, "the pillow" for a man's head after he got where he was headed.

The pipe was brought. The subject was all giggles as he softened the pill over the coconut oil lamp and stuck it firmly into the bowl of the pipe. First he lit a cigarette and it was explained to me that the smoke from raw opium is quite rank and must be "chased" by an inhale from a cigarette in the same way a drinker chases a shot of bourbon with a sip of soda or water. By now I had a slight headache and felt strange. The air was full of opium smoke and, of course, I had been breathing it and I suppose there was some minor effect. But when this addict got his pipe going and offered it to me, I refused. I have never in my life used drugs except for pain and never intend to—not even one puff.

I remained in the crib for almost an hour, until my subject lost interest in me, stopped giggling and put his head on the pillow. I have never seen a man voluntarily make himself completely helpless before, and it was a strange and unsettling experience. My subject, when I left him, could not have prevented me from sticking needles into his open eyes. One man I judged to be about 50 appeared dead. His face was quite gray and the addiction had reduced it to the outlines of a skull. His eyes were open but he wasn't there. He wasn't even close. He had neglected to take his "chaser" out of his mouth after his last bout with the pipe and there was an ash about three inches long that had burned his chin and his lips as it slowly ate up to the end of the cigarette as it lay in his mouth.

When I was in Vietnam to cover the air war I was told of "Air Opium," a civilian airline that was said to handle opium from Laos, Thailand, Vietnam, Cambodia and China. I did not verify this charming little operation, but it was said to use a couple of Twin Beeches, be bossed by an amiable pirate and to handle quite a few millions of dollars worth of the fruit of the poppies on a regular basis. Too bad, it seemed to me, to be dropping all the napalm on the VC. Seemed a couple of spare tanks ought to have been held out for delivery to Air Opium planes if they could be found in the act of loading drugs in some little boondock field. I happen to be against napalm, and would say that its use against Air Opium planes is just about the *only* place I'd really like to see it used, ever.

To be perfectly honest, I do not feel that an American boy, when he is drafted into the armed services or joins voluntarily, is necessarily in for a lot of trouble. If he is unlucky and steps on a mine or gets hit by an ambush, of course, he's in very, very bad trouble. But a look at the casualty rates among American GIs in Vietnam should be reassuring to parents, wives, brothers, sisters and kids back home. It takes four guys back behind the lines to keep one man up front fighting. Those four guys behind the lines—which gives you an 80-20 odds right off the bat—aren't any more likely to get hurt than they'd be tooling along a Hollywood Freeway, or, in fact, climbing into a bathtub. Those good old statistics "prove it." And even the fellow on the front lines, fighting, has a better chance in this war than in any we've ever fought.

If he's hit they go in with a chopper and airlift him out—maybe in a few minutes—and he goes straight to the best medical care there is.

On the brighter side of the picture, a GI has a chance (whether he takes it is up to him) to see some of the most magnificent sights and meet some of the most interesting people in the Orient. He can have a real ball on R and R. Some of those bar girls are as good-looking as movie stars, and not all of them have VD. The services give a man a chance to learn a valuable trade, as many an affluent TV repairman who learned his trade fooling with service radars during the Korean War can tell you. And the GI Bill is almost worth joining up for, in itself, when you consider that college costs about $3,500 a year these days ($14,000 in cold cash as a bare minimum for the four-year hitch), and a GI can get it free. If this sounds as if it were written by the recruiting service, sorry about that. It happens to be the truth.

18   THE OUT-COUNTRY WAR

The out-country war—the bombing of North Vietnam, Laos and the occasional "mistakes" in Cambodia—began in earnest in February, 1965, and has been increasing in intensity (with several pauses) ever since. The bombings began as an effort to interdict the movement of supplies southward over the Ho Chi Minh trail and the many other roads, trails and waterways (including coastal routes in the South China Sea) leading into South Vietnam. This original mission was gradually broadened to include supply depots—fuel dumps, ammo dumps, etc.—where resupply matériel is collected to move south over the jungle trails into Vietcong country. U.S. raids then began to hit at the concentrations of military goods on the outskirts of the Hanoi-Haiphong complex, center of power in North Vietnam.

Officially, the raids had a two-fold purpose—to prevent fresh supplies of men and matériel reaching the Vietcong, and secondly, to punish North Vietnam, to show them that they had a price to pay in increasing destruction of their homeland if they persisted in supporting the war to the south.

A third American purpose doubtless lurks in the background. The North Vietnamese have a well-equipped regular army of over 300,000. To the north is the numberless army of China. If either North Vietnam or China ever commits its regulars in force they will need constant resupply along the routes we are bombing. So our interdiction raids, by showing them they would have a tough time supporting a large regular army in the field, may perhaps dissuade them from the temptation to adventure south.

The interdiction raids were, and still are, based on hitting "choke points"—places where bomb damage is most difficult to repair rapidly, and where the maximum number of trucks and other vehicles will be stacked up. A bridge that crosses a fast-flowing river with high banks is a good choke point. Narrow mountain passes are good choke points.

The North Vietnamese have been ingenious in combating our interdiction bombing. When a bridge is knocked out, they reroute traffic to a shallow place where the river can be forded; or construct a pontoon bridge that can be used at night and swung in against the bank under the trees in the daytime; or they build sunken spans below the surface of the fast-flowing, muddy water. These underwater bridges can carry traffic, yet are not easily seen from the air. Camouflage is extensively used by the enemy. The tops of freight cars are painted in the familiar broken patterns of tans, browns and greens, and are somtimes thatched with branches and palm fronds. Dummy equipment has been placed on SAM sites to divert our bombers from more profitable targets. And maximum use is made of the swarms of laborers—some apparently Chinese "volunteers"—who can fill up bomb craters in a matter of hours.

The key targets are the bridges. Many have been attacked again and again with great loss of our airplanes and pilots and still remain intact. They are the most difficult targets imaginable. They are small—hitting one is like placing a bomb in your living room. They are strongly built. Shock waves and fragmentation from near misses don't affect them. And they don't burn.

They have to be hit by large high-explosive bombs from directly overhead—rockets fired from a distance are too small to be effective. They cannot be attacked from high altitudes—key bridges bristle with SAM emplacements. The higher an attacker flies, the more time a SAM has to lock on and destroy him.

Only one attack point is left—directly over the target under 15,000—right into the teeth of the ack-ack surrounding the bridge. No one knows this better than the North Vietnamese gunners. When a bridge is attacked they often ignore the trajectory of our planes, and simply put up every piece of steel and HE they can muster directly above the bridge, knowing our planes must fly through in order to hit the target. Ack-ack shells, 20 mm, mortars, hand-held rifles—everything goes into the air over the bridge.

What results is the most concentrated AAA barrage in the history of air warfare. Pilots described it to me as "an awesome curtain of exploding steel." Pilot after pilot has looked at this flak storm over the bridges of North Vietnam and not believed it possible for any plane to pass through and survive—and yet pressed on in to strike the target.

The workhorse of the out-country war is Republic's F-105 Thunderchief, which at the time I was in Vietnam was flying over 75 percent of the USAF strike missions to the north. The damage inflicted by the F-105s to North Vietnamese oil, power, communications, marshaling yards and transport systems is greater than that done by any other plane we have. A powerful force of F-105s is stationed over there. They have the most dangerous missions. So many have been shot down over North Vietnam that they are widely known by the rueful name of "Thunderthuds." During certain periods, a plane a day was lost. Some outfits have lost 30 percent of their planes in six months. Many of the F-105 missions are north into the Red River Valley and beyond, hitting the two track and road systems connecting Hanoi with China. The whole Red River Valley is one big nest of triple-A, much of it radar-controlled. If a pilot is able to eject from a flak-hit plane and survive, he is out of reach of the "Jolly Green Giants" helicopter rescue—doomed to capture or death. If you go down north of the Red, chum, *sayonara.*

Since the F-105s are being shot down so frequently that they may become extinct (none are coming off the lines and haven't for years), a description for posterity may be in order. The F-105 is powered by a Pratt & Whitney J-75 (P & W is hard to beat for rugged get-you-home guts). The plane has lines like a giant bullet, certainly the best-*looking* fighter ever built. It was designed to carry an H-bomb inside its streamlined belly, but since no nuclear weapons are being used in Southeast Asia (yet), that space is available for a 2,500-pound-capacity fuel tank to give the bird longer range. Because the F-105s come from Ta Khli and Korat (the divert base is Nakon Phanom, called "Naked Fanny" by the pilots), deep inside Thailand, they need all the go-juice they can get, so a couple of 450-gallon drop tanks are hung under the wings, or a 650 is hung on the centerline.

The F-105 carries a 20mm Vulcan cannon that shoots at the rate of 6,000 rounds a minute. Max gross for takeoff is 52,800 pounds, for which you need water injection, and on a hot day it helps if they can jack the field up a foot or so, and then suddenly retract it, to get you unstuck. The F-105 has no self-sealing tanks and no armor plate, and the North Vietnamese gunners stay at their posts in the face of cannon fire, napalm and 750s. That's a big part of why we sometimes have lost one F-105 a day.

I talked at length to Maj. Jim Kasler, who may well be remembered as the number-one American pilot of this war. He calmly discussed life-and-death operations in the tone of a fellow describing how to put together the grill for a cookout. But his calm evaporated when it was suggested to him that the F-105 was an oversold collection of black boxes.

"That isn't true," Kasler said flatly. "Any other bird would have been hit harder. For one thing, we've got the range. Another fighter would run out of gas in five minutes with both ABs on. For another, we've got the speed. Down on the deck nobody can get past us when we open up. And the plane is hard. I've taken hits of heavy stuff in the wings and nose section. I didn't have to abort the mission. I went ahead and unloaded on target after I'd checked and found I had no serious damage. I think we have the best fighter-bomber in the world."

The F-105 was handy as a hammer in Jim Kasler's hand. Long gone were the days when he had to think his way through sequences and procedures. It had all become automatic for him, like touch-typing for a good stenographer. Kasler had a philosophy of dive-bombing. It centered around the same basic idea football coaches teach: "You get hurt less when you hit the other guy harder than he hits you." The ground gunners try to kill you as soon as you get in range. Regardless of whether you are conservative or aggresssive, they try just as hard.

"I tell my guys that we are there to get the target the first time," Kasler said. "If we succeed, we don't have to go back again. Then they don't get any more shots at us another day. If you enter your run at 15,000 and toggle off at 12,000, your chances of hitting a bridge are not very good. If you press down to 3,500, you are sure of a near-miss at least. I watch my bomb all the way. If I miss, I radio my wingman and give him the correction he should make. By the time our squadron is through with a target mission, somebody has usually hit it."

"But what about 3,500 feet? Isn't that dangerous?"

"I can only tell you our losses," Kasler said. "I've lost four guys out of my squadron. Some of the outfits that stay high have lost twelve. I think it's more dangerous to try to play it safe."

I interviewed Maj. Kasler at Tan Son Nhut about two weeks before he was shot down, and got the details of his most damaging and important raid of the war from him in person. He was a quiet, deadpan guy and he spoke so low I had to lean across the table and strain to hear him in the afterburner roar of the bar crowd.

"It was a cloudy day," Kasler said. "We had a little difficulty finding the tanker in the clouds."

"You refueled in solid clouds?" I asked, surprised.

"No, not solid clouds," Kasler whispered in the roaring club. "There were layers. We tooled around until we spotted the tanker between layers. I'd say we had about a half-a-mile visibility. We all plugged in and got a full load. Then we started north. I was a little concerned because we were in heavy clouds all the way and I wanted the TOT to be on the money."

"What's TOT?"

"Time on target. It's important in a big raid when everybody is converging on a place. If you are early or late, you can louse things up and people can get killed. We try to coordinate it so everybody is zapping in from all angles at once—so the gunners can't get organized on who to shoot at. You've pressed in and dropped your load before they know what happened—and then you're in afterburner and you're getting away as hard as you can." Kasler smiled then, a small tightening of the lips, the eyes not affected. "We never saw the ground until we were three minutes from drop. We broke out of the overcast coming down a long razorback into the

Red River Valley and I picked up the checkpoint I was looking for. We were dead on our nav—three minutes up the river from Hanoi."

"Any flak?"

"Yes," Kasler said softly. "Flak. I guess the news must have leaked that we were coming in full force because I never saw the flak heavier. The whole valley was lit up with little winking lights and it was like driving through a cloud deck—the burst. You can tell what kind of a gun it is by the color and size of a burst. The 37s are white, the 57s are gray and the 85s and 100 millimeters are big, black mothers with red centers. Over to the left, I noticed the Phuc Yen Airfield with a bunch of MiGs parked on it. It was a real clear day. The Red River must have been flooding because a lot of the farmland was under water. Then, up ahead, I saw the city of Hanoi and, over on one edge, just like we'd been briefed, that big area full of oil tanks. I looked at my watch. We'd come in pretty good. We were 10 seconds of TOT—which is about as close as you can hack it."

You've read the papers. You know what happened on that first Doomsday Mission (as the boys call a big balls-to-the-wall raid) against Hanoi oil. The F-105s clobbered the place and Maj. Jim Kasler and his squadron went in very low and hit the target with every bomb they carried, and when they left a column of smoke rose to 40,000 feet. It was visible from the aircraft carrier *Constellation*, 150 miles away in the Tonkin Gulf. The flames that fed that giant column were several hundred feet high. There was a temperature inversion that day and some of the smoke spread out horizontally over hundreds of square miles, making a real "darkness at noon" over the Navy targets at Haiphong. Most of the F-105s that hit Hanoi's oil dumps were satisfied when they'd got rid of their bombs. They hightailed it for home. But not Kasler.

"We all had a load of 20mm cannon ammo in our M-61s," he told me, matter-of-factly, "so we went out looking for targets of opportunity. We ran across a convoy of 25 trucks on a mountain road and we were able to destroy 12 of them before we ran out of ammo. Then we went looking for the tanker, as we were a little low on fuel."

"I assume you found him," I said.

"We found him," Kasler said, and took a mild sip of his beer. "Everybody hooked up, no sweat. Then we went home."

That's Kasler. He describes the highest point in the entire Vietnam war, when the air was full of shrieking steel and any second might have seen him smashed and burning, somersaulting end over end in his big fighter, as though he had watched it on the Late Show.

One of Jim's squadron-mates, whom I talked to later, said Jim was a loner, a guy who you'd see sitting by himself down at the end of the bar, nursing a beer. "I think Jim Kasler is a special kind of a guy," this pilot said. "He was an ace in the Korean War. He got six MiGs there. Then peace came and nobody heard another peep out of him until Vietnam. He was in Bitburg, Germany, and Wheelus Field in Africa, and he volunteered five times for Vietnam. Finally they must have got sick of it. They let him go six months early. You know the rest. He's been up there over the Red River every minute they'd let him, beating hell out of things. I guess you heard of that flap with Gen. Momeyer?"

"Flap?"

"Yeah. Gen. Momeyer told Kasler he'd have to stop going after all these secondary targets. He was too valuable. Hit the primary and come home, the general said. And Kasler didn't buy it. At least, the way I heard it, he didn't. He told the general you took a big risk crossing all that flak along the Red River and, when you made it, you didn't feel like going home until you'd expended all your ammo. You were up there to do damage. And as long as he had a bullet in his gun or a bomb on his rack, he was going to use it—not bring it back."

"What did Momeyer say to that?"

"I don't know," the pilot said. "He could rack Kasler to hell and gone if he felt like it. He's the big boss of all the air strikes in Asia. I don't know what he said. I don't even know if this happened. I just heard it over the grapevine. But somehow I can believe it. It sounds like Kasler. The guy is like an actor. He hasn't had a role to play since Korea when he was out hunting MiGs. He's got a role now. War. I can believe he said that to the general."

Jim Kasler's war had been a semi-secret war. The F-105s that had done the major damage in the deadly flakstorms in North Vietnam had been reported as coming from "somewhere in southeast Asia." The Chinese, the Russians, the North Vietnamese, even bandy-legged little natives in the hills—they knew the F-105s were coming from Thailand. But the United States had a diplomatic understanding with the Thais that we just wouldn't speak of those jets as coming out of Thailand. The Air Force was living up to it grimly, but newspapers and magazines didn't. The cat is out of the bag and has been for many months.

This truth is, we're not going to run out on Thailand. We've committed ourselves to help them to the limit and we're not just talking—we're building. On the Gulf of Siam, on the edge of a deep-water port, we've just completed an enormous air base at a place called Sattahip. The runways are 11,500 feet, long enough to take Strategic Air Command B-52s and, of course, the big KC-135 jet tankers. Fuel and logistical supplies of all kinds can be offloaded at Sattahip and flown to the other big U.S. bases in Thailand: Ta Khli, Korat, Nakhon Ratchasima, Udon-Thani, Muang Ubon and a big new one under construction at Khon Kaen. American civic action teams and Special Forces units (to combat the spreading anti-American "Thai Cong" terrorists now operating in the villages) are beefing up the air bases. A 600-foot aluminum pier is being completed at Sattahip along with ammo bunkers and the harbor is being dredged and deepened.

It has been said that "Thailand breathes through Bangkok," which is its main city located 27 miles up the silted Chao Phraya River from the Gulf. As many as 35 ships at a time must wait to unload in this choked setup. But the U.S. has committed $200,000 as ante money for what may become an aerial second front in Asia. It's not a peanuts operation. It's very big, and the out-country war, as raids against North Vietnam out of Thailand are called, is certainly of crucial importance. That means that the F-105s are not just another little rinkydink out in the boondocks. They are bearing the brunt of stopping the flow of men and supplies from North Vietnam into the hot battle zones to the south!

Did you know that on some "black days" they've lost six F-105s? Did you know that pilots have been so short that men have had to stay on and fly *two tours* into what are generally recognized as the most deadly flak defenses in history? The Red River Valley from the Chinese border down through Hanoi and Haiphong to the coast of the Tonkin Gulf, is one massive asparagus bed of guns: automatic weapons so thick they simply shoot straight up and form a vertical wall of steel for low-flying planes to fly through; 37mm cannon for planes above 5,000 and under 15,000 feet; 57mm for planes around 15,000; 85mm and 100mm guns for planes up to 40,000 feet!! And SAMs are so thickly spotted around North Vietnam that no F-105 pilot is out of range of *some* site, from the moment he crosses the border on a raid until he leaves. Did you know that the SAMs themselves (they hadn't been very effective at first, thanks to our countermeasures) are now more accurate and deadly? Formerly, you could dodge them. They didn't start "hunting you" with their radar control until they'd been roaring along for 1,500 feet or so. Now they start hunting you as soon as they leave their launching pads.

Finally, did you know that if an F-105 pilot is shot down north of the Red River (most of the raids must go north of the Red) he is in a pretty near hopeless position to be rescued? The rescue choppers, known as Jolly Green Giants, are the bravest men we've got. They'll settle down to make a pickup in the face of murderous ground fire. But even the Jolly Greens usually don't try to cross that flak forest that fills the air with steel over the Red River Valley. They cruise at 130 knots. They'd probably never make it.

This, then, is the kind of situation Kasler and the other F-105 pilots flying out of Ta Khli and Korat faced for many months. So many of them have been killed that they've been referred to as "the bloody hats." I talked to one of those veteran pilots named Capt. Bob Becker, who'd been at a "secret base in the Southeast Asia" in the "good old days." There was no water for showers, sometimes none for drinking; the field was either in the grip of a desert heat wave, dry as an old bone, or it was ankle-deep under water in the rains. The temperature was about 100 degrees F. They had two kinds of snakes, the "one-steppers" and the "two-steppers," depending on how many steps you could take before you pitched over on your face after they struck. There was also a "no-stepper," a king cobra type (would you believe 25 feet?) that not only killed you; it hit you so hard it knocked you down. Becker said they feared the tiny little krait the most, however. It was about the size of a big fishing worm and it had to gnaw awhile with its ittie-bittie fangs to get through your skin, but once that happened—one step, brother!

The pilots at these F-105 bases understandably wanted to get the best life insurance they could and they have found that tiger teeth do the job. No self-respecting Thunderchief pilot would dream of going north to dodge shells without his trusty tiger tooth dangling with his dog tags around his neck. The most popular model is the "Super-Jumbo-Man-Eater-Front-Fang-Killer." This baby costs you a cool 20 bucks, but it's said to be proof against all kinds of guns, surface-to-air missiles, VD and the common cold.

To top off the delightful morale-building conditions around the first pioneer bases, there simply wasn't a darned thing to do when a man got a day off. All around those bases were miles and miles of absolutely nothing, except for the primitive nearby towns. You could go to the Dragon Lady's if you simply couldn't deny the call of the flesh, but your chances of getting struck by lightning were better than good. As a matter of fact, one flight surgeon said, "A man was really lucky if he just got *one* form of VD. Often as not, he'd come up with a pair of them, back to back."

I asked what advice the troops were given.

"I just tell the pilots this," the flight surgeon replied. "Go ahead and have your fun, boys. Just remember that if you develop symptoms after you're shot down in North Vietnam, forget the penicillin. It isn't on the room-service list at the Hanoi Hilton. That holds the little bastards."

Intellectually, a man's only recourse on an F-105 base is a book. It would be pleasant to report that the men read Shakespeare to improve their minds on the long, hot nights, but the fact is they read *Dr. No,* if they read at all. Usually, on their night off, they belly up to the bar and slosh down the whiskey like it was going out of style. And who can blame them? They don't do this on the night before a mission, and it has very little to do with their high sense of duty and patriotism. They just know that if they fly up north with a hangover, their chances of coming back alive are even lower than usual. A man has to be blue-blade sharp when he sees one of those white telephone poles leave the launch pad with a billow of red dust and come roaring up, balancing on its blinding tail flame. I heard a playback of a tape made on a mission when such a thing was sighted. I would love to quote the pilot who made the report with some deathless phrase like "Damn the torpedoes! Full speed ahead." But what he actually screamed was, "Oh, shit! SAM!" Actually, this is a pretty effective way to get the other pilots' attention.

The flight mechanics and other ground-pounders around Korat and Ta Khli think very highly of the pilots whose planes they service. Back home, in the land of the big PX, it takes a full day to change some leaky little gasket. At Ta Khli, they'll zap a new one in in 12-½ minutes. If the muggerflugger gets out of sync, they don't down the plane for a week while they send to Japan for a new muggerflugger. They dismantle it to a hatful of bolts and cogwheels, diagnose the ailment, fix it and reassemble the works, and the muggerflugger purrs like a kitten. One pilot said he's seen a plane captain down on the flight line with a bottle of hot beer (cold bear is like diamonds) to hand to his pilot when the fellow totters over the edge of the cockpit after a tough one north of the Red. If a pilot is lost, the flight mech may actually take it so hard he has to be sent home. That's no bull. Combat brings these men very close indeed.

There were some dark days in the past when Gen. LeMay of SAC sent over one of his sternest generals to "Sacumsize" Tactical Air. It was all based on a thing called Management Control System, or MCS, which detailed just about every move everybody made, from how many strokes he used to brush his teeth in the morning to the number of turns he twisted the alarm clock at night. Brownie points if you recorded it all. Bleak fitness reports if you didn't. This was all very well for those pilots of the Strategic Air Command who had been trained under LeMay, to fill out forms from morning until night and love it. But it was no joy for the gung-ho tigers of TAC. "You can tell a fighter pilot," the saying goes, "but you can't tell him much." Which, in a way, is why he is a fighter pilot in the first place. He flies the plane, navigates, strafes, bombs, watches the radar, tunes the radio, does recon—in fact, anything that gets done, this one little guy does. He's an individualist and he's motivated by the red scarf, the screech these monsters make in the sky, the look of a bridge when it fills up the whole windscreen on a bomb run—and he is *not* motivated by brownie points.

It is good to report that they gave up trying to Sacumsize TAC. They have a fighter-pilot-type general running things there now, Gen. Gabriel Disosway, and I was told that the first thing he did at his very first staff meeting as the boss was to announce, in a medium bellow: "MCS has got to go! Now!"

I met Gen. Disosway briefly in his office at Tactical Air headquarters, Langley Field, Virginia, and he lived up to his billing. He crushed my hand heartily. He stared at me with his hot fighter-pilot eyes. He lost no time in letting me know where he stood, which, in a nutshell, was this: "TAC first—all the way!"

So you fighter pilots can stop worrying. You're in good hands with Gen. Disosway as long as you go in on those targets balls to the wall. Never mind the brownie points.

There is, however, a rather serious thing going on in the Tactical Air Command as this is written. *A squadron of pilots is being lost, for various noncombat reasons, every month.* There can be little doubt that some of this is due to the fact that TAC pilots, rightly or wrongly, feel that the U.S. public couldn't care less if they go up over the Red and bust their butts. The public has more interesting things to think about, apparently. At best, they are just bored with TAC's little problems. At worst, they regard them as bloodthirsty hawks. In either case, it's not really an incentive to go up there around those SAM sites when you could— merely by signing your name to an airline contract—be sitting up front in a Northeast Yellow Bird or one of those wild Braniff 707s with the stewardesses dressed like dancing girls (and not a SAM within 10,000 miles).

The thing Americans should remember (whether they are doves or hawks) is that Vietnam isn't the end of these wars. Wars have been going on since the first caveman made the discovery that he could pick up a rock and brain his neighbor with it, and no doubt war will continue for some time to come. You can't fight with H-bombs if you hope to survive. You have to cool it and use little iron bombs, and the way these are best delivered is by little planes that drop them on a pinpoint target—not rain them down all over the forest as SAC does, hoping to hit a VC who might be down there. So there's real reason to worry about these squadrons that are leaving TAC. Like those boys or not, we might need them in the worst way any day now, from now on, all our lives—to keep Communism out of the back yard. It might be a good idea to show them we care—if, indeed, we really do care.

I would like to end this report on Tactical Air in Asia with the most dramatic event that has taken place in the out-country war of the F-105s against North Vietnam. On August 8, 1966, Maj. Jim Kasler was out on a raid against railway bridges and oil-storage yards about 55 miles northwest of Hanoi, in the heavily defended Red River Valley, when his wingman was hit and ejected. Kasler happened to be marginal on fuel (his usual condition) but instead of pulling out for home, he made a quick run to the tanker and hurried back to fly a Rescap (rescue combat air patrol) over his downed squadron-mate. By now, the whole neighborhood was shooting at him with everything from rifles to 100mm, and this time, on his 75th mission, the Kasler luck ran out. He took a crippling hit with a big shell, and he had to get out before the plane disintegrated. He got a good chute and landed. The other F-105s in the area heard him radio that his leg was broken. Then his "beeper"—the radio homing device that brings the Jolly Greens to the rescue—began to come over loud and clear. There was still a chance, although he was so far north that it was very thin, to get Kasler out . . .

Back at supreme headquarters at Tan Son Nhut airfield, near Saigon, the big boss of all American air power in Southeast Asia, Gen. Momeyer, got the news that Jim Kasler was down. This was the same general who'd ordered Kasler to stop going after secondary targets; the man Kasler had, in effect, defied on this issue. How would he now react? Gen. Momeyer reached over and lifted the command mike and reportedly said: "I want Maj. Kasler back. I don't care how many planes it takes. Now, get on it!"

And then, suddenly, the mighty power of the U.S. Air Force closed ranks to look after its own. Even the Jolly Green Giant choppers, who don't normally try to cross the Red River, muttered out of their secret forward bases and headed for the USAF's number-one boy, the Thunderchief himself, and be damned to the flak guns. Flying all around them, for low-and-slow protection, were the big, black prop-driven Skyraiders that can fire rockets, drop bombs, shoot guns, fling napalm, and that have endurance to stay around and fight for hours, if need be. They would escort the choppers in across the deadly river and then take on any ground gunners who tried to bar to door.

Meanwhile, the word went out by radio to high-flying doublesonic Phantom jets that were cruising in the North on other missions to stop what they were doing and divert to Kasler's aid. If MiGs appeared and tried to shoot down the Jolly Greens and the escorting Skyraiders, our own Phantom jocks would come smoking in and take on the MiGs.

And that MiG CAP of Phantoms would need fuel, so giant KC-135 tankers, which normally would have been on the ground or orbiting well to the south, were ordered to get as close to Kasler as they possibly could to provide aerial filling stations for anybody who was short.

The command and control of the mass rescue attempt was being commanded by Gen. Momeyer personally, at Tan Son Nhut, but he wasn't leaving this vital matter to chance. A propjet Hercules flying command post was ordered to the area to take over "on-scene" control if he was needed because of radio difficulties.

Last, and perhaps most thrilling of all, the F-105 Thunderchief guys out of Ta Khli, Jim's home base—his comrades in arms—were told the Chief was down and were given Gen. Momeyer's blessing to do what they could. They reacted like a hand jerked off a hot stove. Every pilot and every plane that could get in the air out of Ta Khli left for the Red River Valley. Shortly, the sky over Jim Kasler's bailout position was so full of screaming jets it looked like an air meet. There were so many that they had a hard time not running into one another. The massive combined thunder of their jets could be heard for many miles in all directions. The Jolly Greens arrived with their escort planes under this howling protective canopy. They were low on fuel, having come so far. They tooled around the area at low altitude getting shot at, looking desperately for Kasler. He was not to be seen. His beeper had stopped. The grim fact was this: He'd been taken prisoner. Nothing anyone could do, even though the bulk of U.S. power was there trying, could get him out. The furious rescue attempt failed.

Maj. Jim Kasler is now a prisoner in Hanoi. His fate is in doubt. Several things bode well for him, however. First and foremost, Kasler didn't hit many civilians, and the reason was that he not only was *briefed* for military targets and *singled out* such targets, he always came down so low and close that he couldn't *hit* anything but military targets.

TV pictures have shown the Hanoi surgeons actually operating on Kasler, and these pictures have appeared in the United States. So the North Vietnamese are taking care of the Thunderchief. They probably aren't organizing any Kasler fan clubs in Hanoi, but on the other hand, they may very well have a grudging respect for this great bomber pilot who took heavy antiaircraft hits three times, before the final blow that felled him, and kept right on coming, boring into the heart of the fury.

The U.S. Air Force has a tradition of naming new air

bases after its great heroes, and some day it's possible that when a jet fighter comes screaming in for a landing, his words on the radio may be: "Hello, Kasler Tower. Air Force jet on final . . ."

And, of course, if there are peace talks, there's a chance that Jim Kasler will be home, safe and sound, in person. A lot of people sure hope so.

Capt. Jim Mitchell, another F-105 pilot I talked to at Tan Son Nhut, has 100 missions under his belt now and is back home out of the sleetstorm. Jim was up to 92 and had only eight more to go when we talked. "I hope I don't get zapped in the last eight," Jim told me. "It's a very scary place up there over the Red. I'm hyperventilating when I come into the target area. The excitement is something I can't even begin to describe. It is the most exciting thing I guess a human being could experience, diving through the flak at a target. It's best if you have the lead, because you don't see the stuff that is bursting behind you. It seems relatively safe—until you get hit. But it looks pretty bad to the number-two man. He's flying down into all those big red explosions that missed the leader. The sky seems to be so full of it you couldn't possibly escape."

Jim Mitchell was a thoughtful guy. He said he had always been more or less reluctant to speak up, but now he had changed. "I figured that when the top brass was around I'd be smart to listen instead of talk. But when you go out day after day and you see your friends shot down and killed, and you know you could be next, it does something to you. You somehow figure you've got the right to speak."

Mitchell said a pilot is less scared when he goes on raids every day. "If you lay off for a few days and then go up, you wake up very early on the morning of the mission and can't get back to sleep. You wish to God you didn't have to go. But you go. The reason is that somebody has to fly those rough missions into North Vietnam. If I don't fly mine, another guy in my outfit will have to fly it."

After returning from Vietnam, I was looking at TV one night and a drawing of Jim Mitchell appeared on the screen. He had been shot down over North Vietnam on his 99th mission, the announcer said, but had been rescued by the Jolly Green Giants. Jim then appeared in person. "I've got one more to go," he told the announcer. "Then I go home."

"I hope he makes it," my wife said.

"I hope he has a busted blower," I said. "Before takeoff."

(I heard later that the Air Force had miscounted, and Jim didn't have to go again. The mission he had been shot down on actually turned out to be his 100th and last. If you read this, Jim: *Mabu Hi!*)

19   THE FLYING MARINES

Marine F-4C fighter-bomber squadrons out of Danang also fly missions into the North. I talked to one of their pilots who had flown approximately 45 missions in support of Marine troops south of the DMZ, and who was now flying into North Vietnam doing armed recon, flying recon air cover for photo planes and hitting bridges and supply lines in North Vietnam and along the Ho Chi Minh trail.

"Supporting the Marine ground troops was a good mission," he told me. "But all the while we were doing it, we were anxious to hit north of the DMZ. You have to hit enemy supply to break their backs. The war could go on for years if you don't take out the supply lines.

"Every pilot in our squadron wanted the chance to get on a big mission up north—to hit a big target like a POL dump or a bridge or a SAM site, or to get a crack at a MiG. But I'll tell you this: the minute you get north of the DMZ and get a look at the ack-ack, you start getting second thoughts.

"There's a huge difference in the intensity of the ground fire between South and North Vietnam," the Marine pilot said. "And it's not just the triple-A and the SAMs that bother you; you can see where that is coming from and you get a chance to take it out. But the small arms fire—everything from rifles to 12.7mm automatic weapons—is deadly. You can't see where it's coming from, and the amount of metal they can throw up over a target is so great it's just bound to hit something. The enemy knows that to hit with any accuracy, we've got to come in fairly low and right over the target. So every troop in the area just fires whatever he's got straight up into the air. It makes for quite a barrage and they've been very successful with it.

"You might say," he concluded, "that the excitement and anxiety level is considerably higher in the North than it is in the South."

Once the Danang F-4C squadrons began flying north of the DMZ, their operations were conducted on a much larger scale. Many more aircraft participated in the North Vietnam raids than in the close support missions in the south. There were continual flights of four F-4Cs departing Danang.

"One strike involved more than 100 aircraft," the Marine pilot told me. "Our squadron flew escort for an ECM (electronic countermeasure) airplane, which in turn was flying cover to distract a possible MiG intercept of the F-105s and F-4Cs hitting a SAM site and barracks complex about 45 miles west of Hanoi. There was also a bridge involved."

"Did they get the bridge?"

"They got it."

I asked the Marine lieutenant about attacking bridges.

"They're not very hard to *hit*," he told me, "but the ordnance isn't always effective. It takes a lot of good solid hits—either right on the bridge or directly under the span—to take a bridge out. You can't count on near-misses to do the job."

He described one mission involving a two-span bridge, about 50 yards long and wide enough to accommodate six-by-six trucks.

"We were a flight of four F-4Cs as part of a larger strike force. Our ordnance that day was six 500-pound bombs and four packs of 2.75-inch rockets, 19 to a pack. There was no triple-A around the bridge, but there was moderate small arms fire.

"We came in at 500 knots at a 30-degree angle to the bridge, avoiding the worst of the ground fire deployed along the road leading to the bridge, from 7,000 feet AGL (above ground level). We dropped our bombs at 3,000 AGL and got the hell out. Each plane made four passes. We scored a total of five hits on the bridge—I hit it twice myself—and took it out completely. Part of the span floated down the river and the rest dropped in the gorge.

"The easiest way to get a bridge," the Marine lieutenant told me, "is to come in right down the line—right down the approach road leading to the bridge. That way you can walk your bomb load down the length of the span and you've got a better chance of scoring direct hits. But most of the ground fire comes up from the area around the road, which is why we mostly come in at an angle."

"Do you use your 2.75-inch rockets on the bridge?"

"No. They are useless for that purpose. We use the rockets to suppress ground fire when we can pinpoint it."

"How do you feel about getting shot down and captured?"

"That's a funny thing. If you go down in North Vietnam, your chances of being picked up by the chopper boys aren't really too good, but at least the North Vietnamese will treat you fairly well. In South Vietnam, on the other hand, your chances of being picked up are excellent. But if the Vietcong catch you they will kill you. They have no facilities for keeping prisoners."

Typical of the Marine pilots fighting in Vietnam is George H. Witchell of Pitman, New Jersey. Witchell flew with a Marine Corps F-4 fighter-bomber squadron in Vietnam during the latter half of 1965, and is now a member of the Piper Aircraft Company's Navajo sales team.

George Witchell originally learned to fly at the Bridgeport, New Jersey, airport when he was 18 years old. He had always been fascinated by airplanes—building models as a boy and spending his weekends standing around the field watching takeoffs and landings. During his three years in college—two at Miami University in Ohio and one at Rutgers—he accumulated 150 hours of student pilot time in Piper Colts, Super Cubs and Tri-Pacers.

On June 3, 1961, at the age of 20, Witchell enlisted in the Marine Corp's Aviation Cadet Program (MARCAD). He was sent to the Naval Air Station (NAS) at Pensacola. Witchell flew the propeller-driven Beech T-34 Mentor and North American's T-2A Buckeye jet trainer, getting 30 hours of dual instruction and putting in 120 hours of solo time.

From Pensacola, Witchell was sent to Meridian NAS, Mississippi, for more jet training. There he flew 100 hours, split evenly between dual and solo, in the T-2A.

He completed the initial phase of his training at Beeville NAS, Texas, where he flew 100 more hours—about 35 of them dual—in Grumman's F-9F-8 Cougar and F-11A Tiger advanced jet trainers. He got his wings and his second lieutenant's bars on December 21, 1962. At this point Witchell had been in flight training for 18 months and 18 days, was 22 years old, and had yet to fire a gun or drop a bomb.

After his graduation at Beeville (and 30 days' leave, which he spent in Wenonah, New Jersey, getting married to Kathryn Langston), Witchell joined Marine Fighter Attack Squadron VMFA 513 at the El Toro, California, Marine Corps Air Station. When Witchell arrived at El Toro, VMFA 513 was flying Douglas F-4D (now F-6A) Skyrays, but three months later the Skyrays were replaced by the new McDonnell F-4 Phantoms.

Witchell trained for 20 months at El Toro, practicing carrier landings on the *Coral Sea*, and going through the gunnery phase of his training: air-to-air missile firing and tactics, using the Sparrow and Sidewinder missiles ("The Sparrow is a very effective missile," says Witchell. "It has 360-degree capability and trails much better than the Sidewinder."); and air-to-ground gunnery practice at the Fallon, Nevada, Ordnance Range using practice bombs and 2.75-inch rockets.

In October of 1964, Witchell's squadron got its orders: Report to Atsugi NAS, Japan, and bring your weapons.

So VMFA 513—16 McDonnell F-4 Phantoms—left El Toro and flew to Atsugi, via Honolulu's Kaneoi Bay MCAS and Wake Island, with "normal full fuel—internal and external tanks." When he arrived in Atsugi, Witchell had been in training for three years and three months.

In Japan, Witchell's squadron spent another six months in air-to-air and "extensive" air-to-ground training. Of this period in his Marine Air Corps career, Witchell says, "We became gradually aware we were going into action in Vietnam. Every pilot wanted to go. Our morale at that point was very high. Yes—you might say we were gung-ho. We had been in training for more than three years, and we were as trained as men could get. In fact, we had reached a peak, and we weren't getting much out of our training anymore."

In late April, 1965, VMFA 513 was ordered aboard *USS Constellation* for two weeks of carrier qualification, then to Cubie Point NAS, Subic Bay, Manila, for two weeks of training missions. By the end of May the squadron was ready and orders were cut: Proceed to Danang.

George Witchell had now been in training for exactly four years and had flown 1,350 hours in six different aircraft for the Marine Corps. He was 25 years old, a first lieutenant, and as ready for combat as a human being could be.

During the five months VMFA 513 operated out of Danang, Witchell flew 87 missions—seven more than the average for his squadron. About half Witchell's missions were flown in support of Marine Corps ground troops on search-and-destroy missions in the northern sector of South Vietnam. The other half involved missions into North Vietnam: armed reconnaissance, recon-air cover for RF-101 and F-8U photo and ECM airplanes, and armed strikes against bridges and supply lines.

In October, 1965, VMFA 513 was relieved (it had been deployed overseas for a year). Witchell flew his F-4 from Danang back to Atsugi NAS, and was flown from Atsugi in a P2V to Iwa Kuni MCAS where an Air Force C-135 jet transport brought him back to El Toro, California.

At this point, George Witchell, who had just made captain, exercised his option to retire from the Corps. Why?

"Since I was a reserve officer," Witchell said, "I had fulfilled my five-year obligation. I decided I'd had enough and I got out."

How did he feel about the Vietnam war once he became a civilian again? Witchell's answer was thoughtful and carefully worded.

"When we went out there," he said, "I was excited about going . . . mostly because it was a chance to put all that training to work for what I, at that time, considered a questionable cause.

"After my tour of duty in Danang—after meeting and talking with the Vietnamese pilots we came in contact with, and listening to their stories about Vietcong atrocities—after seeing for myself what's happening there—I felt that my small part was worth the time and the 25 pounds I lost.

"In fact," Witchell concluded, "I felt very good about it and I still do. I think it's great that a country like the U.S. will back up with force what it says it believes. You can't sit behind your fortress and let things like that happen just because it's 10,000 miles away."

20 THE JOLLY GREEN GIANTS

South of the Red River, our shot-down pilots are often saved, thanks to a tough bunch of helicopter crews operating out of advance bases in Thailand close to the North Vietnam border. They drive a big long-range chopper by Sikorsky called the HH-3E. It has a speed of 130 knots, a range of 266 miles, an endurance of 6½ hours, armor plate, a 240-foot hoist for its forest penetrator, and is fitted with UHF, VHF, FM, HF and SSB radio. It is painted with brown-gray-green jungle camouflage.

Normally, the HH-3E has a crew of four: pilot, copilot, crew chief and paramedic. This gang is known everywhere as the Jolly Green Giants. They are among the bravest men who fight in this war. A Jolly Green Giant HH-3E has to proceed to a rescue pickup at the relatively slow speed of 130 knots across many miles of enemy country. Then, to make the actual pickup, it has to sink right down to the treetops and hover there. The North Vietnamese usually wait for the chopper to get his hoist down and his paramedic on the ground; *then* they fire. They concentrate on the front of the machine, trying to kill the pilots. The urge to pull pitch and get the hell out of there is almost irresistible—but the Jolly Greens stick it. Even if they get hit, they stick it.

A pilot was shot down in North Vietnam while I was in the rescue center at Tan Son Nhut, and I had a grandstand seat at a drama that is being played daily in the North. The plane that went down was an F-105. The wingman had seen the pilot eject and had heard him radio that he had landed but had a broken leg and needed help at once. The wingman was low on fuel and couldn't wait to be relieved by another jet in the area (the usual procedure if you have the fuel). So he radioed the downed pilot's position back to the rescue center, then left to find a tanker.

Now the rescue operation began, directed from Tan Son Nhut. Four A-1 Skyraiders out of Thailand were immediately scrambled toward the coordinates given by the wingman, and they started north at full bore. A Jolly Green Giant chopper was launched out of another Thailand base and took up a course toward the downed man. The plan was for the A-1s to get there first and suppress any ground fire to make it safer for the big chopper. But the show was only beginning. The downed pilot was just south of the Red River, and this is MiG country. So a gaggle of F-4 Phantoms on station close by were diverted to fly a MiG CAP over the A-1s. If jet MiGs were to pounce the slower, propeller-driven A-1s, our F-4s would pounce *them*.

It is difficult for radio waves to get in and out of the deep valleys of the North Vietnamese mountains (where the pilot presumably was), so a C-130 flying command post, fitted with sophisticated radar and radio gear, was vectored north to take close-in charge of the rescue and to relay radio signals back to Tan Son Nhut. A KC-135 jet tanker was also moved in to serve as a filling station for the MiG CAP.

This entire complex operation was organized and in the air about six minutes after the first word was received that a man had gone down. It was thrilling to sit there and watch the power of the U.S. Air Force pulled in so swiftly from all directions and coordinated into a team to get one man out of a faraway jungle valley deep in hostile territory. I wish I could report they did it. But there was a tragic ending. When the wingman returned to the scene after having hit his fuel tanker, he radioed that he had been in error on his first coordinates. The F-105 had gone down *north* of the Red River. This meant that the Jolly Green Giants could not get to the pilot with the amount of fuel aboard.

Then the voice transmission from the downed pilot was lost. Then his location beeper quit.

The whole rescue operation, in just a minute or so, changed from hopeful to impossible. The chopper couldn't reach the man, and it was pretty obvious that loss of radio and beeper contact meant the North Vietnamese had captured him. In a hopeless situation you don't hang around and hope. You give up and come home.

However, if there is even a skin-of-the-teeth chance of getting men out, the Jolly Greens are prone to take it. A mission into Laos flown by Aircraft Comdr. Bob Weekly is a good case in point. A Navy F-4 Phantom had been shot down near the Ho Chi Minh trail, and its pilots were somewhere in the Laos jungle. Nobody knew if they were alive or dead. There was no beeper signal. Two A-1 Skyraiders were tooling around at low altitude, looking for signs of the pilots, and Weekly was churning toward the spot in his HH-3, together with his copilot, Lt. Dick Sans; his crew chief, Sgt. Joe Barnes; and his pararescue man, A1C L. W. Kellerman. A C-54 air command post (this was before 130s were used) was in the area directing things. The A-1s were receiving moderate ground fire, which did not bode well for an approach by the chopper.

The situation was confused by the fact that four A-1s had

been over at night, dropping flares and the little white para-chutes were draped over bushes and trees. In order to tell if a white chute was from a flare or had been used by one of the Navy men, the Skyraiders went right down on the deck, flying slowly, looking for harnesses. They finally gave up and told the command post C-54 it was hopeless. No personnel chutes, no guys.

All this time Bob Weekly had been orbiting at altitude out of range of the guns. Weekly was unwilling to leave without having a go at the thing himself. He put it up to his men, since it was going to be dangerous, and they were already short on fuel.

"We've got 15 minutes of loiter time left," Weekly said on the intercom. "There are two men down there. Do you guys want to go down and make a real slow pass? There may be a lot of ground fire."

The crew said they would do it. Weekly let down while the A-1s roared around in circles, waiting to fire if anybody fired at the chopper. Nobody did. Weekly made a slow pass over the mess of white chutes. Nobody showed.

"There's no ground fire," Dick Sans said. "Why don't we hover from chute to chute and blow the trees apart with our downwash, so if there's a harness we can see it."

"Okay," Weekly said. "But that's it. We're just about out of loiter time."

They went very low and flailed the trees and looked for a harness attached to a chute. Nothing. They were now down in minimum fuel for return to their base. "Pull pitch," Weekly said to his copilot. "We've had the course."

At this point a voice came over the radio. "There's a guy out in a clearing!" said one of the A-1 pilots. "He's waving a red flag."

It was one of the Navy pilots. The chopper hovered over him and lifted him to safety on the sling. When he was secure, the crew asked him why the hell he hadn't come out before. He answered that he'd been afraid to show. Weekly gave him a few pungent words of advice about the wisdom of hiding under the trees when the only hope he had of living was down to its last drop of reserve fuel.

"How about your buddy?" they asked him.

"He's over there," he said, pointing to some trees.

They were now below the fuel needed to return to their base, but they hurried over and lashed the trees with the downwash and saw a harness on the ground but nobody in it. "He's down there someplace," Kellerman, the pararescue, said. "I'll go on down and have a look around."

They lowered Kellerman on the hoist and he raced around the edge of the clearing, floundering in the undergrowth. Back under the trees he came upon the other Navy pilot. He had a broken leg and was bleeding, but he was not in shock. His survival gear was intact; he could have signalled an hour earlier by firing his flare pistol. Why hadn't he done it? Weekly shook his head, almost sorrowfully, as he told the story. "He'd given up," he said. "And Charlie, in *this* man's war, if you give up, you got to be doggoned lucky to get home!"

Kellerman picked the man up and carried him to the clearing. The crew chief lowered a stokes litter. Kellerman strapped the man to it, and they hauled him up. Then Kellerman himself was lifted back into the chopper. By this time the fuel was so low that there was no hope of returning to their base. The only possibility was an Army Special Forces camp about 35 miles away.

"This was where it got hairy," Dick Sans told me. "The weather was bad. We climbed up and got through a solid overcast at 6,000 feet. Mountains were all around us in the clouds. The A-1s stuck with us and led us to a hole in the clouds. We followed them down through a mountain pass full of Vietcong and landed in the Special Forces camp. But there was no doctor there, no fuel, and our Navy pilot was bleeding. We had 20 minutes of fuel remaining. The Special Forces guys said there was another camp about 15 miles away. Weekly put it to the crew again. Did they want to try for it? They said they did."

Weekly took off and flew up through the weather. They were in bright sunshine, but the undercast was dark as night. They flew the number of minutes they thought it would take them to reach the other camp, and called on the radio: "Do you hear our engines?"

"Yes," came the reply. "Turn left."

They turned left.

Suddenly the radio yelled: "You're going right over us now!"

Weekly instantly started a letdown through the clouds. He broke out into haze and rain at 300 feet. The Special Forces camp was in sight; 30 seconds later they settled into it. A doctor came in about 15 minutes. Fuel enough to get them to the next forward operating base was brought in 55-gallon drums. There they got a few more barrels of fuel and flew to still another FOB. *There* they got enough fuel to take them back to their home base.

"The Navy boys didn't forget us," Sans said. "When they got back to their carrier, they had four cases of Crown Royal sent to us." In addition to the booze, everybody got a Silver Star, which is one of the best medals you can win.

It wasn't really an extraordinary save. It was probably a lot less hairy than most. But it gives you an idea of the kind of guys who go by the name of Jolly Green Giants. Nobody, but nobody!, badmouths the Jolly Greens—unless he wants to get five propelled by an outraged right arm in his teeth.

21 YANKEE STATION

"I thought I saw a glimmer of light," Lt. Comdr. Glenn McGeorge radioed to his element leader, Comdr. Bud Ingley, as the two of them flew their tiny Skyhawk bombers on instruments through the inky darkness of North Vietnam. "Okay to drop a flare?"

"I didn't see anything," replied Commander Ingley, "but go ahead."

McGeorge toggled a magnesium flare and it settled under its parachute, lighting up the main north-south supply route, Highway One, and in the sun-bright glare there stood revealed a long convoy of trucks loaded with war supplies. Instantly the air around the jets lit up with tracer fire as the truck-guard gunners let loose. The two little Navy bombers broke hard, in formation, and rolled in on the lead truck of the convoy, 20mm cannon winking. There was a sudden fierce glare of fire.

"Got him," Ingley said shortly. "That corks the front. Let's get Tail-End Charlie."

The two jets tilted steeply into the high darkness above the falling flare, racked over almost inverted and came smoking down on a reverse course. Again their cannon stammered in the heavy, leisurely manner of 20mms, and the last truck in the convoy shuddered, heeled over on its side and burst into flame.

"Call the Blue Tails!" Ingley told his wingman. "We got those jokers locked in now."

McGeorge got on his radio to the carrier *Constellation*, 100 miles away, making her standard racetrack pattern in the throat of the Gulf of Tonkin, giving the coordinates of the truck target; Comdr. Dave Leue, boss of the Blue Tail Fly Squadron, sitting in the ready room, got the message, and his guys headed for their Skyhawks on the run; and in the same spread of seconds, Bud Ingley was coming in very low, directly over the column of trapped trucks, walking his 20-mm bullets from one end of it to the other. The black gap between the two burning end trucks lit up with the fury of fire fed by gasoline and ammo, and even as Leue's bombers were flung off the steam cats of the *Constellation* the light from the burning target became visible on the bridge of the carrier across 100 miles of ocean.

"We clobbered them that night," Bud Ingley said. "What we didn't have the ammo for, the Blue Tails did. And after the fire really got going, its light showed us an entire second convoy that had pulled off the road; they were trying to hide under some trees. When we found them, we hit them—and they went up in flames. I'd say we destroyed about 36 trucks that night. Conservatively. It might have been more."

This incident illustrates what goes on with the jets that fly off Yankee Station and that hit North Vietnam with about half the total number of strikes the United States directs against that battered country. (The Air Force out of Thailand and, to a small extent, out of Danang, accounts for the other half of the strikes.)

Yankee Station has had little or no publicity. Few people in the United States would know what you were talking about if you mentioned it. Yankee Station is not a siding in Back Bay, nor a rock 'n' roll radio station playing Colonial music. It's a position in the South China Sea about 100 miles northeast of Danang where American aircraft carriers cruise around in a methodical pattern and launch and recover fighter and bomber airplanes that are hitting North Vietnam. Yankee Station is really a patch of ocean. But the jets that come from this patch of ocean are uniquely bothersome and deadly to the North Vietnamese. First reason is that they work so close to shore that they are always within a few minutes' flying time from a hurry call to hit a target (the Air Force planes in Thailand are hundreds of miles and many minutes away). For example, when Bud Ingley and Glenn McGeorge found that convoy of trucks, they were able to call in the Blue Tail Fly Squadron and destroy them all in just a few minutes.

These Navy carriers (there are usually at least two or three working on Yankee Station simultaneously) are right on the North Vietnam doorstep, day and night. They have air-tight security, since spies cannot infiltrate them (as they sometimes do in a shore base). There are no problems about sailors getting local belles in trouble or busting up bars, since there are 100 miles of deep water between the crew and such temptations.

The carrier on Yankee Station is a mobile, privileged sanctuary. It can be replenished from home with whatever it needs to fight. It can go anywhere in the world on short notice. It is immune from sneak missile attacks, since it is always moving. No capricious foreign government can order it closed (as can happen to a land base). The carrier can control its food, water, health and recreation very tightly. There are no mosquitoes to give you malaria. And because the carrier is isolated and there is really no recreation but "work," the crews "amuse" themselves by working an average of 15 hours a day. They stay "on the line" for 30 to 35 days and then take 10 days or two weeks off for repairs and rest and relaxation.

The air war waged by the carriers on Yankee Station is one of the most efficiently fought operations in the Vietnam conflict, and what is particularly interesting is this: Just a few years ago, people were screaming, "Junk those obsolete, vulnerable, impotent carriers in favor of ICBMs and long-range B-52s!"

That song has left the Top Ten! Navy aircraft carriers have now proved their worth in this Vietnam war—and their potential for any wars of a similar type that might erupt sometime in the foreseeable future. I spent 23 days aboard the *USS Constellation* during the summer of 1966, and now I would like to take the readers aboard this mighty ship and show you, close up and at first hand, how it really is to fly off a carrier in a high-performance jet.

The *Connie* is a sea-going airfield that can move around at

35 knots; houses more than 5,000 officers, men and tech reps; can hurl jets off her four steam cats like shooting beans; carries enough power to flatten targets just as flat as the Strategic Air Command's massive intercontinental bombers and missiles; can launch and recover day or night in very lousy weather; has a flight deck of 4½ acres; carries dozens of planes—fighters, bombers, photo-recon, radar picket, onboard delivery and planeguard helicopters.

In a nutshell, this carrier and others like her are the most complex, dangerous, glamorous and exciting weapons in the world. The labyrinth of passages, ladders, rooms, shafts, vents and ducts is so complex that it would take one man months to set foot in every space on board—if, indeed, he could find them all. Men spend their entire tour of duty on a big carrier like the *Connie* without being familiar with anything but the tiny fraction of her interior that they must frequent in their jobs. There was actually a large room on the *Kitty Hawk* that had no doors at all. It was a great, hollow, black void for months before somebody cut a hatch in it and started using it!

There are all kinds of crazy things going on aboard a carrier. Would you believe that "jet-fuel bugs" grow in the tanks of JP-5 and must be carefully eliminated before the fuel is put in the planes, lest they cause the engine to stop in midair? Would you believe that Russian long-range jet bombers pay a visit to all American carriers in midocean between Hawaii and Japan, and when the call "Snooper X!" goes out over the ship's command public-address system, we zap Phantom jets up there to fly within spitting distance of the Russians and escort them while they are in the area? I had expected hackles would bristle at a time like this. Not necessarily. Our guys have taken to holding up the latest *Playboy* foldout Playmate of the Month in their cockpits for the Russians to admire from their bombers through binoculars! Maybe this kind of thing, and not diplomats in striped pants, is the avenue that will lead us to world peace. We'll overcome them with Playboy bunnies!

I sat in the Silver Fox Ready Room (A-4 Skyhawks led by Comdr. Jim Morin, USN, on the *Connie*) and watched movies with them as we steamed toward our combat station. The film fare was, it must be admitted, a bit dated. Groans, sounds of wonder and suggestions of a fairly earthy sort were frequently heard above the whirring of the projector and the sound track of the film. If a man was particularly moved, he might take off his baseball cap and hurl it at the screen. Carrier pilots do not take themselves seriously. "Stay loose" is a general slogan on a carrier. If a man tended to tighten up on Yankee Station, he'd strip his emotional threads and crack up in a short time.

Frantic little situations of a life-or-death nature happen daily to carrier pilots. Comdr. Jim Morin was leading a Skyhawk raid over the delta of North Vietnam looking for mobile missile sites to destroy, when one of the men in his group, Lt. Paul Moore, took a .37mm shell through his wing that blew a gaping hole in the wing tank and set jet fuel streaming back in a hissing white froth. Luckily, it didn't catch fire! Then a second shell smacked Moore's Skyhawk in the belly and severed a main fuel line, and the fuel pump, upstream of the break, was merrily pumping the precious stuff overboard like a fire hose. To top off his difficulties, Lt. Moore had just finished strafing an enemy stronghold, was down to 800 feet and his engine flamed out.

"My main idea was to get as far away from there as I could," Paul Moore told me. "It isn't considered desirable to make a crash landing in the vicinity of folks you have just been strafing. They tend to be antisocial."

Moore must have been a fairly cool head, for he managed to get his jet engine restarted in midair as he settled like the well-known rock toward the boondocks. But he found himself with certain handicaps. The throttle had been jammed at 83 percent rpm—just enough to keep the airplane flying at around 200 knots—and it was 150 miles back to the carrier.

"I headed for the ocean," Moore said. "If you can reach the water before you jump out, your chances of being picked up by a destroyer or a helicopter are good. If you jump out over North Vietnam, forget it. Those little buddies ring the church bells when they see a chute blossom and everybody and his brother grabs a hoe and takes off after the foreign devils!"

Flying close to Paul Moore, Comdr. Morin summoned a Navy tanker plane that was orbiting on station high above the carrier. It came screaming down from the heights and got in line in front of Moore's now nearly fuelless Skyhawk. The problem was unique. Moore had no throttle, no speed brakes. He could not gradually ease up and jab his probe into the basket. If a hookup was to be made, the tanker *had to back into Moore!*

A third pilot, the executive officer of the squadron, now slid in alongside the tanker and the stricken jet and "talked the tanker back, inch by inch, until the connection was made." But trouble came almost instantly. Moore, flying at a steady 200 knots, was now about five knots faster than the "backing" tanker. He started to overrun it, jamming the drogue up at a 35-degree angle and moving fearsomely in for a low-speed collision.

"Speed up!" Moore shouted frantically to the tanker pilot. *"Speed up, goddammit!"*

The tanker goosed throttle and pulled free. Things were almost hopeless, but Moore tried again; and this time, thanks to the help of the exec in the plane off to the side, he made a hookup and began taking fuel. This was a day, however, when he couldn't do anything right. The added fuel made him heavier. The added weight made him slower. He couldn't get a single additional rpm above 83 percent. His speed sagged to 190 knots. This was too slow for the tanker—heavy with fuel—and the tanker had to pull away. Even then, Moore was in deep trouble. He had enough fuel to fly home, but not enough power to carry it and maintain altitude. Twenty miles short of a search-and-rescue (SAR) destroyer and with 75 feet of altitude and sinking, Moore took the only course left: He punched out. He got a good chute just above the surface, hit with a giant geyser of seawater and got trussed up like a Christmas turkey in his shroud lines.

"We carry an emergency hunting knife in a shoulder holder," Moore told me. "I got mine out. I shudder to think what would have happened if it had slipped out of my hands before I cut myself free of those shrouds."

Jim Morin called out a gaggle of Skyraiders to fly a Rescap (rescue combat air patrol) over the downed flyer, because this was Indian country. An enemy junk could have hurried over and captured Moore, without protection from the sky. Some time later, Moore was taken aboard a destroyer and returned to his carrier. It was all in the day's work. He was out flying raids again the next day, good as new—except, perhaps, for a couple of gray hairs he hadn't had before.

Now, for a moment, let's look at the big picture of operations on Yankee Station. The three big attack carriers often work as a team, and the planes from all three ships—more than 200 of them—go off in coordinated waves in strikes against a single target, sometimes going back time after time, for days, until that particular target is simply battered to a pile of dust and rubble.

On June 15, 1966, three carriers on Yankee Station, the *FDR*, the *Constellation* and the *Oriskany*, working together, attacked the industrial complex around Than Hoa—railway yards, a thermal powerplant, oil supplies, flak sites, a massive concentration of North Vietnamese power—in continuous waves. All the various planes were used. The Phantom jets, which are doublesonic, went in first at terrific speed, firing rockets to suppress the flak. Following them came a "gang bang" of little Skyhawks, which screamed in at treetop level, pulled up, sighted the target, rolled in and bombed. They did it in a screeching melee, from all angles, making it very hard for the defending gunners to concentrate on any one plane. Then the Grumman A-6 Intruders, which look like pregnant bumblebees, but have the most deadly and sophisticated electronics bombing system in the world, lugged in loads of bombs (these funny-looking birds can carry 15,000 pounds of bombs in one load!) and pinpointed the big structures. The smoke and flame from this massive, continuous, hour-after-hour, day-after-day destruction raid could be seen for 100 miles in all directions. When it was over, the Than Hoa complex was simply leveled, finished!

Raids like this are undertaken, from time to time, when it is decided to eliminate a target for good and all. They are devastating. Their destruction would have to be seen to be believed. Dry-bones communiques detailing numbers of items hit and numbers of sorties flown simply do not tell the story at all. Yankee Station happens to be one of the most important offensive bases of operations in this whole war, and nobody even knows the place exists, except a few experts who follow these matters closely.

Having lived on the *Constellation* for many days, I got a fairly good idea of how she works and why she is such a deadly fighting machine. Two innovations make the carrier the efficient weapon she is: (1) the canted deck and (2) the steam catapult. In the good old days of the straight deck, it was necessary to raise a high barrier of powerful steel cables amidships, directly in front of landing planes. If a plane overshot the low arresting-gear wires or came aboard in some kind of difficulties, it wound up in the barrier, often burning brightly. Now it's different. The planes land at a small angle to the fore-and-aft line of the ship, on a so-called "angle deck." This deck is open at the end. If you can't make it, or if you miss the arresting wires, you simply add power and go around for another try. Also, with the canted deck, you can work planes much faster. As soon as they are down, they unhook and jazz their engines, taxiing out of the way. They couldn't do this on a straight deck. The barrier had to be lowered. They then taxied over it. Then it had to be raised again. All of which took time. It is possible to bring jets aboard safely every 40 seconds with a canted deck and a smooth-working team.

The steam catapult is important because it makes possible a much more rapid launch. The principle is quite simple. Enormous reservoirs of steam are stored up by the boilers. This steam is then released suddenly, in powerful surges, to fling a jet down the groove and off into the sky. There is no delay while pressure is built up. You've got the pressure on tap, ready for use. If the *Constellation*, for example, got word from one of its Super Fudd radar picket planes that there was an incoming raid of Communist jets, there would still be time to launch a strike of nearly all flyable planes on the ship before the raiders arrived to attack. There are four steam cats. Sometimes, when things are going well, two planes can be in the air off the cats simultaneously—bow and waist. You can clear the whole deck in an incredibly short time. In fact, one of these red-rush launches is about the noisiest, fiercest exhibition of man and machinery in action known in war.

A carrier launch or recovery, however, is a very tight operation, time-wise. In the words of a carrier pilot, "We have no fuel to fool." If there is an emergency on the deck and the air around the ship is full of "low-state" jets, things can get desperate—I mean that word literally—in a few minutes. The jets come back to the ship from strikes with just enough fuel for a couple of extra passes. There are, of course, tanker planes standing by for guys who have to get a drink immediately or ditch. And there is always the land field at Danang as an alternative. But even so, planes can run out of fuel and go in the water.

Life aboard the *Connie*, except for Flight Quarters, was confining and often boring to me. I turned into a chow hound like everybody else. I went down to the ship's store and bought pogie bait (candy) by the carton and dropped in about six times a day at the Fighter Pilots' Mess on the galley deck up forward. This mess is a place where you can go in your flight coveralls, your hair matted with sweat and not be thrown out (as opposed to the Senior Officers' Mess below the hangar deck aft, where you have to be in uniform). The food was plentiful, fattening and superb. It was served by a bunch of Filipino boys, one of whom wore a red ribbon around his ear for some personal reason (nothing to do with Benny Boys; these kids were he-men) and he could fry an egg any way you wanted it to a lovely, golden perfection. There was an urn full of hot chocolate in the lounge and beside it, there was a huge container of heavy, doughy buns with sweet icing and raisins which I would munch on at odd hours. I began looking like Col. Blimp in no time at all.

The guys I kind of pity on an aircraft carrier are the tech reps. They are the ones, often middle-aged, who stay on board for the nine months of the cruise to fix the complex electronics and other gadgetry that modern planes are fitted with. They sit at the table eating; they look glum and lonely—at least some of them. They share an overcrowded cabin with perhaps a bunch of wild young CPOs or ensigns who play rock 'n' roll half the night. They spend their working time studying through manuals, examining dials and ailing connections, and if the cotton-picking black boxes don't do what they are supposed to do, everybody and his brother bitches and screams at the tech rep. If the black boxes *do* perform well, the pilot comes back and says, "Well, I sure was on the money today!" I would rather be a tech rep than an elevator operator, but that is about as far as I will go.

I was interested in the moral issues of the war, and I noticed that the pilots were too. The *Connie* has a large library stocked with the latest books on Vietnam, and the pilots of the Skyhawk squadrons (Silver Foxes and Blue Tail Flies), with whom I spent most of my time, were toting these books around and reading them in their spare time. I think it is safe to say that, almost without exception, the pilots I talked to were heartily in favor of the war, felt no compunctions at all about bombing things in North Vietnam and held the standard GI opinion: "We have to stop Communism here—or face it later, closer to home." Considering the really grave danger they were facing in bombing North Vietnam, it would not have been easy for them to go into that flak storm holding any other views.

I experienced tragedy too on the *Constellation*. Comdr. Chuck Peters, a huge man of six feet four or more, weighing over 200 pounds, was the executive officer of the Silver Fox Squadron (who wore green baseball caps and green scarves). Chuck was courteous, brave, likeable in every way and it was not surprising that he was known to his squadron mates as "The Jolly Green Giant." He had survived a crash landing in the ocean at night, when his plane hit at 218 knots, in what seems close to miraculous. The plane was badly smashed up and Chuck Peters was in it, stunned. He realized he was sinking. His ankle was broken and he was badly shaken, but he did what anybody who has ever tried to get out of a torso harness dry, standing up in a lighted room, will tell you is almost superhuman. He got out of that tight webbing with those fiendish metal buckles while he was under water—and he fought his way out of the cockpit and swam up to the surface. All his survival gear was attached to the torso harness, so he lost it. Luckily for him, one of the wing tanks was empty. It ripped off when the plane hit the water and was floating nearby. Chuck grabbed hold of it and held on in the darkness. At one point, he told me, "Something came up behind me and nibbled on my ass. It felt like something big—but not hungry. And I guess it wasn't, because it went away." Six hours later, he was rescued by a destroyer.

Comdr. Jim Morin left the *Constellation* on June 30, 1966, Comdr. Chuck Peters took over as CO of the squadron the next day, July first. Coming back from a strike over North Vietnam, when he was nearly over the ocean, Peters took a heavy hit on his Skyhawk. The plane began to burn. He stayed with it, trying to get away from the shore guns. Then it began to go out of control.

"I'm ejecting!" Peters radioed.

He passed over a Communist-held island. The plane now began to somersault, end over end, a mass of fire. He ejected and his parachute blossomed. As he drifted toward the water, his squadron-mates screamed around him like angry hawks ready to gun down anybody who tried to fire at him. Then the parachute hit the sea—but Chuck did not fight free this time. He must either have been dead or unconscious. He sank from sight. His loss was a sad thing. He was one of the Navy's finest.

Before I close this piece, I would like to pay my respects to Capt. Bill Houser, who was skipper of the *Connie* when I was aboard and who was my genial host. Bill Houser didn't look like the captain. He looked like the commander of the air group. He was tall, lean, fit-looking—the kind of a guy who'd beat your eyebrows off at handball any Tuesday. His pomposity quotient was zero. When he talked to the crew after a serious accident or important event, he held it to the facts, spoke in a businesslike but friendly way and then shut up.

When we put in at Yokosuka, Japan, for fuel and repairs, before going into combat, Capt. Houser turned the crew loose ashore with his blessing to whoop it up. Each division had its own party. Capt. Houser was invited to them all. He went to them all. I went along to one of them and we arrived when the boys were on their 17th beer apiece. A big old chief hit me on the back in a friendly way and I thought he'd broken a vertebra. Then he shoved a beer in my hand and roared for me to drink it. Gasping slightly, I did.

Then they brought in the lovely Chinese strip-teaser. She wore high-heeled blue sandals, a kind of glittery medallion at a crucial point and *nada mas*. A hurried and excited consultation was held with her, and she was seen to smile warmly and nod her assent. Then she came forward—rather demurely, I thought, for a stripper—grasped my old head firmly in her dainty little hands, thrust it between her naked breasts and shook them gently and warmly against my ears. The sound of approval was awesome in the room. Then she did the same to Capt. Houser. A less sophisticated man might have stood on his dignity or ducked around coyly. The captain took it with smiling aplomb, and the cheers shook the whisky bottles behind the bar.

Then the captain was called upon to make a speech and what he said was classic. "Your beer is fine," he said. "Your hostess is even better." (Wild hoots of approval.) "I have only one thing to say to you. When we get out at sea in combat and any of you want to talk to me about anything—you know where my office is. I don't keep the door locked." This is exactly the way to talk to sailors with (or without) 17 beers.

A few days later, when I was standing in Primary Flight

Control with the air boss and Captain Houser, we spied "Sweet Willie" Williams waving one of his large fists in a typical explanatory motion under the nose of one of the other Red Shirts. He was wearing the red cloth helmet with a radio transceiver in it, as the key men do on a flight deck.

Ken Enny, the air boss, picked up his mike, and said, "Hey, Willie. What's the trouble?"

Williams knew Ken's voice, of course, and he stared up at us with his hot, brown glare. "Nothing, Commander!" he said.

"I've got the captain here with me," Enny said. "I don't want you to screw up while he's watching."

Sweet Willie's burning stare shifted to the skipper and his voice boomed in over the wall speaker: "Tell that old rate grabber we're onto him," he said. "We know he's eager as a bride on the wedding night—but give him my congratulations anyhow."

I was a junior-grade lieutenant in the Navy at one time and I would have never dreamed of calling my skipper a rate grabber. I took a deep breath, wondering what Capt. Houser would do.

He picked up Ken Enny's hand mike and said, "Thanks, Willie. I appreciate those good wishes."

I learned, then, what it was all about. Capt. Houser had just been elevated to admiral by the powers in the Navy Department and would move onward and upward to take over duties as chief of strategic planning for the Navy in the months to come. That was what Willie meant by "rate grabber."

I had my first contact with the Navy's side of the out-country war in Yokosuka, Japan. This was when *Constellation* was on her way to Dixie Station from Pearl Harbor. We had put into Yokosuka for fuel and last-minute precombat maintenance. *Constellation*'s sister carrier, *Kitty Hawk,* was also at Yokosuka. She had just come off the line at Yankee Station, where her air group had been hit very hard. The purpose of the conferences was to point out mistakes that had been made—and try to prevent them from happening again. There had been heavy losses of RA-5C Vigilantes, shot down on recon missions. The *Connie* Vigilante pilots, as a result of the talks, decided to fly a very cool profile—"Not risking those big $17,000,000 birds for a 25-cent target," was the way one old pro phrased it. There are times when risks must be taken, but there are also times when it is better to skirt a place and leave it for a "gang bang" (a wild pounce by a bunch of free-firing, free-dropping Skyhawks).

"In any mission," Comdr. Charlie Smith, boss of *Constellation*'s Vigilantes, said to me, "you get out of it what you put into it. I know that's obvious. But people sometimes forget it. I mean this. If you study every scrap of information available on the target you are after, and check with the latest reports from guys who've been over there, and then you study the terrain and the deployment of the defenses as best you know them, you can plan a safer show. And you can bring back better pictures. In our business you don't flap a red scarf around your neck, rush down, kick the tire and light the fire. Not if you want to come home with the good stuff."

At the time *Kitty Hawk* had been on Yankee Station, the Navy was still in the process of learning the deadly lessons of the SAMs. They were finding out that you were safer if you stayed under the SAM envelope (below 3,000 feet) but that when you did that, you opened yourself up to ground fire from automatic weapons. Hence you not only had to stay very low but ride behind the ridgelines too. Or else you had to jink, and the RA-5C jinks "majestically"—which is not the safest way to jink.

One of *Kitty Hawk*'s A-6 Intruder pilots, Lt. Bill Westerman, was shot down in a freakish manner. Westerman and his bomber-navigator, Brian Westin, were out on a napalm run over North Vietnam. (Why was this sophisticated bird being used to drop napalm on hootch lines? I don't know, but I think it had something to do with the bomb shortage.) At any rate, a farmer standing in a field shot Bill Westerman in the left shoulder with a rifle. This was the only hit the plane sustained. "I instinctively pulled back on the stick," Lt. Westerman said. "Brian said I was getting too high, up in the SAM envelope. I was feeling nauseous. Things began to go dark. Brian took over by reaching across me (the pilot and BN sit side by side in an A-6) and turned us toward the sea. He flew it and at the same time he managed to get out a two-ounce bottle of brandy we carry for emergencies. I drank that and felt a little better."

But Westerman was bleeding, and shock was setting in. He was alternately losing and regaining consciousness, coming in and out of the dark. Accompanying the stricken plane was

Comdr. R. J. Hayes, the third commanding officer the A-6 outfit had had in six months. About 30 miles offshore it became evident that Westerman would not be able to fly the plane aboard. Though Westin, the BN, could maintain level flight, he could not perform the complex task of making a carrier landing, which is tricky business even for a seasoned pilot. The decision was made for Westerman and Westin to bail out while Hayes circled overhead. It is normal practice for the pilot to bail out last, but Westin wasn't taking any chances on Westerman blacking out after he, Westin, had jumped. He insisted that Westerman go out first, which Westerman did.

Westin then punched out and was picked up, after firing a flare, by a rescue chopper. Westin directed the pilot to the spot where he thought his injured buddy might be floating, and they sighted him. He had become separated from his life raft. They settled low. Westerman looked up and smiled but he was obviously exhausted. The helo crew dropped the sling. But the violent turbulence of the whirling rotors washed so powerfully down on the wounded pilot that he could not help himself readily. Brian Westin grabbed an old-fashioned Mae West (he'd already taken off his own Mark 3 Charlie flotation gear and torso harness) and was lowered by the sling to help his buddy. Working under such conditions requires an unusual amount of effort due to the sea motion, the fact that the gear is soaked, and the general fury of the downwash whipping everything to a foam in front of your face. After some trouble, Westin got the pilot hooked up properly and saw him lifted safely to the rescue helicopter.

Meanwhile, the rescuer—Brian Westin—was in trouble. He'd put on the old Mae West improperly in his hurry. When it inflated, instead of holding his face out of the water as it was designed to do, it was forcing his face under the waves. "I tried to get into a makeshift sling they had lowered to me," Westin said. "For a few minutes I was suffocating and about to drown. I think I almost gave up. But finally I managed to blow up my anti-G suit—and with it and the Mae West to support me, I waved the helo off to take Bill to medical aid. The secondary sling was too small for me to fit into."

Westin wanted his buddy to get to medical aid before he lost too much blood. The helo dropped a smoke flare to mark the spot and took off. Five minutes later (the longest of his life, Westin felt) another helo arrived with the right kind of sling. They took him aboard. After they hauled him up a crewman pointed to the water at something. He said it was a shark. Westin never saw it. For his part of the rescue of the wounded pilot, Westin received the Navy Cross.

The air war has, of course, been escalating. Rivers in the North have been mined by Navy P2V Neptune bombers so that traffic—both war goods and civilian goods—will be hampered and the economy slowed down. Navy ships have been bombarding the shores of North Vietnam and 175mm long-range cannon have been firing into North Vietnam across the Demilitarized Zone. The new steel mill north of Hanoi—the pride and joy of the North Vietnamese—has been heavily bombed. It was one of the most important industrial innovations since Ho Chi Minh came to power. There has been talk of mining or bombing Haiphong harbor, to deny this key port to Russian ships arriving with war supplies. But opponents of this idea have pointed out the danger of drawing Russia into the war on a massive scale if this is done—and they have stated too that the loss of the harbor might not stop the supplies anyhow. They could be offloaded onto beaches, using small craft, as has already been done by both sides successfully in the past.

The North Vietnamese have made every effort to counter our bombing by dispersal of their oil in 55-gallon drums spaced at intervals along back roads, and have also stored them in bomb craters. We have bombed and strafed these dispersed stores of oil with considerable success—particularly the drums stored in craters, which have been ignited by dive bombing and strafing with 20mm cannon.

The North Vietnamese are reported to be trying very hard to get the Soviet Union to send them SA-3 Guideline missiles to replace the SA-2s now deployed there. If this should take place it could be extremely serious. The SA-2s are the SAMs that have been used without much effectiveness against our planes heretofore. They are not as sophisticated as the new super SAMs, so to speak, the SA-3s—which have longer range, more sophisticated guidance, and are much more difficult to avoid. There has been increasing pressure in Congress, by Senator Stewart Symington, for one, to bomb the airfields in North Vietnam—to knock out the MiG-21s that have been increasingly active lately—but our high command has been slow to do this. Perhaps on the theory that if we knock out the MiGs the Soviets may just decide to send those new super SAMs as a further escalation of the war.

Our B-52s are now flying bombing missions out of the recently completed superbase (11,500-foot runways) on the Gulf of Siam near Sattahip—just one hour from their targets as compared with a 12-hour round-trip mission out of Guam. A program is under way to replace the F-105 fighter-bombers with twin-jet F-4s for the runs against North Vietnam targets. The F-105s have suffered heavily and are, in fact, going to be in short supply eventually—so the substitution of the faster F-4 Phantoms is really looking ahead; it's an attempt to make the replacement in an orderly fashion rather than on a crash basis.

American ingenuity has made an urgent attempt to outwit the attacks on our fighter bombers by North Vietnamese surface-to-air-missiles. Special planes fitted with countermeasure gear have been sent along with the fighter-bombers to "fake out" the ground guidance systems of the SAM sites. This little caper, known as "Wild Weasel," has been only partly effective. The North Vietnamese missile men have, in their turn, been playing games with the Wild Weasel planes, trying (and sometimes succeeding in faking *them* out. Another electronic countermeasure (ECM) plane has been the Douglas RB-66, which has been used to pave the way for bombing planes by going in first and screwing up the acquisition radars of the ground missile sites.

In the meantime, the smaller Lockheed F-104 Starfighters—known as "the razorblade on a pregnant hatpin" because of its needlelike fuselage and tiny seven-foot wings (so sharp they cut like a dull butcher knife if you run your finger along the leading edge)—have been used to strike at Communist Pathet Lao activities in nearby Laos out of their Thailand base at Udon. The C-130 Hercules propjets—fitted with seven rapid-firing machine guns pointing out the side and also beefed up with armor plate—are also flying out of Udon-Thani against targets in Laos. This is known as the AC-130 and is a kind of Magic Dragon—faster than the old DC-3 Dragon Ship of the Mekong Delta, but not having the rotating Gatling guns.

For a long time we did not admit that we were using Thailand as a base from which to attack North Vietnam. Now the lid is off. We have openly stated that our planes are coming from Thailand and will continue to come from there. The tension is increasing almost daily. How far it will go is anybody's guess. President Johnson is under great pressure to bring the North Vietnamese to the conference table before reelection time comes around. The military people are strongly urging him to give them more and bigger targets "to smash them flat and get it over."

22 GOTT MIT UNS

No book on war, air or otherwise, would be complete without a short acknowledgement to the greatest ally of all men and all nations when it comes down to the serious business of killing or maiming other people: God. The first beetle-browed beady-eyed caveman, no doubt, when he heard the thunder rumble, knelt down and muttered reverently, "Oh, Great Grunting One, help me dismember that bastard Woo Goo and his family that live down the cliff a piece!" Man, as everyone knows, prays to a God we refer to as Him, just as codfish presumably pray to a Giant Codfish and triangles pray to The Big Triangle. We men are the most potent people we know, so it was natural for us to decide officially, as I believe you will find in the Bible some place, that God made us in His image.

So when there's war in the air, our holy men pray to God to help us, whoever we are, to knock off the enemy, whoever they are. This may be a bit confusing to God, since all these prayers are coming up simultaneously to Him from the various bellicose nations, and everybody on all sides, is firmly convinced that God, when it's explained to him what miserable slobs the others are, will certainly help *us*.

The business of praying to God for help in war is not confined to holy men. Politicians do it, on national TV, if possible, and some pilots do it before climbing into the cockpit with a load of bombs intended for a bunch of people who may or may not have the foggiest notion who is fighting whom over what. I recall very well a famous book written during World War II by a famous American colonel, Bob Scott, which was called *God Is My Copilot*. Scott's book was made into a movie and I saw it sitting with a bunch of Navy fighter pilots on a Grumman Hellcat base in Florida in 1944 (I was a jaygee at the time) and the high point of the film was when the Jap Zeros attacked and Dennis Morgan, a handsome young movie star of the period (with the help of his copilot, of course) mowed them down like flies. The Navy fighter pilots in the audience were having hysterics because it was obvious that the Jap Zeros were really Navy SNJs (or Army AT-6s if you like) painted with big Jap Meat Balls, and the Jap pilots (whose faces were shown snarling at all times in the closeups) were those of middle-aged character actors with Fu-Manchu mustaches. Later, I heard that Col. Scott was working on a sequel to his big best-seller. The title of the new work, according to the scuttlebutt, was to be *Christ Is My Crew Chief.*

Another dramatic highlight in World War II was the chaplain who, in the heat of combat, was said to have shouted, "Praise the Lord and pass the ammunition!" Or maybe I'm confusing this with a popular song by that title. At any rate, God must have wondered what was coming off down there, since according to the Bible, He gave Moses specific instructions up on the mountain concerning the results of passing the ammo. "Thou shalt not kill" is what it says God said in the Sixth Commandment, and that's a sentence that even a patriotic priest in a tight spot will have a hard time weaseling out of.

I've been told, in the past, by religious men who'd been explaining to me about God, that it might be all very well for me to go on with my flippant little arguments, but wait until the heat came on me and I'd see. "There are no atheists in foxholes!" they informed me, with a triumphant glitter in their eyes. I asked then if they meant by that that the men had *been* atheists before they got in the foxholes, and they said that was the general idea. I asked what changed the atheists into believers and they said, "Harvey, when a man is faced with death he takes a little different view of things."

"You mean he's scared into it?"

"No—he realizes that nobody can be without God, particularly near death."

"You mean he's coppering his bets?"

"Harvey," they said, "wait until you get in a tight spot yourself and maybe you won't be so smartassed about all this."

I didn't continue with the discussion. There was no point in saying that the God I pray to doesn't fly copilot for anybody, isn't impressed by patriotic priests, knows a Johnnie-come-lately self-interested convert when he sees one, and doesn't change the rules for any of these folks in life, nor alert St. Peter to hand them the keys to the kingdom when they come knocking on the pearly gates.

I have not noticed quite so much calling upon God in the war in Vietnam as we had in World War II. (I wasn't in the Korean War so I don't know what happened there.) Of course, our President and the politicians mention God in their major speeches, but it isn't the big thing it used to be. It seems more a matter of protocol—of touching all the bases like the man running for office who carefully greets all those present, by name: ladies and gentlemen, distinguished guests, the members of Fire Company Seven, Fourth Precinct, God, it is a great privilege to be here, etc. . . . I think this may be a step forward, if, as the Bible seems to intend, brotherly love and not bloodshed is the idea behind that great book. Not that I really expect brotherly love to overcome the love of bloodshed, but it's refreshing to see that the chaplains and the politicians and the fighting men on both sides who believe God or Allah or Karl Marx is there helping them kill aren't having so many movies made about them.

It may be that when we get a more clean-cut war, in which we can be sure we are doing the right thing, that we'll start calling on God again. But then again, people really may have changed. They may have begun to take God seriously—not just give lip service to Him on Sunday or remember to call on Him from the foxhole when the bad guys are closing in.

23 THE HAVES VS. THE HAVE-NOTS

It is no longer possible to have a war without people knowing how rough it is, and the reason, of course, is TV. A headline in the newspaper announcing that so many people got killed someplace is trivial in its impact—even if lots of people got killed—compared to a close-up full-color movie of a burning village with screaming, terror-stricken people and pitiful bloody corpses huddled in a ditch. That gets to you.

Similarly, a written report of some political speech, or the doings in a legislative session of the government, is seldom read in its entirety by the masses of the people. But they'll watch a hot argument on TV between Sen. Fulbright, say, and Dean Rusk. They'll listen when Barry Goldwater says, with obvious anger (and approval), that bombing a Russian supply ship in Haiphong harbor would be "just too damn bad!" The American public, in spite of itself, is being given a first-hand look at the marvels of politics, combat, Great Men in Office and other matters they once only read about. Our population, in short, is getting savvier and savvier. It is getting harder and harder for a power-hungry politician or labor leader or businessman to pull the wool over their eyes.

TV is the reason. TV is perhaps the salvation of the world, depending upon how freely and completely it covers the myriad of events in all walks of life as they evolve from moment to moment in this swift kaleidoscope of marvels and horrors we live in. The spate of bang-bang Western shows, James Bond, sex and violence, soap operas, bird-brained panel games, giveaway contests and other antics addressed to millions of bored, tired and frustrated Americans of both sexes and all ages is, in itself, perhaps a very valuable outlet for otherwise short-circuited misery and rage. TV may well be a God-sent answer to a very screwed-up swarm of people, and it may, through *showing* us and not telling us, put a brake on the population explosion, expose war as it *really* is (pretty awful), and prevent evil people from getting a grip on the masses of their countrymen.

Which gets me to the matter of the hawks and doves. Hundreds of millions, perhaps billions or even trillions of words have been uttered or written since this Vietnam war broke out—often in intense passion—by both sides of the argument. Nobody, it would seem, has succeeded in convincing anyone.

I certainly do not expect to change anybody's mind in this short chapter. I would, however, like to add my two cents just for the hell of it. It seems to me that the reason for wars, since the beginning of time, is quite simple. It is a fight between the Haves and the Have-Nots. Somebody had a good hunting ground, a nice dry cliff full of nice dry caves, a stock of beautiful stone axes, a bunch of good-looking or hard-working females, or maybe a combination of all these things—and somebody else didn't have them, but wanted them. So they maybe tried to get them by sweet talk or trickery, and if that failed, somebody got up and made a speech about those foreign devils on the other side of the valley, and how the world couldn't be safe for their offspring until they were wiped out. Everybody roared approval. They passed around the stone axes and the war was on.

It's been going on ever since, for the same basic reasons. The cover story, of course, changes as time passes. Religion was a great cover story for centuries. It's losing its kick at the moment, but may have a resurgence. (The Moslems and the Hindus, quite recently, indulged in a huge blood bath in India that resulted in the death of quite a few people, because somebody was accused of sneaking into a temple and making off with a hair from the beard of some ancient prophet.) The Crusades, organized in the Middle Ages by Christians to go over and stamp out the Mohammedans in Turkey and other places in the Near East, was a cover story dreamed up by a bunch of bored English adventurers who wanted an excuse to loot, rape, burn and raise hell. (They got the stuffing kicked out of them, as it turned out, and crawled back bloody and battered, or remained in the East, face down in the sun under the circling kites.)

The latest cover story for conflict is the communism-capitalism hassle going on between the Haves (us) and the Have Nots (the underdeveloped nations, of which Red China is the most dangerous). The stakes are money, influence, land, power, trade routes, resources, control—just as they always have been. The nice dry caves are world living space; the stone axes are hydrogen bombs; good hunting grounds are minerals, grain fields, fishing waters, forests; the good-looking females are, by our present standards, better looking than the stone-age cuties.

I suppose the reader now expects me to recommend turning over the things the United States has fought and worked so hard for to the deserving underprivileged hordes all over the world. This, I think, would be like committing national and international suicide. It would be like King Lear turning over his kingdom to his no-good daughters. In no time at all we'd be sitting out on the street.

Why are we in Vietnam today? We are there to establish a permanent power base in Southeast Asia against the Chinese, when they get over hassling among themselves and start moving south. The United States is presently a world leader, and I believe we intend to keep it that way. We do not intend to let our power and influence slip away—anywhere in the world—if we can possibly prevent it. And we are prepared to fight, if necessary, to hold onto what we've got and get more. In Vietnam. In South America. Anywhere. We are a Have nation, and we intend to continue to be a Have nation. Without any doubt at all, the Have-Not nations—and there are many—will make every effort possible to pull us down off the top of the mountain by whatever means they can. Communism happens to be their current cover story for that effort.

I understand the Communists. They are human beings, just like us. They want the dry caves, the stone axes and the pretty girls. I'm an American and I want those things myself and I want them for the country. But, I happen to feel that you can't hog it all if you want to hold the lead. That's one reason why I'm in favor of helping other nations get on their feet—because if we don't, sure as God made little apples, there'll be another world war. Che Guevara wrote in his handbook, *On Guerrilla Warfare,* "If a government has come to power through some form of popular vote, whether fraudulent or not, and if that government maintains at least the appearance of constitutional law, a guerrilla uprising cannot be brought about until all possible avenues of legal procedure have been exhausted." We should mark this statement and mark it well. We should never put an adversary in the position of having nothing to lose, because when anybody is put in that position he becomes very dangerous indeed. He becomes, in fact, a terrorist who may strike—and probably will strike—at the time and place of his own choosing, and stamping him out, if he is determined and furious, as we see in the Vietcong in this war, is extremely difficult. For years we have been increasing the pressure of the world's mightiest industrial and military power on a bunch of little brown men wearing cut-up truck tires for shoes and carrying their food in little rice bags, and everybody knows how fiercely and bravely they've resisted. How did this come about? We broke Guevara's rule. Diem, backed by us (and maybe we had the best intentions!), put the Vietnamese people in a position where all possible avenues of legal procedure were exhausted. They had nothing to lose.

When we succeed in pacifying Vietnam militarily, if we

ever do, the problem will then be squarely in front of us. How do you maintain your position as world leader and give the masses in Vietnam, and in fact in all the other underdeveloped or oppressed countries, a break—at one and the same time? If we succeed in solving that one, not only our future, but the future of mankind itself will be very bright indeed.

ABOUT THE AUTHOR

Born in Pittsburgh, Pennsylvania, in 1913, FRANK HARVEY
was raised on a farm in the Allegheny Mountains. After
graduation from Columbia University in 1937, he worked
as a copy editor for Bethlehem Steel for six years and
then entered the Navy. After his discharge, he worked in
advertising agencies in New York until he became a
flying reporter for *Argosy*. His varied background reflects
his adventuresome spirit—he's flown twice the speed of
sound and gone around the world on $300, in addition
to his daredevil stunts as an amateur pilot.

Mr. Harvey, now a free-lance writer, has written many
articles and stories for such magazines as *The Atlantic,
Saturday Evening Post, Esquire, True* and *Popular Sci-
ence*. His novels include *The Lion Pit* and *Nightmare
County*. Mr. Harvey and his wife live in Hackettstown,
New Jersey.